ROI at WORK

Best-Practice Case Studies from the Real World

 **ASTD Press**

**Jack J. Phillips and
Patricia Pulliam Phillips**

ASTD Press is n internationally renowned source of insightful and practical information on workplace learning and performance topics, including training basics, evaluation and return-on-investment (ROI), instructional systems development (ISD), e-learning, leadership, and career development.

Ordering information: Books published by ASTD Press can be purchased by visiting our website at store.astd.org or by calling 800.628.2783 or 703.683.8100.

Library of Congress Control Number: 2004099190

ISBN-10: 1-56286-404-
ISBN-13: 978-1-56286-4 4-0

Edited by Karen Eddlema , LOGOS Scientific Communications
Cover design by Max Nigi to
Text design by Pen & Palet Unlimited

Printed by Victor Graphics, I c., Baltimore, Maryland, www.victorgraphics.com

Contents

Preface

Since the publication of volume 1 of ASTD's *In Action* series entitled *Measuring Return-on-Investment,* the interest in measuring the return-on-investment (ROI) in training and performance improvement has grown exponentially. Volume 1 filled an important void in the training literature. Published in 1994, it remains one of ASTD's all-time bestsellers. Volume 2, published in 1997, demonstrated further progress with measuring ROI for a variety of programs. Volume 3, published in 2001, added more examples of ROI application to the literature. In 2002, the first casebook representing ROI applications exclusive to the public sector was published.

This publication includes current case studies that are at the forefront of measurement and evaluation. It introduces even more examples of how ROI is being applied in a variety of industries including telecommunications, financial services technology, automotive, and pharmaceuticals. The authors of these case studies are diligently pursuing accountability in training and performance improvement programs. Through their writing, they share their experiences with a process that continues to be at the leading edge of measurement and evaluation.

Target Audiences

This book should interest anyone involved in training, human resource development (HRD), human resources, and performance improvement. The primary audience is practitioners who are struggling to determine the value of programs and to show how programs contribute to the strategic goals of an organization. They are the ones who request more real-world examples. The same group also expresses concern that there are too many models, methods, strategies, and theories, and too few examples to show if any of them makes a difference. This publication should satisfy practitioners' needs by providing successful examples of the implementation of comprehensive evaluation processes.

The second audience comprises instructors and professors. Whether they choose this book for university-level students who are pursuing degrees in HRD, internal workshops for professional HRD staff members, or public seminars on HRD implementation, this casebook will be a valuable reference. It can be used as a supplement to a standard HRD textbook. In our workshops on ROI in training and performance improvement, we use casebooks as supplements to other books supporting our trademarked ROI Methodology. This combination of text and casebook offers the technical details of the measurement and evaluation process along with examples of practical applications, which together show participants that the measurement and evaluation process makes a difference.

A third audience is composed of researchers and consultants who are seeking ways to document results from programs. This book provides additional insight into how to satisfy clients with impressive results. It shows the application of the leading process on ROI evaluation for training and performance improvement—a process based on sound theory and logical assumptions. The methodology prescribed in these examples follows a set of standards that ensure reliable, valid results.

The last audience is made up of managers who must work with HRD on a peripheral basis—managers who are participants in HRD programs to develop their own management skills, managers who send other employees to participate in HRD programs, and managers who occasionally lead or conduct sessions of HRD programs. In these roles, managers must understand the process and appreciate the value of HRD. This casebook should provide evidence of this value.

Each audience should find the casebook entertaining and engaging reading. Although in some cases the case authors faced challenges with securing ideal response rates to follow-up, as well as achieving desired thresholds, in others, the studies show programs to be successful beyond expectations. In all cases, lessons were learned and improvements in the programs and the evaluation were made. Discussion questions appear at the end of each case to stimulate additional thought and discussion. One of the most effective ways to maximize the usefulness of this book is through group discussions, using the questions to develop and dissect the issues, techniques, methodologies, and results.

The Cases

The most difficult part of developing this book was to identify the "best" case studies—those that proved to be flawless. We did find that there were many willing authors with successful applications. We pared down our selection based on challenges faced and overcome, lessons learned, as well as on the variety of programs and industries represented. All selected case studies have adhered to the standards supporting the ROI Methodology. We are pleased with the studies presented in this volume and believe that those who have followed the progress of ROI use would agree that these are by far the best to be published.

Although there was some attempt to structure cases similarly, they are not identical in style and content. It is important for the reader to experience the programs as they were developed to identify the issues pertinent to each particular setting and situation. The result is a variety of presentations with a variety of styles. Some cases are brief and to the point, outlining precisely what happened and what was achieved. Others provide more detailed background information, including how the need for the program was determined, the personalities involved, and how their backgrounds and biases created a unique situation.

In some cases, the name of the organization is identified, as are the individuals who were involved. In others, the organization's name is disguised at the request of either the organization or the case author. In today's competitive world and in situations where there is an attempt to explore new territory, it is understandable why an organization would choose not to be identified. Identification should not be a critical issue, however. Though some cases are slightly modified, they are based on real-world situations faced by real people.

Case Authors

It would be difficult to find a more impressive group of contributors than those for this casebook. For this volume we wanted to present the best work available.

We were not disappointed.

The authors presented in this book are experienced, professional, knowledgeable, and on the leading edge of HRD. Collectively, they represent practitioners, consultants, researchers, and professors. Individually, they represent a cross-section of HRD. Most are experts and some are well known in the field. A few are high-profile authors who have made a tremendous contribution to HRD and have taken the opportunity to provide an example of their top-quality work. Others have made their mark quietly and have achieved success for their organizations. All of them are or will be highly successful in their field.

Best Practices?

In our search for cases, we contacted the most respected and well-known organizations in the world, leading experts in the field, key executives in HRD, and prominent authors and researchers. We were seeking examples that represent best practices in measurement and evaluation. Have they been delivered? We will leave that up to you, the reader. What we do know is that if these are not best practices, no other publication can claim to have them either. Many of the experts producing these cases characterize them as the best examples of measurement and evaluation in the field.

Suggestions

We welcome your input. If you have ideas or recommendations regarding presentation, case selection, or case quality, please send them to us at ROI Institute, Inc., P.O. Box 380637, Birmingham, Alabama, 30543, or send them via email to patti@roiinstitute.net.

Acknowledgments

Although this casebook is a collective work of many individuals, the first acknowledgment must go to all the case authors. They are appreciated not only for their commitment to developing their case studies, but also for their interest in furthering the development and implementation of ROI evaluation in their organizations. We also want to acknowledge the organizations that have allowed us to use their names and programs for publication. We realize this action is not without risk. We trust the final product has portrayed them as progressive organizations interested in results and willing to try new processes and techniques.

We would also like to thank Joyce Alff for her continued support and tireless effort to make all of our publications successful. Many thanks go to Suzanne Lawlor who provided assistance in the initial stages of producing this casebook. Also, much appreciation goes to Francine Hawkins who continues to support us in all of our efforts.

A special thanks goes to ASTD for their continued effort to provide the most current research and practice to the training profession.

Jack J. Phillips
Patricia Pulliam Phillips
May 2005

Introduction ————————————————————————————————

These cases present a variety of approaches to evaluating training and performance improvement programs in HRD. Most of the cases focus on evaluation at the ultimate level—return-on-investment (ROI). Collectively, the cases offer a wide range of settings, methods, techniques, strategies, and approaches. They represent manufacturing, service, and governmental organizations. Target groups for the programs vary from all employees to managers to technical specialists. Although most of the programs focus on training and development, others include organization development and performance management. As a group, these cases represent a rich source of information about the strategies of some of the best practitioners, consultants, and researchers in the field.

In every case it is possible to identify areas that could benefit from refinement and improvement. That is part of the learning process—to build on the work of other people. Nevertheless, all case studies follow the fundamental guiding principles that support the ROI Methodology. Although the implementation processes are contextual, the methods and techniques can be used in other organizations.

Table I-1 represents basic descriptions of the cases in the order in which they appear in the book. This table can serve as a quick reference for readers who want to examine the approach for implementing a particular type of program, audience, or industry.

Using the Cases

There are several ways to use this book. The book will be helpful to anyone who wants to see real-life examples of the ROI for training and performance improvement initiatives. Specifically, the editors recommend the following four uses:

1. This book will be useful to HRD professionals as a basic reference that demonstrates practical applications of measurement and evaluation. A reader can analyze and dissect each of the cases to develop an understanding of the issues, approaches, and, most of all, possible refinements or improvements.

2. This book will be useful in group discussions in which interested individuals can react to the material, offer different perspectives, and draw conclusions about approaches and techniques. The questions at the end of each case can serve as a beginning point for lively and entertaining discussions.

3. This book can serve as a supplement to other training and performance improvement or evaluation textbooks. It provides the extra dimensions of real-life cases that show the outcomes of training and performance improvement.

4. Finally, this book will be extremely valuable for managers who do not have primary training and performance improvement responsibility. These managers provide support and assistance to the HRD staff, and it is helpful for them to understand the results that HRD programs can yield.

It is important to remember that each organization and its program implementation are unique. What works well for one may not work for another, even if they are in similar settings. The book offers a variety of approaches and provides an arsenal of tools from which to choose in the evaluation process.

Follow-up

Space limitations necessitated that some cases be shorter than the author and editors would have liked. Some information concerning background, assumptions, strategies, and results had to be omitted. If additional information on a case is needed, the lead author can be contacted directly through the means identified at the end of each case.

Table I-1. Overview of case studies by industry, programs, and target audience.

Case	Chapter Number	Industry	HRD Program	Target Audience
AT&T Learning	2	Networking and telecommunications	New process training	Contract specialists
Central Plains Rural Electric Cooperative	3	Utility company	Leadership development	All utility employees
National Security Agency	4	Federal government	ASTD HPI Certificate program	Internal performance consultants, training professionals
Wachovia Mortgage Corporation	5	Financial services	Sales training	Mortgage consultants, sales managers
Bank of America	6	Financial services	Instructional design foundations	Bank associates responsible for learning development
Nations Hotel Company	7	Hotel management	ROI of coaching	Learning and development team, hotel executives
Ireland-Based Pharmaceutical Company	8	Pharmaceuticals	ROI of management training	Senior management, group leaders, HR department
TechnoTel, Inc.	9	Telecommunications equipment manufacturer	Impact of effective meeting skills	Managers and project leaders
BMW Manufacturing Company	10	Car manufacturing company	Measuring ROI of leadership program	Managers, coordinators, supervisors, level II–IV associates
Global Car Rental	11	Car rental company	Leadership development	First-level managers
Financial Services Company	12	Financial services	E-learning program for the sales academy	Sales associates

Chapter 1

MEASURING ROI

Jack J. Phillips and Patti P. Phillips

Measuring the return-on-investment (ROI) in learning and development (L&D) and performance improvement has earned a place among the critical issues in the human resource development (HRD) field. For almost a decade, ROI has been on conference agendas and the subject of professional meetings. Journals and newsletters regularly embrace the concept with increasing print space. At ASTD, a 500-member professional organization has been organized (the ROI Network) to exchange information on ROI. More than a dozen books provide significant coverage of the topic. Even top executives have stepped up their appetite for ROI information.

Measuring ROI is a topic of much debate. It is rare for any topic to stir emotions to the degree the ROI issue does. Return-on-investment is characterized as flawed and inappropriate by some, and others describe it as the only answer to their accountability concerns. The truth probably lies somewhere between. Understanding the drivers for the ROI Methodology and the inherent weaknesses and advantages of ROI makes it possible to take a rational approach to the issue and implement an approximate mix of evaluation strategies that includes ROI.

Although the interest in the topic has heightened and much progress has been made, it is still an issue that challenges even the most sophisticated and progressive L&D departments. While some professionals argue that it is not possible to calculate the ROI, others quietly and deliberately proceed to develop measures and ROI calculations. The latter group is gaining tremendous support from the senior management team and is making much progress. Regardless of the position taken on the issue, the reasons for measuring the return still exist. Almost all L&D professionals share a concern that they must eventually show a return on their learning investment. Otherwise, funds may be reduced or the L&D department may not be able to maintain or enhance its present status and influence in the organization.

The dilemma surrounding the ROI process is a source of frustration for many senior executives—and even within the L&D field itself. Most executives realize that learning is a basic necessity when organizations are experiencing significant growth or increased competition. They intuitively feel that there is value in providing learning opportunities, logically anticipating a payoff in important bottom-line measures

---

Adapted from *Return on Investment in Training and Performance Improvement Programs,* 2nd edition, by Jack J. Phillips, Butterworth-Heinemann, Boston, 2003, with permission from Elsevier.

such as productivity improvements, quality enhancements, cost reductions, and time savings. Yet the frustration comes from the lack of evidence to show that the process is really working. Although the payoffs are assumed to exist and learning programs appear to be necessary, more evidence is needed or funding may be adjusted in the future. The ROI Methodology represents the most promising way to show this accountability using a logical, rational approach.

Current Status

One thing is certain in the ROI debate: It is not a fad. As long as there is a need for accountability of learning expenditures and the concept of an investment payoff is desired, ROI will be used to evaluate major investments in learning and performance improvement.

A fad is a new idea or approach or a new spin on an old approach. The concept of ROI has been used for centuries. The 75th anniversary issue of *Harvard Business Review (HBR)* traced the tools used to measure results in organizations (Sibbet, 1997). In the early issues of *HBR*, during the 1920s, ROI was the emerging tool to place a value on the payoff of investments.

With increased adoption and use, ROI is here to stay. As highlighted in table 1-1, today more than 2,000 organizations are routinely developing ROI calculations for learning and performance improvement programs.

Specific applications began in a manufacturing sector, where ROI was easily developed. It migrated to the service sector, health care, the public sector, and now the educational sector is interested in ROI. Recent applications involve measuring the ROI for a graduate degree program, in-service teacher training, and continuing education programs at universities. The use of ROI in training organizations continues to grow. Among those included on *Training* magazine's 2004 list of the top 100 organizations, 75 percent are using the ROI Methodology (*Training*, 2004). A major study by the Corporate Executive Board indicated that ROI is the fastest growing metric in learning and development (L&D). It is also the metric that has the widest gap between actual use and desired use, underscoring the many misconceptions about ROI (Drimmer, 2002).

It is estimated that 5,000 studies are conducted each year globally by the organizations using the

---

Table 1-1. Summary of the current status of ROI use.

- The ROI Methodology has been refined over a 25-year period.

- The ROI Methodology has been adopted by more than 2,000 organizations in manufacturing, service, nonprofit, government, and educational settings.

- Some 5,000 studies are developed each year using the ROI Methodology.

- One hundred case studies have been published on the ROI Methodology.

- More than 2,500 individuals have been certified to implement the ROI Methodology in their organizations.

- Organizations in 40 countries have implemented the ROI Methodology.

- Fifteen books have been developed to support the process.

- A 500-member professional network has been formed to share information.

ROI Methodology. This number is based on the number of organizations that have participated directly in the certification for the ROI Methodology. At least 100 of these studies have been published in various case books and reference books on ROI. Some of these are included in journals and trade magazines. Many of the published ROI studies have very high ROI values, representing some of the most successful studies. High ROI values are achieved only when the learning program is needed, addresses a specific performance gap, and is applied and supported in the workplace.

At least 2,500 individuals have attended a five-day workshop to learn how to implement the ROI Methodology. Most of the individuals who have followed through with projects have become certified in ROI implementation. These individuals develop a particular project as part of a weeklong workshop, plan the evaluation, and communicate it to team members. The certification focuses on building competencies in 10 skill areas shown in table 1-2 (Phillips, 2004). These certification workshops have been conducted in most major cities in the United States and in more than a dozen other countries.

Table 1-2. Ten skill sets for certification.

- Planning for ROI calculations

- Collecting evaluation data

- Isolating the effects of training

- Converting data to monetary values

- Monitoring program costs

- Analyzing data, including calculating the ROI

- Presenting evaluation data

- Implementing the ROI process

- Providing internal consulting on ROI

- Teaching others the ROI process

Measuring ROI is becoming a global issue. To date, 40 countries have implemented the ROI Methodology, among them being Ireland, England, the Netherlands, Italy, Germany, Denmark, South Africa, Chile, Peru, Australia, New Zealand, Singapore, Malaysia, Japan, India, and Canada. Implementation is defined as a particular organization establishing a consulting practice for the ROI Methodology in partnerships to present workshops and provide consulting services. Also, as part of this implementation, an article on the ROI Methodology is usually featured in a prominent human resources and training and development publication in that country.

To date, 15 books have been developed to support the ROI Methodology; five complete casebooks are dedicated to the process, two of which are the all-time bestselling books for ASTD Press.

Perhaps one of the most highly visible signs of acceptance of the ROI Methodology is the ASTD ROI Network, which now claims over 500 members. Founded in 1996, the ROI Network was formed by a group of practitioners involved in implementing the ROI Methodology. The purpose of the organization is to promote the application and use of ROI and exchange information on ROI tools, templates, prac-

tices, and applications. In 2002, the Network was acquired by ASTD and operates as the ASTD ROI Network. The Network shares information through newsletters, email distribution lists, chat rooms, and conferences (ASTD.org).

Without a doubt, the ROI Methodology is now becoming a mainstream tool to show the bottom-line impact of human resources, L&D, and performance improvement initiatives.

Why ROI?

Why has ROI gained acceptance in so many industries in so short a time? Although the viewpoints and explanations may vary, some things are very clear. The key issues are outlined in the sections that follow.

Increased Budgets

While declining in some organizations (and virtually eliminated in others), for the most part, training and development budgets continue to grow year after year. As expenditures grow, accountability becomes a more critical issue. A growing budget creates a larger target for internal critics, often prompting the development of an ROI evaluation methodology. The function, department, or process showing the most value will likely receive the largest budget increase.

The Ultimate Level of Evaluation

The ROI Methodology adds a fifth level to the four levels of evaluation, which were developed almost 40 years ago (Kirkpatrick, 1975). Table 1-3 shows the five-level framework. At Level 1 (reaction and planned action), satisfaction from program participants is measured, along with a listing of how they plan to apply what they have learned. At Level 2 (learning), measurements focus on what participants learned during the program using tests, skill practices, role plays, simulations, group evaluations, and other assessment tools. At Level 3 (application and implementation), a variety of follow-up methods is used to determine if participants applied what they learned on the job. At Level 4 (business impact), the measurement focuses on the changes in the impact measures linked to the program. Typical Level 4 measures include output, quality, costs, time, and customer satisfaction. Level 5 (ROI) represents the ultimate level of evaluation. The ROI measurement compares the program's monetary benefits with the program costs. For many, the

Table 1-3. Five-level framework for evaluation.	
Level	**Brief Description**
1. Reaction and Planned Action	Measures participant's reaction to the program and outlines specific plans for implementation
2. Learning	Measures skills, knowledge, or attitude changes
3. Application and Implementation	Measures changes in behavior on-the-job and specific application and implementation
4. Business Impact	Measures business impact of the program
5. Return-on-Investment	Compares the monetary value of the results with the costs for the program, usually expressed as a percentage

evaluation cycle is not complete until the Level 5 evaluation is conducted.

ROI Is a Familiar Term

The business management mindset of many current L&D managers causes them to emphasize economic issues within the function. Today's chief learning officer (CLO) is more aware of bottom-line issues in the organization and more knowledgeable of operational and financial concerns. This enlightened manager often takes a business approach to L&D, with ROI being part of the strategy.

ROI is a familiar term and concept for these managers, particularly those with business administration and management degrees. They have studied ROI in their academic preparation in which ROI is used to evaluate the purchase of equipment, construction of a new facility, or acquisition of another company. Consequently, they understand and appreciate ROI and are pleased to see the ROI Methodology applied to the evaluation of learning and performance improvement.

Accountability Trend

There has been a persistent trend toward greater accountability in organizations all over the globe.

Every support function is attempting to show its worth by capturing the value that it adds to the organization. From the accountability perspective, the L&D function should be no different from the other functions—it, too, must show its contribution to the organization.

Top Executive Requirement

ROI is now taking on increased interest in the executive suite. Top executives who watched their training and learning budgets continue to grow without the appropriate accountability measures have become frustrated and, in an attempt to respond to the situation, have turned to ROI. Top executives are now demanding ROI calculations from departments and functions where they were not required previously. For years, training and development managers convinced top executives that the impact of training couldn't be measured, at least at the monetary contribution level. Yet, many of the executives are now aware that it can and is being measured in many organizations. Top executives are subsequently demanding the same accountability from their training and development functions.

ROI Best Practices

With the acceptance of ROI as a mainstream measurement tool for most L&D functions, the debate has shifted from *whether* ROI should be conducted to *how* it should be conducted on a consistent, standardized basis. As a result, best practices for ROI have been identified. Table 1-4 shows the best practices collected from data involving several hundred organizations using the ROI Methodology. These are the organizations that have specifically determined to implement the ROI Methodology and have sent one or more individuals through ROI certification. The best practices reflect their use of the ROI Methodology and reveal the comprehensive, integrated approach that is feasible, realistic, and achievable within most budget constraints.

Barriers to ROI Implementation

Although progress has been made in the implementation of ROI, significant barriers inhibit the implementation of the concept. Some of these barriers are realistic, but others are myths based on false perceptions. Each barrier is briefly described in the following sections.

Table 1-4. ROI best practices.

- . The ROI Methodology is implemented as a process improvement tool and not a performance evaluation tool for the learning/development staff.

- ROI impact studies are conducted very selectively, usually involving 5 to 10 percent of programs.

- A variety of data collection methods are used in ROI analysis.

- For a specific ROI evaluation, the effects of learning/development are isolated from other influences.

- Business impact data is converted to monetary values.

- ROI evaluation targets are developed, showing the percentage of programs evaluated at each level.

- The ROI Methodology generates a micro-level scorecard.

- ROI Methodology data are being integrated to create a macro scorecard for the learning/ development function.

- The ROI Methodology is being implemented for about 3 to 5 percent of the learning/development budget.

- ROI forecasting is being implemented routinely.

- The ROI Methodology is used as a tool to strengthen or improve the learning/education process.

Costs and Time

The ROI Methodology does add cost and time to the evaluation process of programs, although the added amount is not excessive. A comprehensive ROI process can be implemented for 3 to 5 percent of the overall training budget. This barrier alone often stops many ROI implementations early in the process. The additional investment in ROI could perhaps be offset by the additional results achieved from these programs and the elimination of unproductive or unprofitable programs.

Lack of Skills and Orientation

Many learning and performance improvement staff members neither understand ROI nor do they have the basic skills necessary to apply the process within their scope of responsibilities. Measurement and eval-

uation is not usually part of the preparation for the job. Also, the typical learning program does not focus on results, but more on the learning process. Staff members attempt to measure results by measuring learning. Consequently, a tremendous barrier to implementation is the change needed for the overall orientation, attitude, and skills of the L&D staff.

Faulty Needs Assessment

Many existing programs are not based on an adequate needs assessment. Some programs have been implemented for the wrong reasons based on management requests or efforts to chase a popular fad or trend in the industry. If the program is not needed, the benefits from the program will be minimal. An ROI calculation for an unnecessary program will likely yield a negative value. This is a realistic barrier for many programs.

Fear

Some L&D departments do not pursue ROI because of fear of failure or fear of the unknown. Fear of failure appears in many ways. Designers, developers, facilitators, and program owners may be concerned about the consequences of a negative ROI. They fear that ROI will be a performance evaluation tool instead of a process improvement tool. Also, the ROI process will stir up the traditional fear of change. This fear, often based on unrealistic assumptions and a lack of knowledge of the process, becomes a realistic barrier to many ROI implementations.

Discipline and Planning

A successful ROI implementation requires much planning and a disciplined approach to keep the process on track. Implementation schedules, evaluation targets, ROI analysis plans, measurement and evaluation policies, and follow-up schedules are required. The learning team may not have enough discipline and determination to stay on course. This becomes a barrier, particularly if there are no immediate pressures to measure the return. If the current senior management group is not requiring ROI, the learning team may not allocate time for planning and coordination. Also, other pressures and priorities often eat into the time necessary for ROI implementation. Only carefully planned implementation succeeds.

False Assumptions

Many L&D staff members have false assumptions about the ROI process that keep them from attempting ROI.

Typical of these assumptions are the following:

- The impact of learning cannot be accurately calculated.
- Operating managers do not want to see the results of L&D expressed in monetary values.
- If the CEO does not ask for the ROI, he or she is not expecting it.
- "I have a professional, competent staff. Therefore, I do not have to justify the effectiveness of our programs."
- Learning is a complex but necessary activity. Therefore, it should not be subjected to an accountability process.

These false assumptions form perceptible barriers that impede the progress of ROI implementation.

Benefits of ROI

Although the benefits of implementing the ROI Methodology may appear obvious, several distinct and important benefits can be realized. These benefits are outlined in the following sections.

Measure Contribution

The ROI Methodology is the most accurate, credible, and widely used process to show the impact of learning. The learning team will know the specific contribution from a select number of programs. An ROI study will determine if the benefits of the program, expressed in monetary values, have outweighed the costs. It will determine if the program made a contribution to the organization.

Establish Priorities

Calculating ROI in different areas can show which programs contribute the most to the organization, allowing priorities to be established for high-impact learning. Successful programs can be expanded into other areas—if the same need is there—ahead of other programs. Inefficient programs can be redesigned and redeployed. Ineffective programs can be discontinued.

Focus on Results

The ROI Methodology is a results-based process that brings a focus on results with all programs, even for those not targeted for an ROI calculation. The process requires instructional designers, facilitators, partici-pants, and support groups to concentrate on measurable objectives: what the program is attempting to accomplish. Thus, this process has the added benefit of improving the effectiveness of all L&D programs.

Earn Respect of Senior Executives and the Sponsor

Developing the ROI information is one of the best ways to earn the respect of the senior management team and the sponsor (the person who really cares about the program). Senior executives have a never-ending desire to see ROI. They will appreciate the efforts to connect training to business impact and show the actual monetary value. It makes them feel comfortable with the process and makes their decisions much easier. Sponsors who often support, approve, or initiate training and development or performance improvement programs see the ROI as a breath of fresh air. They are able to see the value of the learning in terms they understand and appreciate.

Alter Management's Perceptions of L&D

The ROI Methodology, when applied consistently and comprehensively, can convince the management group that learning is an investment and not an expense. Managers then can see L&D as making a viable contribution to their objectives, thus increasing the respect for the function. This is an important step in building a partnership with management and increasing management support for L&D.

These key benefits, inherent with almost any type of impact evaluation process, make the ROI process an attractive challenge for the HRD function.

The ROI Model

The calculation of ROI follows the basic model illustrated in figure 1-1, which shows how a potentially complicated process can be simplified with sequential steps. The ROI model provides a systematic approach to ROI calculations. A step-by-step approach keeps the process manageable so that users can tackle one issue at a time. The model also emphasizes that this is a logical, systematic process that flows from one step to another. Applying the model provides consistency from one ROI calculation to another. Each step of the model is briefly described here.

Figure 1-1. The ROI process model.

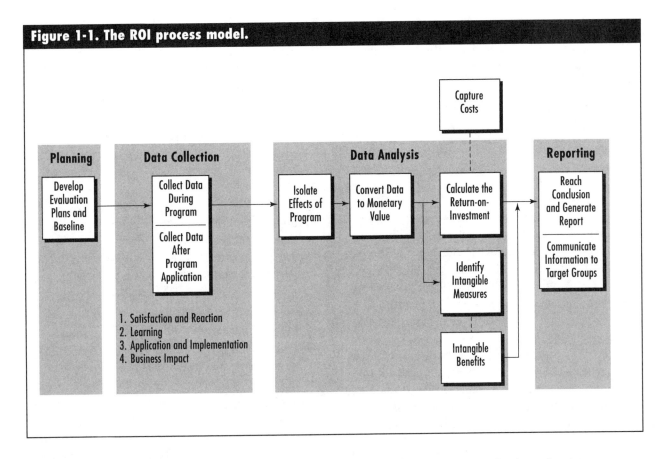

Planning Evaluation

Three specific elements are important to evaluation success and are outlined in this section. They are purpose, feasibility, and objectives of the L&D programs.

Purpose

Although evaluation is usually undertaken to improve the L&D process, several distinct purposes can be identified. Evaluation is planned to:

- improve the quality of learning and outcomes
- determine if a program is accomplishing its objectives
- identify the strengths and weaknesses in the learning process
- perform a benefit-cost analysis for an L&D program
- assist in marketing L&D programs in the future
- determine if the program was appropriate for the target audience
- establish a database that can assist in making decisions about the programs
- set priorities for funding.

For most programs, multiple evaluation purposes are pursued.

Feasibility

During the planning stage, the feasibility for a business impact or ROI study should be examined. Relevant questions to address are:

- What specific measures have been influenced with this program?
- Are those measures readily available?
- Can the effect of the program on those measures be isolated?
- Are the costs of the program readily available?
- Will it be practical and feasible to discuss costs?
- Can the impact data be converted to monetary value?
- Is the actual ROI needed or necessary?

These and other questions are important to examine during the planning process to ensure that the evaluation is appropriate for the program.

Objectives of Programs

L&D programs are evaluated at different levels as described earlier. Corresponding to the levels of evaluation are levels of objectives:

- reaction and satisfaction objectives (Level 1)
- learning objectives (Level 2)
- application objectives (Level 3)
- impact objectives (Level 4)
- ROI objectives (Level 5).

Before ROI evaluation begins, program objectives must be identified or developed. Program objectives link directly to the front-end analysis. The objectives form the basis for determining the depth and the level of evaluation. Historically, learning objectives are routinely developed. Application and impact objectives are not always in place, but they are necessary for the proper focus on results.

Tied very closely to setting objectives is the timing of the data collection. In some cases, pre-program measurements are taken to compare with post-program measures and, in some cases, multiple measures are taken. In other situations, pre-program measurements are not available and specific follow-ups are still taken after the program. The important issue is to determine the timing for the follow-up evaluation.

Evaluation Plans

To complete the planning process, three simple planning documents are developed: the data collection plan, the ROI analysis plan, and the project plan. These documents should be completed before the evaluation project is implemented—ideally before the program is designed or developed. Appropriate, upfront attention can save much time later when the data is actually collected. The documents are usually included in the published case studies.

Collecting Data

Data collection is central to the ROI Methodology. Both hard data (for example, output, quality, cost, and time) and soft data (for example, job satisfaction and customer satisfaction) are collected. Data can be collected using a variety of methods including the following:

- *Surveys* are taken to determine the extent to which participants are satisfied with the program, have learned skills and knowledge, and have utilized various aspects of the program.
- *Questionnaires* are usually more detailed than surveys and can be used to uncover a wide

variety of data. Participants provide responses to several types of open-ended and forced-response questions.

- *Tests* are conducted to measure changes in knowledge and skills (Level 2). Tests come in a wide variety of formal (criterion-referenced tests, performance tests and simulations, and skill practices) and informal (facilitator assessment, self-assessment, and team assessment) methods.
- *On-the-job observation* captures actual skill application and use. Observations are particularly useful in customer service training and are more effective when the observer is either invisible or transparent.
- *Interviews* are conducted with participants to determine the extent to which learning has been utilized on the job.
- *Focus groups* are conducted to determine the degree to which a group of participants has applied the training to job situations.
- *Action plans and program assignments* are developed by participants during the program and are implemented on the job after the program is completed. Follow-ups provide evidence of program success.
- *Performance contracts* are developed by the participant, the participant's supervisor, and the facilitator who all agree on job performance outcomes.
- *Business performance monitoring* is useful where various performance records and operational data are examined for improvement.

The important challenge in data collection is to select the method or methods appropriate for the setting and the specific program, within the constraints of the organization.

Analyzing Data

Isolating the Effects of Learning and Development

An often overlooked issue in most evaluations is the process of isolating the effects of L&D. In this step of the process, specific strategies are explored to determine the amount of output performance directly related to the program. This step is essential because there are many factors that usually influence performance data after an L&D program is conducted. Specific strategies taken in this step will pinpoint the amount of improvement directly related to the program, resulting in increased accuracy and credibility of ROI calculations. The following techniques have been used by organizations to address this important issue:

- A control group arrangement is used to isolate learning's impact. With this strategy, one group participates in a program, but another, similar group does not. The difference in the performance of the two groups can be attributed to the program. When properly set up and implemented, the control group arrangement is the most effective way to isolate the effects of L&D.

- Trend lines are used to project the values of specific output variables as if the learning program had not been undertaken. The projection is compared to the actual data after the program is conducted, and the difference represents the estimate of the impact of learning. Under certain conditions, this strategy can accurately isolate the impact of learning.

- When mathematical relationships between input and output variables are known, a forecasting model can be used to isolate the effects of learning. With this approach, the output variable is predicted using the forecasting model with the assumption that no learning program is conducted. The actual performance of the variable after the program is conducted is compared with the forecasted value, which results in an estimate of the impact of learning.

- Participants estimate the amount of improvement related to the L&D program. With this approach, participants are provided with the total amount of improvement, on a pre- and post-program basis, and are asked to indicate the percentage of the improvement that is actually related to the program.

- Supervisors or managers estimate the impact of learning on the output variables. With this approach, supervisors or managers are presented with the total amount of improvement and are asked to indicate the percent related to learning. The estimates are adjusted for the error of the estimates.

- Experts provide estimates of the impact of learning on the performance variable. Because the estimates are based on previous experience, the experts must be familiar with the type of program and the specific situation.

- When feasible, other influencing factors are identified and the impact estimated or calculated, leaving the remaining, unexplained improvement attributed to learning.

- In some situations, customers provide input as to the extent to which training or learning has influenced their decision to use a product or service. Although this strategy has limited applications, it can be quite useful in customer service and sales training.

Collectively, these techniques provide a comprehensive set of tools to tackle this important issue.

Converting Data to Monetary Values

To calculate ROI, business impact data collected in the evaluation is converted to monetary values and compared to program costs. This requires that a value be placed on each unit of data connected with the program. Several techniques are available to convert data to monetary values:

- Output data is converted to profit contribution or cost savings, based on the unit contribution to profit or the unit contribution to cost reduction. Standard values for these items are readily available in most organizations.

- The cost of quality is calculated, and quality improvements are directly converted to cost savings. Standard values for these items are available in many organizations.

- For programs that result in saving employee time, the participants' wages and employee benefits are used to develop the value for time. This is a standard formula in most organizations.

- Historical costs, developed from cost statements, are used when they are available for a specific variable. In this case, organizational cost data establishes the specific monetary cost savings of an improvement.

- When available, internal and external experts may be used to estimate a value for an improvement.

- External databases are sometimes available to estimate the value or cost of data items. Research, government, and industry databases—usually available on the Internet—can provide important information for these values.

- Participants estimate the value of the data item. For this approach to be effective, participants must be capable of providing a value for the improvement.

- Supervisors and managers provide estimates when they are both willing and capable of assigning values to the improvement.

- Soft measures are linked mathematically to other measures that are easier to measure and value. This approach is particularly helpful when establishing values for measures that are very difficult to convert to monetary values but have linkages to other measures.

- L&D staff estimates may be used to determine a value of an output data item.

This step in the ROI model is necessary for determining the monetary benefits from a learning program. The process is challenging, particularly with soft data, but can be methodically accomplished using one or more of these strategies.

Tabulating Costs of the Program

The other part of the ROI equation is the program cost. Tabulating the costs involves monitoring or developing all of the related costs of the program targeted for the ROI calculation. Among the cost components that should be included are

- the cost to design and develop the program, possibly prorated over the expected life of the program

- the cost of all program materials provided to each participant

- the cost for the instructor or facilitator, including preparation time as well as delivery time

- the cost of the facilities for the learning program

- travel, lodging, and meal costs for the participants, if applicable

- salaries, plus employee benefits of the participants who participated in the learning program

- administrative and overhead costs of the L&D function, allocated in some convenient way.

In addition, specific costs related to the needs assessment and evaluation should be included, if appropriate. The conservative approach is to include all these costs so that the total is fully loaded.

Calculating the ROI

The ROI is calculated using the program benefits and costs. The benefit-cost ratio (BCR) is the program benefits divided by cost. In formula form it is:

$$BCR = \frac{\text{Program Benefits}}{\text{Program Costs}}$$

The ROI calculation uses the net benefits divided by program costs. The net benefits are the program benefits minus the costs. In formula form, the ROI becomes:

$$ROI\,(\%) = \frac{\text{Net Program Benefits}}{\text{Program Costs}} \times 100$$

This is the same basic formula used in evaluating other investments for which ROI is traditionally reported as earnings divided by investment.

Identifying Intangible Benefits

In addition to tangible, monetary benefits, most learning programs will have intangible, nonmonetary benefits. The ROI calculation is based on converting both hard and soft data to monetary values. Intangible benefits include such items as:

- increased job satisfaction
- increased organizational commitment
- improved teamwork
- improved customer service
- reduced complaints
- reduced conflicts.

During data analysis, every attempt is made to convert all data to monetary values. All hard data such as output, quality, and time are converted to monetary values. The conversion of soft data is attempted for each data item. However, if the process used for conversion is too subjective or inaccurate and the resulting values lose credibility in the process, then the data is listed as an intangible benefit with the appropriate explanation. For some programs, intangible, non-monetary benefits are extremely valuable, often carrying as much influence as the hard data items.

Reporting Data

The final step in the ROI model is reporting. This very critical step often lacks the proper attention and planning to ensure that it is successful. This step involves developing appropriate information in impact studies and other brief reports. The heart of the step includes the different techniques used to communicate to a wide variety of target audiences. In most ROI studies, several audiences are interested in and need the information. Careful planning to match the communication method with the audience is essential to ensure that the message is understood and appropriate actions follow.

Operating Standards and Philosophy

To ensure consistency and replication of impact studies, operating standards must be developed and applied as the process model is utilized to develop ROI studies. It is extremely important for the results of a study to stand alone and not vary depending on the individual conducting the study. The operating standards detail how each step and issue of the process will be addressed. Table 1-5 shows the 12 guiding principles that form the basis for the operating standards.

These guiding principles not only serve as a way to consistently address each step, but also provide a much needed conservative approach to the analysis. A conservative approach may lower the actual ROI calculation, but it will build credibility with the target audience.

Implementation Issues

A variety of environmental issues and events influence the successful implementation of the ROI Methodology. These issues must be addressed early to ensure that the process is successful. Specific implementation issues that can lead to ROI success include the following:

- a policy statement concerning results-based training and development
- procedures and guidelines for different elements and techniques of the evaluation process
- meetings and formal sessions to develop staff skills with the ROI Methodology
- strategies to improve management commitment and support for the ROI Methodology
- mechanisms to provide technical support for questionnaire design, data analysis, and evaluation strategy
- specific techniques to place more attention on results.

Final Thoughts

Although there is almost universal agreement that more attention is needed on ROI, it is promising to note the tremendous success of ROI. Its use is expanding. Its payoff is huge. The process is not very difficult or impossible. The approaches, strategies, and techniques are not overly complex and can be useful in a variety of settings. The combined and persistent efforts of practitioners and researchers will continue to refine the techniques and create successful applications.

Table 1-5. The guiding principles.

1. When a higher-level evaluation is conducted, data must be collected at lower levels.

2. When an evaluation is planned for a higher level, the previous level of evaluation does not have to be comprehensive.

3. When collecting and analyzing data, use only the most credible source.

4. When analyzing data, choose the most conservative among the alternatives.

5. At least one method must be used to isolate the effects of the solution.

6. If no improvement data is available for a population or from a specific source, it is assumed that little or no improvement has occurred.

7. Estimates of improvements should be adjusted (discounted) for the potential error of the estimate.

8. Extreme data items and unsupported claims should not be used in ROI calculations.

9. Only the first year of benefits (annual) should be used in the ROI analysis of short-term solutions.

10. Costs of the solution should be fully loaded for ROI analysis.

11. Intangible measures are defined as measures that are purposely not converted to monetary values.

12. The results from the ROI methodology must be communicated to all key stakeholders.

Chapter 2

This case was prepared to serve as a basis for discussion rather than to illustrate either effective or ineffective administrative and management practices.

CONTRACT SPECIALIST EMPOWERMENT

AT&T Learning

Jane M. Ray and Lynne E. Motto

System enhancements and process improvements are a fact of life for a large networking and telecommunications company. Although training is done to support the introduction of these new tools and processes, identifying the impact training has on improving the business is challenging. One group of process engineers, however, was able to provide clearly defined goals for reducing the interval within the contract cycle, allowing for the calculation of monetary savings for the company and ROI for the training organization.

Background

Networking and communications companies in the United States have been facing stiff competition for many years. Protecting revenue, generating net new revenue, and maintaining customer satisfaction have been a major focus. To support those goals, AT&T has been rigorously streamlining processes, increasing automation, and moving work closer to field operations in an effort to get services provisioned and billed earlier. In particular, the sales centers within AT&T have been affected by these activities.

Searching for opportunities to work more effectively, the contract and billing process team identified an opportunity to gain efficiencies within the sales centers that support custom contracts. These contracts are for high-profile clients and receive intense scrutiny from the time the contract is created and signed by the client until the contract is signed by the sales center vice president (SCVP), making the offer official. Process engineers recognized an opportunity to shorten the time period between client signature and SCVP signature by bringing certain functionality into the sales centers.

A new process introduced in March 2004 directly affected the contract specialists (CS), a small group of individuals based in the sales centers throughout the United States. This new process permitted SCVPs to sign custom contracts in the sales centers rather than sending them to headquarters for review, authorization, and signature. Contract specialists were introduced to the functions in the post-customer-signature (PCS) system, which was being used by an organization at AT&T headquarters. The CS received contract information from the sales teams, reviewed the documents to ensure that specific information was entered and that specific elements were in the contract, and then entered the documents into PCS. The documents were transmitted electronically to billing managers for final review and approval. Then, the CS assembled a package for the SCVP to review and sign.

AT&T's ability to support good customer contracts had the support of many senior SCVPs. This support was valuable to the learning organization as we progressed through the project. The CS's role was viewed as a critical, integral part of the whole customer experience. A certification plan was created for the CS, and this training event was to be the first part of a companywide campaign that would introduce the plan.

Business Impact

An average interval for custom contracts from client signature to SCVP sign-off was 12 days. Using the new process, expectations were that there would be no degradation in cycle time and that a two-day reduction would be realized at the beginning of the rollout (10 to 12 days within the first month of the rollout) and a reduction of four days by the year's end. This would be a 33 percent improvement from client signature to SCVP signature, with the long-range impact being accelerated billing. The client organization had benchmarking data to support this information and a team that would track the data during the campaign.

A second area of focus was on contract quality. Contract quality after implementation of the new process and system was to be maintained or improved for the remainder of the year. Additionally, because contracts would now be transmitted electronically to headquarters for review, the company would save at least $170,000 yearly in postage.

The Learning Solution

Because AT&T Learning was contacted early in the program, it was possible to review all the methods and procedures, gain access to the new system, and observe a controlled introduction (CI) session offered by the process engineers to a small number of CS. This group of selected individuals performed user acceptance testing on the new system for two months in preparation for general availability.

The target audience for this training event was 50 people. There was a one-month window in which to deliver the training. In addition to attending the process review and CI session, AT&T Learning interviewed high performers involved in the acceptance testing for feedback as to what was working well, which areas needed strong focus during the instruction, and any recommendations they had to enhance the learning experience.

Based on all the input that the AT&T Learning team gathered, a recommendation was made to create a virtual instructor-led session. A half-day session delivered via a Web meeting was proposed rather than a self-paced, Web-based event. Method and procedure content was supplemented with visuals, graphics, practice exercises, and an end-of-course evaluation. Along with the instructor-led course, there was a self-led component available through which learners could access the PCS system for skill work.

Given the audience size and the fact that this learning event did not need to be maintained after the target audience was engaged, the most cost-effective solution was a distance-learning event. All content was reviewed with pre-identified resources throughout the development cycle. A pilot session was held two weeks prior to the go-live date, and, again, feedback was gathered and incorporated into the course where appropriate.

Scheduling and Delivering the Solution

The client handled communications for the training event. The learning organization prepared a delivery schedule; the client selected learners by region to attend and then sent out notices to the learners. A subject matter expert (SME) attended each training event, and learners had an opportunity to do some hands-on practice in the tool before they were given a system ID and were using it real time. Two days after each training event, an open-mike session was held with the process team to discuss any problems that were encountered during the use of the tool.

Performance Improvement

Although some of the contract specialists currently were reviewing the custom contracts initiated by sales, after the implementation of the new process and tool, the CS would

- analyze the contract packages and validate the information in predetermined critical fields
- create a PCS record
- apply the accept/reject distribution process for each record
- assemble a complete package of documents for SCVP signature
- organize documents for distribution after receiving a counter-signature.

Using these goals, Level 2 course objectives were created and approved by the client prior to development starting. These skill/knowledge objectives were:

- Describe the process for contract package validation before implementation of the PCS system.
- Outline the steps involved in the creation of the PCS record process.
- Identify the criterion that determines a package to be "accepted" or "rejected."
- Determine steps for obtaining counter-signature.
- Distinguish between correct and incorrect documents needed to compile a complete package for SCVP signature.
- Explain the process for compiling documents and identify appropriate email broadcast for post-counter-signature distribution.
- Recognize the process for contract tracking from post-counter-signature distribution to biller load.

Evaluation Design

As part of the front-end analysis of client learning requests, AT&T Learning mandates that Levels 3 and 4 objectives be documented for every project, along with a basic description of how the achievement of these objectives can be evaluated. Based on this information, a measurement plan must be created before the design of the learning event begins. This plan provides detailed instructions for carrying out all the evaluation activities for the project, including

- what data is to be reported at each level of evaluation
- data collection instruments to be developed and administered (surveys, questionnaires, interview guides, performance checklists, and so forth)

- client metric reports to be accessed and data points to be examined
- techniques to be used to isolate the effects of the training on job performance and on specific metrics
- description of how any improvements in the business or performance results can be converted to monetary values
- individuals responsible for the various evaluation activities
- timelines for the activities involved in data collection, analysis, and reporting of results.

Level 4

Because this was an important, high-visibility business project, the client organization and the process teams had already collected detailed baseline metrics relating to cycle time for contract sign-off and to contract defects. Although the learning organization has the goal of measuring the business impact of all learning initiatives, and all groups within AT&T routinely publish a vast amount of metrics on the performance of their systems and work functions, it is not always easy to identify the metrics that closely reflect the work activities to be changed by learning, or to estimate the effect of the training on outcomes to which multiple groups and individuals contribute. But, for the Contract Specialist Empowerment project, validated Level 4 objectives and measurements were readily available from the client organization to show the following:

- the average number of days between the customer signing of a custom contract and the submission of the contract to headquarters for the six months preceding training (the overall baseline to be reduced by the implementation of the new process)
- this same number for each of the three months beginning with the first training session in May
- the percentage of custom contracts meeting all requirements for accuracy and completeness for the same time periods before and after training.

It was significant that these numbers were already published in presentations to AT&T business unit executives in the client organization when AT&T Learning used them in the evaluation report, so the metrics were familiar and validated at a high level. This enhanced the credibility of the learning evaluation results.

The Contract Specialist Empowerment training was one of several factors that would influence contract cycle time and quality. Not only would there be other supports for the new work activities (for example, online documentation and coaching, individual performance incentives and rewards for outstanding performance of this role), but also a significant part of the improvement would result from the new process itself. The client team was in a position to know all the relative contributions of these various influences on contract cycle time and quality at the time the new function was implemented. Their expert estimate was that 30 percent of any reduction in the cycle time could be attributed to the training.

Level 3

To determine if the CS in the sales centers were performing the newly assigned functions, all 50 learners were asked to complete a follow-up survey one month after finishing the learning event. The client organization specifically asked that the follow-up be minimally disruptive to the learners' work; and a short survey that could be taken at any time during the workday best met this requirement. The questions on the survey were reviewed and approved by the client SMEs to verify that they correctly described the key behaviors to be supported by the course.

The survey was accessible via the company intranet, and comprised nine questions asking participants to:

- Use a five-point scale to rate how effectively they were able to perform each of the required activities on the job.
- Explain any difficulties they had in performing these activities.
- Check off which environmental factors (if any) interfered with their performance of the job. Choices included system problems, system usability, confusing or incomplete methods and procedures, lack of on-the-job support, or other.

It was recognized that the formal training delivered by the learning organization was only one enabler of the new behavior. Examinations of how people learn to perform their jobs have shown that, on average, employees attribute less than half of their competency to training. Accordingly, the CS

were asked to estimate what percentage of their ability to perform their new functions came from the training by allocating 100 percent among these supports:

- training in the Contract Specialist Empowerment course
- help from supervisor, peers, or SMEs
- previous experience doing similar work
- online documentation or other performance support tools
- other (to be described by the respondent).

Because AT&T Learning staff have consistently found that surveys get a high rate of response when the request comes from their own group (rather than the training organization), the emails to the learners were sent by the client sponsor. The respondents were assured that all their input would be anonymous, and the survey did not even include a field for the participant's name.

Level 2

Learners' mastery of the course content was assessed by a 12-question test presented online at the end of the course via the learning management system (LMS). Tests were scored automatically and pass/fail status reported to the participant in real time. The LMS calculated test results for all sessions of the course and displayed online reports showing

- number of learners who attempted the test
- number of learners who passed
- average number of attempts before passing
- percentage of learners who passed the test
- high and low scores overall
- average percentage of correct responses.

Level 1

Learner reactions were captured via the standard learner satisfaction questionnaire used for instructor-led distance learning events (table 2-1). Scores were available for individual learners, for particular sessions, and for the course overall.

Evaluation Results

The results showed a strong, consistent, and positive chain of impact at all the levels where evaluation was performed, starting with the 100 percent participation in the training by the CS target audience,

Table 2-1. Responses to the AT&T learning organization's learner satisfaction questionnaire.*

Key Questions	Strongly Agree	Agree	Neutral	Disagree
I am confident I will be able to apply the skills I have learned in this course on my job.	69%	25%	0%	0%
This course effectively addressed the identified learning objectives.	81%	13%	0%	0%
I would consider the course materials relevant and useful.	81%	13%	0%	0%
I consider the instructor effective.	75%	13%	0%	0%
	Excellent	**Very Good**	**Average**	**Fair / Poor**
Overall, I would rate this learning experience:	63%	37%	0%	0%

* Not all participants responded to all items; therefore, the percentages do not add up to 100%.

their positive reaction to the learning experience, 100 percent passing the posttest, successful performance of the new job functions, reductions in process time, achievement of quality targets for contracts, and positive ROI.

Reaction

The learners' immediate end-of-class reaction to all aspects of the learning event was very positive:

- All of them were confident they would be able to apply the skills on the job.
- All agreed (with 81 percent strongly agreeing) that the course met its objective.
- They all found the course materials relevant and useful.
- Sixty-three percent rated the course excellent overall, and the remaining 37 percent said it was very good. This is much higher than the average score on this question.
- Learners' comments indicated that the live demonstration of all steps involved with using the PCS tool was of particular value.

Learning

All learners passed the test, averaging 1.13 attempts. Although the required passing score was 80 percent, the actual average score was 91 percent. Item analysis did not show the learning event was weak in any particular skill/knowledge areas.

Job Performance

A total of 22 participants completed surveys reporting their posttraining job performance. This figure corresponds to a response rate of 44 percent, which the client sponsor felt was adequate to draw conclusions about work behavior—particularly because the target metrics were reflective of the desired performance.

Contract specialists' self-reports of their ability to perform the critical activities for their new role were very positive:

- All of them were able to analyze contract packages, validate the information in the critical fields, and enter the required contract data in the PCS system.
- Ninety-five percent could assemble a complete package of documents for SCVP signature.
- Ninety-one percent could organize documents for post-counter-signature distribution.
- Eighty-seven percent could apply the accept/reject distribution process for each record.

The participants estimated that the greatest contribution to their ability to perform these functions came from the Contract Specialist Empowerment training, averaging 36 percent. Other performance supports were

- help from supervisor, peers, or SME (20 percent)
- online documentation or other performance support tools (19 percent)

- previous experience doing similar work (18 percent).

Two-thirds of the participants reported that they had no difficulties performing these new functions. The other third cited barriers such as:

- incomplete or confusing processes and procedures (mentioned by 14 percent of the respondents)
- insufficient on-the-job support from supervisor, SMEs, and others (9 percent)
- technical problems with the systems (5 percent).

Business Impact

The cycle time for custom contracts from the time the customer signs the contract to the date the contract is submitted to headquarters showed a steady decrease month over month since the training began (table 2-2):

- The average number of days has been reduced from 11.68 to 9.03.
- Cycle time was reduced by 2.65 days.
- Cycle time was reduced by 23 percent.

The client revalidated its estimate that 30 percent of the reduction in overall cycle time from customer signature to submission to headquarters was due to the training provided by AT&T Learning. After applying this isolation percentage, the result was that the reduction in overall custom contract cycle time due to training was 0.80 days.

The results around contract quality were not as consistent and required interpretation by the client's SMEs responsible for analyzing defects. Contract accuracy was significantly above target for May and June but declined to below target in July (table 2-3).

Table 2-2. Cycle time for contracts pre- and posttraining.			
Average Number of Days From Customer Signature to Receipt at Headquarters*			
Baseline	**May**	**June**	**July**
11.68 days	10.96 days	10.72 days	9.03 days

* Contract Specialist Empowerment training began in May.

Table 2-3. Contract quality pre- and posttraining.			
Total Percentage of Custom Contracts With No Defects*			
Baseline	**May**	**June**	**July**
85%	91%	98%	84%

* Contract Specialist Empowerment training began in May.

However, the client SME stated that the decline in the average percentage of accurate contracts in July was largely due to system problems rather than errors by the CS. His statement, based on root cause analysis of contract defects detected, was: "The bottom line is that the quality of the contract specialist work has not degraded by moving some of the functions to the branches. The quality of the CS work is on target and continues to improve."

ROI

Calculating the ROI required AT&T Learning to calculate the fully loaded program costs as well as the benefits attributable to the Contract Specialist Empowerment training.

Program Costs

The total cost of the training program was computed by using the loaded labor rate per employee times the number of hours spent by the AT&T Learning organization to identify requirements, design, develop, deliver, and perform formative evaluation of the course. The total also included prorated expenses for summative evaluation and infrastructure (including the LMS and technology to deliver training via the intranet to the remote audience). The final amount totaled $10,323.

Costs were relatively low because the business requirements, objectives, and measurements were already clearly defined by the client team; much of the course content had already been assembled by the client process team; and there were no travel and living expenses for the instructor for the five sessions of the course because it was delivered via technology to a remote audience.

The $9,600 cost of students' loaded salaries while in training was also included in the total training expenses. This calculation was based on an average of $384 per day per employee, divided by two (because the training was a half-day), times the number of students (50) who attended the sessions.

Including all the expenses described above, the total cost of the training was $19,923.

Benefits

The major financial benefit to be achieved by reducing the time for contract signature can be attributed to the fact that the requested customer services can be provisioned and billed earlier, and revenue can be collected earlier. Because the average annual value of a custom contract can reach $1 million, advancing the billing by even a single day can have significant monetary impact.

A conservative approach was used in calculating the projected benefits:

- The lowest average custom contract value was used to compute a daily value of $1,370.

- Although the average reduction in contract signing cycle time was 2.65 days over all, AT&T Learning staff assumed that only half the contracts achieved this reduction.

- The number of actual contracts signed in only one month was used in the ROI computation, rather than annualized benefits. The month used was the one after the entire CS audience completed training and performing all required functions. This was done because contract volumes fluctuate greatly due to business conditions.

Based on these assumptions, ROI was calculated as follows:

- One hundred seventy-seven contracts processed by the CS were signed in the first fully productive month after training.
- Half of these contracts (88) had a cycle time reduction.
- Average cycle time reduction for these 88 contracts was 2.65 days.
- Average daily value per contract was $1,370. Therefore:

$$88 \text{ contracts} \times 2.65 \text{ days} \times \$1,370/\text{day} = \$319,484 \text{ accelerated billing}$$

- Average savings in postage (because these contracts no longer need to be mailed) was $14,167 per month.
- Total monthly benefit to the business: $333,651.
- Client estimated that 30 percent of this benefit was due to training: $100,095.

Subtracting the $19,923 total cost of the training as described above, the net benefit is $80,172.

$$\frac{\text{Total Benefits} - \text{Program Costs}}{\text{Program Costs}} \times 100 = \frac{\$100,095 - \$19,923}{\$19,923} \times 100$$

$$= 402\% \text{ ROI}$$

Summary of Results

After more than a month using the new tool and process, the business expectations were realized:

- Contract specialists were using the new system and process effectively and were able to reduce cycle time to better than the target set for system rollout.
- Contract specialists are divided into four groups based on the clients they support. All four groups showed at least a two-day improvement in their cycle time numbers.
- Individual CS maintained contract quality. System errors were generated initially but were eventually identified and fixed.
- All contracts are being supported by the system, and postage costs have been eliminated.

Communication Strategy

After the final evaluation report was prepared, the lead Learning Planner and the Metrics Team member who conducted the study presented the results to the following groups, in accordance with the AT&T Learning end-to-end process:

- The managers of the AT&T Learning Planning Team for Operations
- The members of the AT&T Learning Center of Excellence team, which was involved in the design, development, and delivery of the training: This team not only reviews the results, but also they have valuable insights to share about the Level 1 and 2 results. And, because they are generally close to the client organization, they can often provide context around findings at Levels 3 and 4 as well.
- The key client contacts involved in providing the initial learning requirements as well as assisting in the data collection: Because of the visibility of this project, the immediate client contacts included the learning impact data in

an executive presentation. The Contract Specialist Empowerment training was only one part of a major improvement initiative around contract processing.

The reactions from all the participants were highly positive. It was significant that not only did everyone appreciate the good results of the project itself, but they agreed that the lessons learned—the factors that made this learning project and this evaluation study successful—should be applied to other efforts. Indeed, the findings were discussed with the rest of the Learning Planning Team and the Metrics Team so that all could share them. The report was posted on the internal AT&T Learning Planning Website so it could be accessed by other members of the organization.

Lessons Learned

All training project evaluations at AT&T Learning conclude with a review of the methodology used for the project as a whole and the actual experiences during all phases, as well as the results. These discussions include everyone involved from the front-end learning planners through the designers, content and media developers, instructional staff, evaluation team, and training managers, as well as the client contacts. This approach helps to ensure that successes—what worked well—are leveraged on future projects and that problems are reduced.

AT&T Learning received a great deal of support for this project both from the process teams and the client organization. Super-users were identified at the beginning and provided valuable input to the design team. Process team members were available for the training sessions and then sponsored an open-mike call two days after each training event to answer questions about the tool and process.

The client was pleased with the results and has shared them with many at the business unit executive level.

The continuing visibility and criticality of the Contract Specialist Empowerment initiative will be a performance incentive and reward program. All CS groups will be monitored for quality and cycle time improvement. If a specific group is falling below target, individualized plans will be developed to help get that person/group back on track.

Questions for Discussion

1. Given that the target audience was small, the development and delivery costs were low, and it was a one-time learning event, what was the rationale for measuring this project to Level 5 (ROI)?

2. Why was it appropriate to use only one month's posttraining financial results when calculating the monetary benefits?

3. Was the response rate on the survey sufficient to provide evidence of improved job performance? What other methods could have been used to collect additional feedback at Level 3? What could have been done to improve the response rate on the survey that was used?

4. The Level 4 data around contract accuracy showed that the percentage of contracts with no errors actually decreased for the month of July, yet the report concluded that the CS were meeting targets based on an affirmative statement from a SME in the client organization. How would your evaluation team deal with a situation such as this, when the numbers say one thing but an expert reports a different finding?

5. The monetary benefits for this program were calculated based on accelerated billing due to cycle time reduction resulting from faster processing of contracts. What other methods could have been used to compute financial benefits for this project?

About the Authors

Jane M. Ray is a planner with the AT&T Learning organization. She supports the Worldwide Customer Service group that is responsible for all postsales activities (ordering, provisioning, maintenance, and billing). In this position, Ray works with her clients to ensure the development of employees' critical functional skills by linking learning interventions to critical business priorities and demonstrating quantifiable impacts on those priorities. Ray has more than 20 years' experience with AT&T, half of which has been in the training department. She holds a master's degree in the teaching of mathematics from Oakland University. Prior to coming to AT&T, she taught high-school calculus and physics. Correspondence may be sent to AT&T Learning, 55 Corporate Drive, Room 31A21, Bridgewater, NJ 08807.

Lynne E. Motto is a member of the Metrics Team of the AT&T Learning organization. She performs learning impact studies for identified training programs in the operations area, in support of network provisioning and maintenance, customer ordering and billing, as well as for programs that address management and leadership competencies. In her 30-year training career, Motto has been involved in many different content areas, ranging from stock and bond transfer processing through systems engineering and project management, and has handled every function from front-end analysis through design, instruction, and formative evaluation. In the course of her career, Motto has conducted more than 50 evaluation studies. She is a Phi Beta Kappa graduate of Douglass College/Rutgers University with degrees in psychology and sociology. She is a member of American Mensa.

Chapter 3

This case was prepared to serve as a basis for discussion rather than to illustrate either effective or ineffective administrative and management practices.

LEADERSHIP DEVELOPMENT TRAINING

Central Plains Rural Electric Cooperative

Ted Garnett

Organizations, large and small, often have similar needs. The need for leadership, as well as the need for financial responsibility in a limited resource world, transcends organizational size or industry. While leadership development can seem difficult to measure and the ROI of such noble programs may not even be the primary interest or reason for implementing the program, the ROI of those programs is often asked for by boards and CEOs. The ROI can be calculated, and the Phillips ROI Methodology provides more than one way to measure and evaluate such programs. This case outlines the ROI evaluation of a leadership development program in a small, nonprofit organization and also describes some problems involved with the lack of an ROI measurement and evaluation strategy.

Background Information

The Central Plains Rural Electric Cooperative (REC) is a small, rural electrical cooperative located in the Midwest. REC provides power and utility to approximately 8,000 member-consumers and approximately 2,500 miles of electrical line. A cooperative is a business enterprise that is jointly owned and equally controlled by those who use it. It is a form of business with more focus on service to people than on making dollars, though it must, of course, bring in enough money to pay its own way. In a cooperative, membership and joint ownership are open to all that want to use its services; this factor distinguishes a cooperative from other forms of business enterprises. REC is a nonprofit entity because any margins remaining after all expenses (including taxes) are paid belong to the patrons and not to the cooperative enterprise.

The organization was in a transitional period with a newly hired CEO/general manager. The new CEO and the board were interested in drastically improving the culture and the leadership/decision making within the REC. They commissioned a survey of all 32 employees to discover the issues faced by the organization. They learned that the employee population lacked clarity on where the organization was going for the future and did not understand their roles in the REC's new direction, even if it were known.

Much of the old way of doing things was no longer desired, but the CEO and the board believed that they needed an education on new tools and approaches to leading the organization forward. This determination led to leadership development training (LDT) for all employees and implementation of a strategic planning process. The focus was to lay the groundwork for a new way of professional operation and a clearer direction that would include input from the overall employee population, which previously had no opportunity for any input.

The employee demographics range from high-school educated to college degreed. Some had not worked outside REC for decades or ever. Some had rather short tenure, and others had vast experience at other companies or even another rural electrical cooperative. Formal training had never been part of the culture at REC, except for occasional technical or safety training that typically only field or line workers attended.

The Learning Solution

From the initial survey it was apparent that the employees did not have the skills to lead the organization in a new way. The REC senior management considered options for the LDT and decided to outsource to a consultant, using our firm, Performance Resources Consulting. The program was tailored to REC's situation and included three sessions attended by all 32 employees with interactive learning workshops focused on tools for leadership including Leadership Versus Management, Leadership Listening and Communication Skills, and Action Planning. All employees attended these sessions, which stressed that leadership is not a position; it is a verb ("You *do* it"). Stated otherwise, an employee doesn't need to be in a supervisory capacity to help facilitate leadership within the organization. The top 12 employees (those with supervisory responsibilities) also attended a fourth session, Becoming an Effective Leader, which focused on performance management and delegation skills. Sessions were 3.5 hours long and held approximately every four weeks, with half the employees attending in the morning and half in the afternoon.

Evaluation Planning

The identified objectives of the evaluation included the following:

- applying the leadership time management tool
- applying a benefit-cost analysis
- identifying barriers to effective listening/communication
- documenting an action plan
- implementing an action plan
- identifying and improving an area of personal leadership.

Because the senior management had not purchased outside training in the past, Performance Resources Consulting offered to provide a basic Level 5 ROI analysis of the training based on Jack Phillips's ROI Methodology. Management was interested in an indication of the outcome of their financial investment because this program involved the entire organization, was going to cost considerable resources, was fairly visible to the board and outside constituents, and, finally, because it was to be used for the foundation of the strategic planning process for the next three to five years.

Measuring leadership skills can be less tangible than sales skills or other production and metric output oriented skills. We believed we needed to receive some type of feedback from this first-ever training effort to allow the organization to see any benefits and compare them to the costs of such efforts. We also needed to provide that feedback to the organization in a way they could understand and use it for future decision making.

The ROI Methodology provides 12 guiding principles and a framework for six types of measures:

- reaction/satisfaction and planned action
- learning
- application and implementation
- business impact
- ROI
- intangible measures.

It also includes a technique to isolate the effects of the program. This process involves a much more thorough feedback mechanism than is typically used with training participants.

The Data Collection Plan

The approach reflected in the data collection plan (figure 3-1) for this program needed to allow for the broad impacts that leveraging leadership into an organization can accomplish. The approach also

Figure 3-1. Data collection plan.

DATA COLLECTION PLAN

Purpose of This Evaluation: Understand the Basic ROI for Leadership Development

Program/Project: Leadership Development

Responsibility: Facilitator **Date:** _____

Level	Broad Program Objective(s)	Measures	Data Collection Method/Instruments	Data Sources	Timing	Responsibilities
1	**SATISFACTION/PLANNED ACTIONS** • Identify positive participant reactions to materials, content, facilitation • Identify planned actions	• Favorable or unfavorable responses to CEO and facilitator follow-up • Planned actions reported	• CEO follow-up • Questionnaire	• Participants • Participants	• After each session • End of program	• CEO • Facilitator • Facilitator
2	**LEARNING** • Apply Leadership Four-Quadrant time management tool • Apply benefit-cost analysis • Identify the barriers to effective communication and listening • Document an action plan • Implement an action plan and identify results • Identify an area of "leadership" to improve and create an action plan	• Understanding of the four quadrants and application to decisions • Ability to understand the format to calculate benefits and costs • Identify 15 communication barriers including your own top three • Understand the action planning process steps • Identify personal leadership areas for potential improvement	• Participant estimates • Skill practices • Facilitator assessment	• Participants	• During program	• Facilitator
3	**APPLICATION/IMPLEMENTATION** • Utilize the tools to make and implement decisions	• Ratings on questions • Completed and turned in action plans	• Follow-up questionnaire	• Participants	• 15 days after the end of program	• Facilitator
4	**BUSINESS IMPACT** • Identify one business impact directly improved from the use of the training skills/tools	• Varies	• Questionnaire	• Participants	• 15 days after the end of program	• Facilitator
5	**ROI: BREAK-EVEN POINT**					

Comments: _____

Source: Reprinted with permission from the ROI Institute. 2004.

could not depend on established measurement and evaluation measures because the organization was in its infancy with regard to measurement. The CEO and board wanted a credible evaluation of ROI but without expending many resources to accomplish the ROI evaluation. ROI was not a primary driver in the decision process for senior management, but in a limited-resources world it was certainly a consideration worth addressing.

Participants were expected to document an action plan and to begin using some of the tools immediately after the first session of the four-month program. The participants were introduced to the ROI questionnaire by the facilitator and the CEO during the first session so they could be prepared to track and report their outcomes at Levels 1–5. They were again reminded of the questionnaire at each monthly session. The ROI objective was not critical; therefore, it was set at the break-even point (0 percent).

ROI Approach

The data table (see table 3-3 later in the case) shows the approach to analyzing the potentially broad range of data elements to be reported by participants. There was no available control group, and multiple factors came into play during the training period; therefore, trend-line isolation was not feasible. The most efficient approach available for isolation (given no prior leadership metrics or measurement) was a conservative participant estimation process following the ROI Methodology. This isolation method included the following five adjustments in keeping with a conservative approach in estimation:

1. Participants who did not respond to the questionnaire or responded with unusable data were assumed to have no improvement. It is likely that some individuals would have improvements but failed to report them on the questionnaire, but this adjustment keeps maintains a conservative approach.

2. Extreme data and unrealistic claims would be omitted from the analysis although they may be included in the intangible benefits.

3. Because the program was short term in nature, benefits should occur within one year. With this principle in mind, annualized values were used. In reality, a leadership program should be expected to add value for perhaps several years after the training, but it was important to show a year one result.

4. To adjust for error in the estimate, the participant's level of confidence in his or her estimate, expressed as a percentage, would be multiplied by the reported improvement value. Although this adjustment reduces the amount of improvement, it maintains the conservative nature of the process, thereby enhancing credibility.

5. The improvement amount would be adjusted by the amount directly attributable by the participant to the training versus any improvement attributable to other factors, expressed as a percentage.

The method to convert to monetary values relied on participants' estimates as well. Participants were guided in the questionnaire to assign a monetary value to the business impact they identified; indicate if it was weekly, monthly, quarterly, or annually; and identify the basis for their estimates (how they arrived at the value). Some participants arrived at their value by consulting with experts; therefore, expert input could also be considered a conversion approach.

Costs

Costs were fully loaded including costs for participants who did not respond to the questionnaire and the cost of the ROI evaluation. The cost categories included

- total employee salary (calculated by taking the average wage broken down hourly and multiplied by 1.3 for fully loaded benefits, then taking that hourly value times 549 total hours of all participants' time in the program)
- program materials cost
- facilities and general overhead cost (partially an estimate of the value or cost of using the REC's in-house training room)
- training facilitation and ROI evaluation cost.

The total of these fully loaded costs was $24,480.

Evaluation Results

Of the 32 employees, 19 responded to the questionnaire. Some, but not all, reported the results in all six types of data generated by the ROI Methodology. Where no results were reported, no improvement was conservatively assumed. Following are the results of each data category.

Reaction

Participants responded almost completely favorably as indicated by follow-up carried out by the CEO and facilitator and by feedback on the questionnaire. Eighteen of 19 respondents stated they would recommend LDT to others. Several participants reported that the pace, facilitation, and content were enjoyable and there were no reports to the contrary.

Learning

The facilitator provided subjective assessment that all participants engaged in the training and had their questions answered to the extent that they had learned the content. Participants each were required to bring an article on leadership as identified in this program from any publication. They were required to explain their article in the context of the leadership skills and principles being delivered in the program, and all participants successfully demonstrated a learning of the leadership concepts through this exercise. Finally, the program included action plans to be documented by the participants at the beginning, middle, and end of the program, further demonstrating that the participants had learned (and applied) many of the skills in the program.

Application and Implementation

Participants received a questionnaire at the beginning of the program and again at the end of the program. The CEO requested that they return the questionnaires anonymously to the outside consultant for tabulation 15 days after the program. This questionnaire was four pages in length and had been reviewed with the participants at the beginning of the program so they would understand what they needed to contribute and that it would require some time to complete the questionnaire. The questionnaire appears in figure 3-2, on pages 28–31.

Participants ranked their application of the tools on a scale of success from 0 (no success) to 4 (completely successful), and the scores were averaged to identify the application outcomes for the program. Using a scale from 0 to 4, the participants indicated their success in applying the tools to the objectives identified for the program (table 3-1).

Participants also reported using teamwork, delegation, and goal-setting tools not specifically addressed by gathering data in the questionnaire. Participants mostly reported no barriers to application: 14 participants reported no barriers, four reported lack of time to apply, one reported lack of

Table 3-1. Participants' self-assessments of leadership tool application.

Leadership Tool	Average Score	Score Interpretation
Applying effective listening skills	3.95	Completely successful
Applying the Four-Quadrant time management model	3.58	Generally successful to completely successful
Documenting an action plan	3.38	Generally successful to completely successful
Applying an identified area to improve leadership	3.26	Generally successful
Implementing an action plan	2.89	Limited success to generally successful
Applying a benefit-cost analysis	2.83	Limited success to generally successful

trust, and one reported that the training material did not apply to his or her job. Additional support for application that the participants identified centered on their requests for reinforcing skills with a review at a later date and refresher courses or ongoing training of this kind.

Business Impact

Participants were asked in the questionnaire to identify business impacts that were positively influenced by the leadership training program in their own work or that of their work unit. They ranked the measures from 0 (not applicable) to 5 (very significant influence); the results are shown in table 3-2, on page 32.

Participants collected business impact data that was specific to each individual as well. The questionnaire administered at the end of the program asked them to identify a specific organizational benefit for the REC derived from their participation in the leadership development training. Questions 5 through 10 asked them to think about improvements that actually led to increased revenue; increased overall customer service or satisfaction; or

Figure 3-2. Leadership development training evaluation questionnaire.

1. Listed below are the objectives of the Problem Solving/Process Management Leadership program. After reflecting on the program, please indicate your degree of success in achieving these objectives.

Skill/Behavior	No Success	Very Little Success	Limited Success	Generally Successful	Completely Successful
A. Apply the Four-Quadrant time management model.	❑	❑	❑	❑	❑
B. Apply a benefit-cost analysis.	❑	❑	❑	❑	❑
C. Identify the barriers to effective communication and listening.	❑	❑	❑	❑	❑
D. Document an action plan.	❑	❑	❑	❑	❑
E. Implement an action plan and identify results.	❑	❑	❑	❑	❑
F. Identify an area of leadership to improve and create an action plan.	❑	❑	❑	❑	❑

2. Please rate, on a scale of 1–5, the relevance of each of the program elements to your job, with (1) indicating no relevance, and (5) indicating very relevant.

	No Relevance		Some Relevance		Very Relevant
Group (Class) Discussions	1	2	3	4	5
Facilitation/Teaching Content	1	2	3	4	5
Skill Exercises (scenarios, role plays, simulations, and so forth) . .	1	2	3	4	5
Materials/Handout Content	1	2	3	4	5
Articles on Leadership	1	2	3	4	5
Other?_____	1	2	3	4	5

3. Have you used any of the tools discussed in the sessions during or since participation in the program?

Yes ❑   No ❑
Please explain which ones.

_____

_____

_____

4. List the two behaviors or skills that you have worked to improve as a result of the program.

A. _____

B. _____

5. What has changed about you or your work as a result of your participation in this program? (Think in terms of specific behavior changes such as improved communication with employees, better perspective of costs and benefits, employee participation in decision making, improved problem solving, and so forth.)

_____

_____

_____

_____

6. How has your organization benefited from your participation in the program? Please identify specific business accomplishments or improvements that you believe are linked to participation in this program. (Think about how the improvements actually resulted in influencing business measures such as increased revenue, increased overall shipments, improved customer satisfaction, improved employee satisfaction, decreased costs, saved time, and so forth.)

_____

_____

_____

_____

7. Reflect on your specific business accomplishments/improvements as stated above and think of specific ways that you can convert your accomplishments into a monetary value. Along with the monetary value, please indicate your basis for the calculations.

Estimated monetary amount $ _____ .

Indicate if above amount is weekly, monthly, quarterly, or annually.

      Weekly ❑   **Monthly** ❑   **Quarterly** ❑   **Annually** ❑

What is your basis for your estimates? (What influenced the benefits/savings and how did you arrive at the value above?)

_____

_____

_____

_____

8. What percentage of the improvement above was actually influenced by the application of knowledge and skills from the Problem Solving/Process Management Leadership program?

_____ % improvement (0% = none, and 100% = all)

9. What level of confidence do you place on the above estimations?

_____ % confidence (0% = no confidence, and 100% = certainty)

10. Do you think this Problem Solving/Process Management Leadership program represented a good investment for your organization?

Yes ❑   **No** ❑

Please explain. _____

_____

_____

(continued next page)

Figure 3-2. Leadership development training evaluation questionnaire *(continued).*

11. Indicate the extent to which you think your application of knowledge, skills, and behavior learned from the Problem Solving/Process Management Leadership program had a positive influence on the following business measures in your own work or your work unit. Please check the appropriate response beside each measure.

Business Measure	Not Applicable	Applies but No Influence	Some Influence	Moderate Influence	Significant Influence	Very Significant Influence
A. Work output	❑	❑	❑	❑	❑	❑
B. Quality	❑	❑	❑	❑	❑	❑
C. Cost control	❑	❑	❑	❑	❑	❑
D. Efficiency	❑	❑	❑	❑	❑	❑
E. Response time to customers	❑	❑	❑	❑	❑	❑
F. Cycle time of products	❑	❑	❑	❑	❑	❑
G. Sales	❑	❑	❑	❑	❑	❑
H. Employee turnover	❑	❑	❑	❑	❑	❑
I. Employee absenteeism	❑	❑	❑	❑	❑	❑
J. Employee satisfaction	❑	❑	❑	❑	❑	❑
K. Employee complaints	❑	❑	❑	❑	❑	❑
L. Customer satisfaction	❑	❑	❑	❑	❑	❑
M. Customer complaints	❑	❑	❑	❑	❑	❑
N. Other (please specify) _____	❑	❑	❑	❑	❑	❑

Please cite specific examples or provide more details: _____
_____
_____

12. What additional benefits have been derived from this program? _____
_____
_____

13. What barriers, if any, have you encountered that have prevented you from using skills/behaviors gained in the Leadership Program? Check all that apply:

❑ I have had no opportunity to use the skills.

❑ I have not had enough time to apply the skills.

❑ My work environment does not support the use of these skills/behaviors.

❑ My supervisor does not support this type of program.

❑ This material does not apply to my job situation.

❑ Other (please specify):_____

If any of the above checked, please explain if possible. _____

_____

_____

14. What additional support could be provided by management that would influence your ability to apply the skills and knowledge learned from the program? _____

_____

_____

15. What additional solutions do you recommend that would help to achieve the same business results that the Problem Solving/Process Management Leadership program has influenced (or should influence) in your opinion? _____

16. Would you recommend this program to others?

Yes ❑   **No** ❑

Please explain. If no, why not? If yes, what groups/jobs and why? _____

_____

_____

17. What specific suggestions do you have for improving this program? _____

_____

_____

18. Other comments: _____

_____

_____

Business Measure	Average Score	Score Interpretation
Employee satisfaction	3.86	Significant influence
Employee turnover	3.83	Significant influence
Employee complaints	3.71	Significant influence
Efficiency	3.57	Moderate to significant influence
Work output	3.43	Moderate to significant influence
Customer satisfaction	3.17	Moderate influence
Customer complaints	3.00	Moderate influence
Cost control	2.86	Moderate influence
Quality	2.86	Moderate influence
Employee absenteeism	2.40	Some to moderate influence
Response to customers	2.33	Some influence
Cycle time of products	Not applicable	—
Sales	Not applicable	—

Table 3-2. Participants' rankings of the LDT's business impact.

percentage of the identified benefits in the "Est $" column they would have directly attributed to the LDT program. "Confidence" identifies the participants' estimates of how confident they were that the "Improvement" and the "Est $" were exactly correct.

We then multiplied the "Est $" by the "Period" to arrive at the gross benefit amount. By multiplying that amount by the "Improvement" percentage, we were discounting it to isolate for the amount we could attribute directly to the LDT program. Then, we determined the actual benefit value to plug into the ROI equation by multiplying that number by the participants' "Confidence" level.

ROI

Nine of the 19 questionnaire respondents attempted a monetary conversion. A total of $48,720 of benefits was reported by these nine participants. After discounting this amount through the isolation process (asking what percentage was directly attributable to the LDT and then how confident they were in that amount), the program benefits came to $17,426 directly attributable to the LDT. Fully loaded costs came to $24,280.

The BCR was calculated by taking the total attributable benefits and dividing by the costs:

$$BCR = \frac{\$17,426}{\$24,480} = 0.71$$

The ROI is calculated by taking the total attributable benefits less the costs and dividing by the costs:

$$ROI = \frac{\$17,426 - \$24,480}{\$24,480} \times 100 = -29\%$$

The ROI of −29 percent may seem disappointing initially, but it serves to educate us on the importance of the ROI Methodology. The CEO was not taken aback by this report because, in his words, "We didn't do this to make money; we did it because it needed to be done."

Intangible Data

The follow-up questionnaire allowed the participants to identify intangible impacts they perceived to be directly attributable to the LDT program. These were important because they represented business impacts that the participants identified as resulting from the LDT but were not converted to monetary value. The intangibles listed by the 19 questionnaire respondents included the following:

- everyone's realization about the need to be a leader in the organization regardless of his or her position

improved savings—cost savings or time savings. Seventeen participants responded that the ROI of the program was a good investment for their organization.

The specific approach for isolating and converting to monetary value is identified in table 3-3. The "Est $" figure is the amount identified by the participant as the benefit amount from the business impact they chose. The "Period" reflects the number of times per year that they estimated that the benefit occurs. "Basis" is an abbreviated explanation of what they were using to drive their "Est $" amount. "Improvement" relates to the participants' estimate of what

Table 3-3. Data used for isolating the effect of training and determining monetary values.

Est $	Period	Basis	Improvement (%)	Confidence (%)	Good Investment? Yes (Y) or No (N)	ROI
					Y	
$25	12	Can't identify a dollar amount, but I know I've saved REC money with the time I've saved!	50%	50%	Y	$75
		Can't identify a dollar amount, but I know I've saved REC money with the time I've saved!			Y	
$300	52	Member issues resolved without multiple employees saves time.	50%	80%	Y	$6,240
		It impacted time savings, cost savings, quality increases, and productivity increases.			Y	
$25	52	Time spent with members and employees is more efficient.	100%	100%	Y	$1,300
$100	1	It impacted time savings, cost savings, quality increases, and productivity increases.	20%	75%	Y	$15
		It impacted time savings, cost savings, quality increases, and productivity increases.			Y	
$1,000	12	Listening, the #1 Leadership Skill, saved time in communication.	40%	50%	Y	$2,400
		It impacted time savings, cost savings, quality increases, and productivity increases.			Y	
					N	
					Y	
$2,500	1	1.5 hourly rate times 8 hours per month in time savings.	50%	70%	Y	$875
$50	52	Guesstimate.	50%	50%	N	$650
					Y	
$6,000	1	Increased sales, marketing results, communication.	75%	75%	Y	$3,375
$160	52	30 minutes saved per person on four-person crew each week.	60%	50%	Y	$2,496

- focus on better leadership
- better organization and focus on the same goals (mission driven)
- better teamwork
- personal confidence
- improved communication away from work
- less speculation on what's going on, better communication
- organizational unity improved
- increased motivation to do a good job.

The organization deemed these intangibles to be as valuable, or more valuable, than any ROI actually calculated. The consensus of management was that the program was worth doing if only to achieve these results.

Communicating the Results

The CEO and key stakeholders received the information regarding the feedback and ROI analysis. Communication with the CEO and senior management was routine and ongoing throughout the process. Communication about how to complete the ROI questionnaire and what ROI meant was only done at the beginning of the session with reminders as a means of follow-up.

The CEO and board (as well as most of the employees) were satisfied with the LDT program. Even though it had a negative ROI, there was enough value in the program to see the benefits as worth the costs. The ROI calculation was, no doubt, affected by the less-than-optimal response rates in questionnaire returns and the fact that few of those who did return them actually calculated a monetary impact.

Lessons Learned

The ability to provide an accurate ROI within the standards and guiding principles of the ROI Methodology requires the organization to be willing and capable of providing the data for evaluation. In this case, ROI was not a main initiative so there was no real budget allocated and the participants did not allocate or expect to allocate much time to the measurement and evaluation of this program.

Nevertheless, this case study illustrates an example of how the conservative approach to ROI necessitates effort in the education of the ROI process/

evaluation on the part of the participants as well as a commitment from them to track and report business impacts that they can attempt to convert to monetary value.

We can see this lesson illustrated in the following: Recall that only nine of the 19 questionnaire respondents provided data. Only those nine data items were used to calculate the benefits; the rest were assumed to have no benefit. However, five of the 19 respondents indicated that they "knew" there was an impact on time, cost quality, or productivity, but they stated they had no idea of how to identify the amount of money that was worth. The problem here is that they knew there was a monetary value, but they were uneducated in estimating that value. They signaled that there was value but did not provide data on the value of the training to the organization. What can we learn from this?

If we assumed the average benefit amount was attained by those five who clearly stated they knew there was a value, we would be assuming that amount and, therefore, not providing a credible ROI. But, the process is worth looking at for its insight: The range of annualized benefits (after discounting for confidence and direct relevance to the program) was between $15 and $6,240, so we assigned the average of all those nine who did convert to monetary value ($1,936 annualized) to the other five who stated they "knew there was value." Because they specifically stated they knew there to be a financial impact in time, cost, quality, or productivity, we could give them the average annualized amount, which takes us from nine financial data items out of 19, to 14 out of 19. This is still somewhat conservative because even though the last five questionnaire respondents did not specifically say they "didn't see any monetary benefit," we still allocated no improvement to them. They did not say if they saw a benefit or not; they simply didn't respond to that item, so we still assume those are $0, along with all the others who didn't respond to the questionnaire at all.

This assumption analysis simply accommodates our error in not better educating the five people who saw value so they could estimate or convert that value to monetary value. By assuming the average from their peers, the "unofficial," assumed average ROI calculation gives us a look at what could have been. The assumption would be $27,106 in benefits with the same cost of $24,280 for an "unofficial ROI" of +12 percent! This is revealing! By only getting five more data items gathered for a total of 14 data items out of a population of 32 participants, we could see the potential for a positive ROI. It is important to note, however, that this is an unofficial ROI based on an assumption after the data was gathered. You could not credibly report this assumption approach as the ROI of the LDT program. This scenario does show the importance of helping people understand how to assign monetary figures to the perceived value of a training program.

 ## Questions for Discussion

1. What could be done to improve the response rate to the questionnaire? What impact would you predict this would have had on the official ROI of the LDT program?

2. What is the impact of a negative ROI when calculated?

3. In what way would a negative ROI serve as a process improvement tool?

4. How would you present the results of this ROI to your key stakeholders?

5. Which of the guiding principles should be bendable or flexible when presenting a negative ROI? Would it be possible to present this over a two- or three-year period because the costs are fixed in the first four months in order to boost the ROI?

6. Can a Level 5 ROI be used in small companies or with small divisions or departments?

7. When is it best to consider Level 5 instead of a lower level of ROI evaluation?

About the Author

Ted Garnett is an entrepreneur with various business interests in the Midwest and a primary focus as the founder and managing partner of Performance Resources Consulting (PRC), a business process improvement consulting firm based in Cedar Rapids, Iowa. A graduate of the University of Northern Iowa, Garnett holds a bachelor's degree of arts in business administration (human resources and business communications). He is certified in ROI. In addition, PRC is partnered with the ROI Institute, founded by renowned ROI experts Jack and Patti Phillips. Garnett is also certified as a professional in human resources by the Society for Human Resource Management. He holds certifications in employment law and ERISA Benefits/COBRA administration and is certified as a Six Sigma Black Belt in business process improvement through the University of Texas School of Engineering.

Prior to founding PRC, Garnett was employed in private industry in manager and executive HR positions. He was also a manager of the consulting practice for the national McGladrey & Pullen firm. His background includes a decade of business consulting with clients ranging in size from various small companies to *Fortune* 500 companies (John Deere, General Electric, Firestone, NCS Pearson, Rubbermaid) with a focus on accelerating business impact results.

Garnett's awareness of the strategic importance of human capital management and ability to translate these issues to bottom-line business planning creates an approach well accepted by management decision makers. He brings to the table a refined expertise in organization development/training, business process improvement and tracking, performance measurement and evaluation, employee welfare benefits, and HR policy and legal issues. His background in high-turnover industries lends strength to his work in developing and delivering effective training, business planning, employee relations, organizing recruitment and retention strategies, and in the evaluation of organizational communication tools. As a generalist, he is familiar with the broad spectrum of effective business impact planning and implementation, from technical/tactical to global.

Garnett's approach favors direct and candid assessment about results orientation and implementation that will drive execution and ROI. He can be reached at ted@resourcezone.net.

Chapter 4

This case was prepared to serve as a basis for discussion rather than to illustrate either effective or ineffective administrative and management practices.

ASTD'S HPI CERTIFICATE PROGRAM

The National Security Agency
Associate Directorate of Education and Training

*Bernadette Schoukroun and Deborah Wharff
in collaboration with Patti Phillips*

The National Security Agency's Associate Directorate for Education and Training (ADET) faces unprecedented challenges. It must demonstrate in tangible ways how it adds value to the agency's mission through its education and training programs while delivering extraordinary learning opportunities that transcend the classroom. Offering client-centered, results-based performance improvement solutions demands highly talented internal performance consultants. These consultants must develop new analytic competencies to assess their client's organizational performance and workforce skill gaps and articulate the consequences of those gaps to mission outcomes. Moreover, they must identify appropriate solutions for closing those gaps and then evaluate the success of the solutions. To achieve these goals, ADET implemented ASTD's Human Performance Improvement (HPI) Certificate Program. In an effort to ensure long-term payoff on its investment, ADET conducted an ROI forecast evaluation. This case study describes the results of the evaluation as well as lessons learned and explains how those lessons have been applied to a second launch of the ASTD HPI Certificate Program.

Program Background

The National Security Agency/Central Security Service (NSA/CSS) is America's cryptology organization. It coordinates, directs, and performs highly specialized activities to protect U.S. information systems and produce foreign intelligence information. A high-technology organization, NSA is on the frontiers of communications and data processing. It is also one of the most important centers of foreign language analysis and research within the government.

NSA/CSS values continual learning and development for its most important resource—its people. Technology changes at the speed of light, and techniques that are cutting edge today will be antiquated tomorrow. Keeping the NSA/CSS workforce in peak intellectual shape and honing their skills are critical components to the agency's success.

ADET is the organization within NSA/CSS responsible for developing, delivering, and maintaining learning development opportunities and solutions for the workforce. ADET is responsible for oversight of all cryptologic and cryptologic-related training for the entire U.S. Department of Defense. NSA sponsors employees for undergraduate and graduate studies at the nation's top universities and colleges, and selected agency employees attend the various war colleges of the U.S. armed forces.

ASTD's HPI Certificate Program comprised five courses. Each course addressed a key issue concerned with enhancing human performance in the workplace and provided traditional trainers the opportunity to develop the necessary knowledge and skills to move into performance consultant roles. The key performance objectives of the program were to develop the knowledge and skills needed to apply analytic models to determine performance gaps and root causes, to design solution strategies to address the root causes of those performance gaps, and to create a process to evaluate the impact of implemented solutions.

Potential students of the HPI program had to be nominated by their supervisors and were required to commit to participation in all five courses. Twenty-five of ADET's most experienced training professionals were selected for the HPI program. An intended outcome was that, as these individuals began to apply the knowledge and skills acquired from the HPI program and implemented key aspects of the HPI methodology, their customer organizations would ultimately transform into continuous learning organizations. Not only did ADET want to change its culture and the behaviors of its own workforce, it wanted the HPI process to facilitate an agency-wide shift in thinking. The agency culture supported the belief that "training is a panacea for solving workplace performance problems." Through the HPI process, ADET planned to educate its customers about systemic issues and barriers that impeded transfer of learning. The intent was to have the capability to provide analytic data that showed how organizational processes, policies, and other managerial behaviors might stand in the way of improved employee performance.

Evaluation

The HPI program launched in January 2003 and concluded in October 2003. The participants attended the five HPI courses, completed individual action plans, and applied new knowledge and skills learned to an actual project. Supervisors played a pivotal role before and after the training by facilitating the transition of knowledge and skills to the workplace. The investment in the HPI program was considerable not only due to the program costs, but also because of the participants' time spent in the program and the time of the ADET staff, which were significant cost factors.

By implementing the HPI process, ADET intended to improve critical measures of success to its mission, including reduction in costs and time associated with inappropriate or ineffective solutions. ADET leaders recognized that service to their clients ultimately affects critical measures important to the entire cryptologic and intelligence community.

With this in mind, coupled with the considerable investment in the HPI training program, ADET leaders required a comprehensive evaluation process to ensure that an appropriate return on that investment was achieved. The evaluation process included a forecast of the impact of the HPI program. Three important evaluation objectives were addressed:

1. Demonstrate the potential value of ASTD's HPI Certificate Program.

2. Identify barriers to applying knowledge and skills learned.

3. Identify opportunities for program improvement.

Program Objectives and Measures

Program objectives are typically derived from a formal needs assessment, which then drives the evaluation. ADET did not conduct a formal needs assessment; however, it did recognize the need to improve customer satisfaction and process cycle time. Customer feedback and evaluation data from traditional training programs compelled ADET to rethink its strategies and approaches to serving its customers, especially by providing more appropriate solutions for closing the performance gaps. Table 4-1 summarizes ADET's objectives for the ASTD HPI Certificate Program and measures by which those objectives were evaluated.

Data Collection Methodology

The comprehensive approach for data collection process included four primary elements: defining the program objectives and measures by which to

Table 4-1. HPI program measures of success as defined by ADET.

	Broad Objectives	Measures
Satisfaction Objectives	Positive reaction and satisfaction with the knowledge and skills presented in the program	At least 80% of participants rate the following the high score (5 out of 5) on the PEAK survey: • Relevance • Percent knowledge/skills expect to use • Frequency of use • Trade-off of benefits • Overall course rating.
	Planned action	Participants complete action plans at the end of each course defining specific actions they will take when returning to the job.
Learning Objectives	Increase in knowledge and skills learned in the program	Ninety percent of participants score themselves as having expertise at the intermediate or above level on the post-program skill inventory.
	Confidence to use the knowledge and skills	Participants indicate an ability to apply information and concepts as defined by improvement in ability to use knowledge/skills prior to program versus at the end of program as shown on PEAK survey.
Application Objectives	Extent of use of skills and knowledge learned in the program Extent of application of specific actions defined by participants Barriers to application Enablers to application	Extent of use of the following skills as defined in the ASTD objectives: • Implement and communicate model/process to determine performance gaps • Apply models to determine performance gaps and their root causes • Reconcile requests for solutions with real organization goals • Manage implementation of the solution • Troubleshoot the implementation of the solution • Recommend the right solution (beyond training) to fit the identified performance gaps.
Impact Objectives	Improved customer satisfaction*	Customer satisfaction is improved as defined by: • Perception of ADET • Quality of services • Implement consultants' solutions • Solution impact on customer needs (time, costs, quality, productivity) • Confidence in ability of ADET • Repeat use of ADET • Frequency of use of ADET • Overall satisfaction with ADET.

(continued next page)

* Customer satisfaction data collected during the forecast evaluation was to serve as baseline data by which to compare follow-up results.

Table 4-1. HPI program measures of success as defined by ADET *(continued)*.

	Broad Objectives	Measures
Impact Objectives *(continued)*	Reduced costs	Costs associated with inappropriate solutions are reduced or eliminated.
	Reduced time	Less time is needed for developing and implementing performance improvement solutions.
ROI	25%	

determine whether the objectives had been achieved, determining the data collection methods, identifying the sources of data, and determining the timing of data collection.

Data was collected using five methods:

- the Program Evaluation and Assessment Key (PEAK) form (ADET's standardized end-of-course questionnaire)
- pre- and post-program skill inventory
- participant forecast questionnaire
- supervisor forecast questionnaire
- a customer questionnaire that was used to gather baseline data on current Level 3 behaviors and their current impact on productivity, quality, time savings, and cost savings (Level 4).

Participants were asked to complete action plans at the end of each course; however, participants failed to complete their action plans as requested. To overcome this problem, a question was added to the participant and supervisor forecast questionnaires to gather planned actions that would have been captured through the action planning process.

ADET selected three data sources based upon which groups could provide the most credible data for the measures:

- *Participants:* The participants served as the sole source of data for Level 1 evaluation. Level 2 data was collected from participants using the pre- and post-program skill inventory and the survey. Using the forecast questionnaire, participants provided data on the extent to which they expected to apply the knowledge and skills learned in the program as well as the expected impact measures that would

result from their use of the new knowledge and skills. They were asked to describe potential barriers and enablers to the application of knowledge and skills. In addition to providing expected impact measures, participants were asked to estimate the monetary value of those impact measures if in fact they did improve.

- *Supervisors:* The participants' supervisors were also asked to provide input on the extent to which they expect participants to apply what they learned in the program. They provided input on specific actions they expect participants to take as a result of the program. They were asked to describe potential barriers and enablers to the application of knowledge and skills. In addition to providing insight into Level 3 expectations, supervisors were asked to forecast key impact measures that would improve as a result of the knowledge and skills learned in the HPI program. Supervisors were also asked to estimate the monetary value of these improvements.

- *Customers:* The customers served as a source of data for the six Level 3 behaviors defined in the ASTD objectives. Customers provided baseline data regarding the current extent to which ADET consultants applied the specific behaviors. Customers were also asked to provide the extent to which the ADET program helped them improve productivity, quality, costs, and time.

Table 4-2 presents a summary of the success with data collection. As shown, 25 employees participated in the HPI program. The response rate was less than 100 percent for all data collection attempts, especially for the forecast questionnaire, which was emailed to participants after the program was completed.

Table 4-2. Questionnaire response rates.

	PEAK	Partcipant Forecast Questionnaire	Supervisor Forecast Questionnaire	Customer Survey
Course 1	22/25 (88%)			
Course 2	10/25 (40%)			
Course 3	22/25 (88%)			
Course 4	18/25 (72%)			
Course 5	21/25 (84%)			
End of Program		6/25 (24%)	4	27/54 (50%)

Data Analysis Procedures

Data analysis included four key steps: converting data to monetary value, tabulating fully loaded costs, identifying intangible benefits, and comparing the monetary benefits to the costs (the ROI calculation). Each step was carefully considered. Typically, a step is included to isolate the effects of the program on impact measures; however, because the forecast assumed that respondents were inferring the impact of the particular program, this step was omitted. A planned post-program follow-up that was to occur six to nine months following HPI did include the isolation step.

Converting Data to Monetary Value

Ten techniques to convert data to monetary value were possible; however, four were considered: standard values, historical costs, participants' estimates, and supervisors' estimates. The decision as to which technique to use was dependent on the measure(s) identified that would improve as a result of the program. The primary Level 4 measures identified by ADET as those that would improve due to the HPI program were

- customer satisfaction
- costs associated with inappropriate solutions
- time associated with developing performance improvement solutions
- time associated with implementing performance improvement solutions.

Because this was a forecast study, additional measures to improve were identified by the participants and supervisors. Anticipated measures to be improved as a result of the HPI program as identified by participants and supervisors included

- reduced cost due to less redundancy
- reduced cost due to less contractor support and more ROI
- increased use of technology
- reduced number of courses offered
- reduced training time for participants and adjuncts.

For the forecast evaluation, participant and supervisor estimates were used to convert these measures to monetary value. All estimates were adjusted for error using participant and supervisor confidence levels.

ADET customers provided data that served as their baseline level of satisfaction with ADET. To determine whether to proceed with converting customer data to monetary value, ADET staff applied a four-part test (Phillips, 2003):

1. Is there a standard value?
2. If not, is there a technique available to convert the measure?
3. Can we convert the measure with our current resources?

4. Can we convince senior management in two minutes or less that this is a credible value?

Ultimately, it was decided not to proceed with data conversion on customer data because of a lack of resources at the time of the forecast study.

Tabulating Fully Loaded Costs

The fully loaded costs were used in the forecast. Table 4-3 presents the details of the cost. Not all participants responded to data collection efforts, but costs for all 25 participants were included.

Identifying Intangible Benefits

Intangible benefits are those that are not converted to monetary value or are benefits derived from the program that are not planned. Intangible benefits identified for the HPI program include the customer satisfaction measures as well as employee satisfaction.

Table 4-3. Costs of the HPI program.

	Hours of Work	Costs
HPI Program Costs		$ 84,250.00
Program Expenses		3,000.00
Course Manager 1	50.0	
Course Manager 2	50.0	
Course Manager 3	60.0	
Evaluation Plan Development Costs		
Evaluation Consultant		
— Customer Consulting Survey (40 hours)	96.0	
— Pre/Post HPI survey (Level 2/3) Development	97.0	
— Meetings hours		
Senior Executive	2.0	
Letter to Customers	3.0	
Letter to HPI Participants	3.0	
Planning Executives		1,500.00
Action Planning Workshop	20.0	
Focus Group (September 15)	28.5	
Action Planning Questionnaire	3.0	
Preparation for Action Planning Workshop	22.0	
Total Hours	434.5	
Loaded Hourly Rate $49.03		
Total Cost for Hours of Work		21,303.54
Overhead (space and so on)		4,092.00
Student Class Hours (25 Students)	3,000.0	147,090.00
Total Program Cost		**$ 261,235.54**

Calculating ROI

A 25 percent ROI target was established for the HPI program. Because of the comprehensive nature of the program and the changes that should take place as ADET transformed from a training organization to a performance consulting organization, it was deemed necessary to raise the ROI target to one above the level of typical investments.

Evaluation Results

Each course was evaluated using the PEAK questionnaire. Level 2 evaluation included a pre- and post-program skill inventory. A forecast questionnaire was administered to participants and supervisors to forecast Levels 3 and 4. The ROI was calculated based on the estimated monetary value of the forecasted improvement in measures. The results of the evaluation were positive; however, opportunity for improvement exists at all levels.

Level 1

Each of the 25 participants was asked to complete the PEAK questionnaire at the end of each course. Response rates varied; however, course 2 had the lowest response rate with only 40 percent (10) of the participants completing the PEAK. It was discovered that participants did not respond to course 2 PEAKs because they either left early on the last day of the course or they were extremely dissatisfied with the facilitator's effectiveness.

Although the PEAK questionnaire asked a number of questions useful to ADET about the program, specific questions represented target measures: relevance to the job, the participants' intent to use knowledge and skills learned, planned action, investment perception, and overall satisfaction with the course. The objective for Level 1 was that 80 percent of the respondents would rate each course with a measure of 5 on a 5-point scale. The reaction to the courses did not meet the 80 percent high-score target, but evidence existed that respondents perceived the courses as relevant, they did intend to use what they learned, they perceived their time as having been wisely invested by attending each course, and they liked the courses. Perhaps these measures served no predictive value, but they did reflect positively on the course from the respondents' perspective.

Program Relevance to the Job

The findings showed that participants agreed that the courses were relevant; however, the 80 percent response to the top score (extremely relevant) was not achieved on this measure for any course. Responses showed that course 2, Analyzing Human Performance, was the least relevant of the courses. Although 60 percent of those who did respond to the course 2 PEAK indicated that the course was extremely relevant, only 10 of 25 participants responded to the question. Course 2 was one of the most critical courses in the HPI program because it provided an opportunity for participants to learn to identify performance gaps and their root causes—a fundamental premise of performance consulting. Lack of relevance indicated little if any actual use of these skills, thereby limiting the success of a transition from training to performance consulting for ADET. Overall, the five courses presented in the HPI program were relevant to the job of participants (figure 4-1).

Intent to Use

The second measure of success at Level 1 was the intent to which participants plan to use what they have learned in the HPI program. Intent to use was defined as the percentage of knowledge and skills participants planned to use and the frequency with which they planned to use them. As in the case of program relevance to the job, no course achieved the 80 percent high-response target on these measures. Respondents indicated that course 4 had the highest percentage of knowledge and skills that would be used, with 82.3 percent suggesting they would use at least 75 percent of what was learned.

Based on responses from those who completed the PEAK, course 2 resulted in the most frequently used set of knowledge and skills with 80 percent of the respondents indicating they would use the skills on at least a weekly basis. However, in all cases, the respondents indicated some intent to use knowledge and skills learned. Overall, the knowledge and skills learned in the HPI program would be used to some extent, but the large number of nonresponses to items on course 2 was disconcerting.

Planned Action

Planned action was considered a critical Level 1 measure. Planned action helps participants create a road map for applying new knowledge and skills. Participants were asked to complete an action plan at the end of each course; however, only one action plan was submitted. Qualitative remarks on the PEAK indicated, in many cases, projects to which HPI skills could be applied had not been identified at the time of the course offerings. Using the participant and supervisor forecast questionnaires, the participants and supervisors were asked to identify planned actions resulting from the entire program. Table 4-4 lists selected planned actions identified by participants and their supervisors. As previously mentioned, the response to the forecast questionnaire

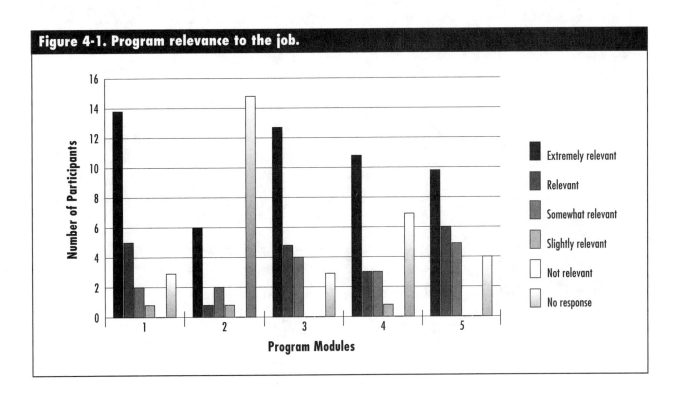

Figure 4-1. Program relevance to the job.

Table 4-4. Some planned actions identified by participants and their supervisors.

Participants' Planned Actions (N = 6)	Supervisors' Expectations (N = 4)
• Conduct an ROI study.	• Create a comprehensive report that defines the program's objectives/goals that will serve as the basis for program planning.
• Help customers become goal-achievement focused versus training focused.	
• Imbed evaluation within in-house and contract training programs.	• Educate/communicate HPI to colleagues.
• Improve the quality of training we currently provide.	• Identify cadre of center personnel to lead customer engagement.
• Increase use of technology in training programs.	• Identify process issues.
• Manage needs assessment process for customer.	• Identify technology and other human barriers to efficiency.
	• Improve technology use.
	• Conduct a curriculum planning session and define the path to program and curriculum design.

was well below what was desired; however, it was understood that results from those responding would reflect only that small sample, and would not be generalized to the larger group.

Investment Perception

Implementation is more likely to occur when participants perceive investment in a program as positive. Although the 80 percent high-response target was not achieved on this measure, overall, respondents could see the value of investing in the HPI program. To measure investment perception, participants were asked to rate the tradeoff between their time away from the job versus the benefits of program participation. As shown in figure 4-2, course 2 ranked the lowest in regard to investment perception. This is reinforced if the nonrespondents were considered as perceiving the courses as having no benefit.

Overall Satisfaction

Table 4-5 summarizes the ratings for overall satisfaction of the five courses offered in the HPI program.

Level 2

Evaluation at Level 2 answered two critical questions:

1. Do participants understand what they are supposed to do and how to do it?

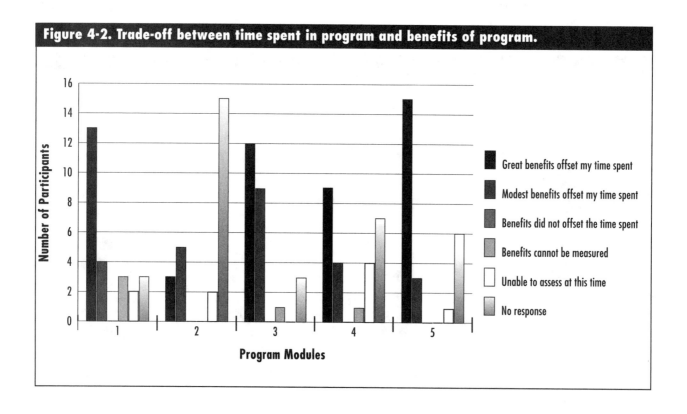

Figure 4-2. Trade-off between time spent in program and benefits of program.

Legend:
- Great benefits offset my time spent
- Modest benefits offset my time spent
- Benefits did not offset the time spent
- Benefits cannot be measured
- Unable to assess at this time
- No response

(Y-axis: Number of Participants; X-axis: Program Modules)

Table 4-5. Overall satisfaction ratings for the courses.					
	Course 1 (N = 22)	Course 2 (N = 10)	Course 3 (N = 21)	Course 4 (N = 17)	Course 5 (N = 22)
Excellent	63.6%	10%	57.1%	70.6%	54.5%
Good	36.4%	90%	38.1%	29.4%	31.8%
Fair	0%	0%	4.8%	0%	9.1%
Poor	0%	0%	0%	0%	0%
Very Poor	0%	0%	0%	0%	0%

2. Are they confident about applying their newly acquired knowledge and skills when they leave the classroom?

Increase in Knowledge and Skills

Prior to the launch of the HPI program, pre-program surveys were sent to the 25 participants. The pre-program surveys included an inventory of 10 critical skills. The objective set for learning was to achieve an increase on the post-program skill inventory over the pre-program skill inventory as indicated by 90 percent of the participants stating they were at the intermediate or above level of expertise.

Even though the 90 percent objective was not met, there was some evidence of increased knowledge and skills, based on the pre- and post-program skill inventory comparisons. The pre-program and post-program surveys were distributed to the 25 participants; of those 25, 23 (92 percent) responded to the pre-program survey and 10 (40 percent) responded to the post-program survey. Because of the conservative nature of the ROI Methodology, an assumption was made that there was no increase in the ability to apply the skill sets taught in the HPI program for the 15 nonrespondents.

Confidence to Use Knowledge and Skills

Success in confidence to use the knowledge and skills is measured by an increase in the participants' perceived ability to apply information/concepts after completion of the course compared to their ability before the course. This measure was taken via the PEAK questionnaire.

Figure 4-3 shows the responses to the questions on the participants' confidence to use newly acquired information/concepts. Respondents rated their ability to apply knowledge and skills learned before and after the program. Nonrespondents were assumed to lack the ability to apply these knowledge and skills.

Some of the courses had lower than desirable response rates. The low response reinforced the need to ensure that participants were made aware of the importance of their participation in the evaluation process.

The improvement in the skills identified in the skill inventory did not hit the 90 percent target. There were increases in all skill sets, however, indicating that knowledge and skills were gained to some extent during each course. Scores on the PEAK survey regarding pre- and post-program ability to apply knowledge and skills learned also increased, suggesting that respondents did have the confidence to apply what they learned in the HPI program.

Level 3

This evaluation was intended to provide end-of-course results and to forecast Levels 3, 4, and 5 results. Along with participant and supervisor forecasts of the extent of use of knowledge and skills learned in the HPI program (Level 3), customers were surveyed to gain an understanding of the extent to which ADET consultants currently apply the behaviors in which they were being trained. The results showed that participants and their supervisors expected participants to apply all the knowledge and skills gained in the

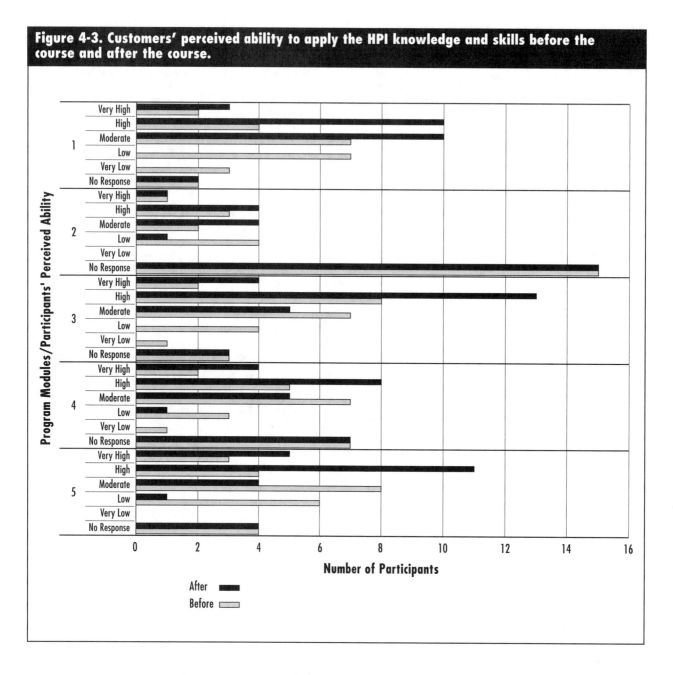

Figure 4-3. Customers' perceived ability to apply the HPI knowledge and skills before the course and after the course.

program to some extent. Customers suggested that current practice in the desired behaviors was limited. Barriers and enablers were identified that would prevent or support the transformation process, thereby filling the gap between current behaviors and anticipated application of knowledge and skills learned in the HPI program.

The ASTD HPI Certificate Program involved six primary behavioral objectives. After completing the program, participants should be able to:

1. Implement and communicate the model/process to determine performance gaps.

2. Define and communicate root causes of performance gaps.

3. Reconcile requests for solutions with real organization goals.

4. Manage implementation of the solution.

5. Troubleshoot the implementation of the solution.

6. Recommend the right solution (beyond training) to fit the identified performance gaps.

Three data sources provided information about the extent to which program participants were expected to apply their new skills/behaviors: the participants themselves, their supervisors, and the customers. To forecast the extent to which participants would apply these behaviors, participants and their supervisors were asked to identify the extent to which those behaviors/skills would be implemented following the course. Some supervisors had a higher target than the participants did.

Customers were asked to rate the extent to which ADET consultants currently applied the six skill sets. As shown in table 4-6, customers perceived the participants to be applying the desired behaviors/skills to a little or no extent. This provided the basis for improvement through the transfer of the HPI skills. Unfortunately, the customer data was brought to light after the program began. Although the gap could be closed by applying what was learned in the HPI program, having recognized this gap at the outset would have helped participants and their supervisors better recognize the need for their full participation in the transformation process.

Using the mode for each measure for participant, supervisor, and customer responses as the plot points, figure 4-4 further illustrates the gap between

current state and expected state with regard to the application of knowledge and skills learned in the HPI program.

Supervisors expected participants to use knowledge and skills learned to a great extent with the exception of managing and troubleshooting implementation. Participants indicated that they would use knowledge and skills learned to some extent. Customers indicated that ADET consultants used the desired HPI behaviors to no extent with the exception of determine performance gaps and reconcile requests.

Barriers

Participants and supervisors were asked to identify the potential barriers that could inhibit the application of knowledge and skills learned in the program. Culture, goals, and expectations appeared to be the overriding themes, hence the need to address alignment of the HPI program objectives with ADET strategic direction.

Culture change is an organization's greatest challenge. It requires unlearning old processes, understanding the need for new processes, learning the

Table 4-6. Customers' perception of actual use of HPI knowledge and skills.

	To No Extent ⟶ To a Great Extent					Mean	Mode
	1	2	3	4	5		
1. Implement and communicate a model/ process to determine performance gaps (N = 22)	6 27.2%	4 18.2%	1 4.5%	7 32.0%	4 18.1%	2.95	4
2. Define and communicate root causes of performance gaps (N = 21)	6 28.5%	3 14.3%	4 19.0%	5 24.0%	3 14.3%	2.81	1
3. Reconcile requests for solutions with real organizational goals (N = 21)	5 24.0%	4 19.0%	3 14.3%	6 28.5%	3 14.3%	2.90	4
4. Manage implementation of the solution (N = 21)	7 33.3%	2 9.5%	4 19.0%	6 28.5%	2 9.5%	2.71	1
5. Troubleshoot the implementation of the solution (N = 21)	7 33.3%	3 14.3%	4 19.0%	6 28.5%	1 4.8%	2.57	1
6. Recommend the right solution (beyond training) to fit the identified performance gaps (N = 21)	7 33.3%	2 9.5%	2 9.5%	7 33.3%	3 14.3%	2.86	1 and 4

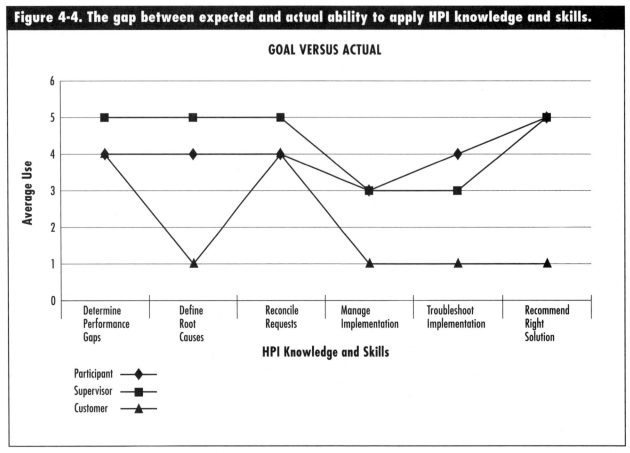

Figure 4-4. The gap between expected and actual ability to apply HPI knowledge and skills.

GOAL VERSUS ACTUAL

NOTE: A five-point scale was used, where 1 = no extent of use, 5 = great extent of use. Customer data = current state; participant and supervisor data = expected state.

new processes, then integrating and sustaining those processes. The HPI program was in essence a culture change process. ADET had operated as one type of organization for a period of time; the leadership was now taking steps to change to another type of organization. The results of the HPI evaluation project reinforced the need to focus on three specific questions:

1. Is there a real need for the change? If there is, whose need is it?

2. Are all stakeholders aware of the need?

3. Do all stakeholders understand the process through which this need will be addressed?

Barriers such as resistance to change, diversity of thought on future direction, and the current status of processes could be addressed if there were a clear understanding of why change should take place.

Common goals make any transformation process flow smoothly. By understanding the need for change,

common goals could be established. When the goals were understood by all stakeholders, priorities could more easily change. The first step in removing barriers such as customer lack of understanding and acceptance, competing demands and priorities, and lack of time was to establish clear goals and objectives—those in which all stakeholders buy in.

Enablers

Participants and supervisors were also asked to identify issues that would support the application of the new knowledge and skills learned. The enablers parallel the barriers and could be captured in the same three categories: culture, goals, and expectations. Some of the enabling factors would require a shift in the culture or structure of ADET. Others supported the notion of common goals and formal policy. Addressing the barriers and enablers to application of the knowledge and skills learned in the HPI program would support the transition from a training function to a performance consulting function.

Anticipated barriers and enablers to the application of knowledge and skills learned in the HPI program were categorized into three areas: culture, goals, and expectations. There was a concern that the culture would not support the transition from training to performance consulting. As such, participants and supervisors agreed that clear goals were necessary to ensure a successful transition. Establishing clear goals would assist in setting new priorities for work. Formalizing expectations through the development of policy would further support the transition and would communicate the commitment of management to making this change.

Level 4: Impact

This evaluation was intended to forecast the impact the application of knowledge and skills learned in the HPI program would have on key measures. Four specific objectives were defined at Level 4:

1. Enhanced customer satisfaction

2. Reduced costs associated with inappropriate solutions

3. Reduced time associated with developing and implementing performance solutions

4. Other measures at Level 4 identified during the forecast.

The customer survey provided baseline data on customer satisfaction measures that should improve as a result of participants applying knowledge and skills learned in the HPI program. The results showed that customers still perceived ADET as a training organization, but that they were somewhat satisfied with the current level of service. Participants and supervisors responding to the forecast questionnaires identified measures relative to productivity, quality, cost, and time that would be improved as a result of applying knowledge and skills learned in the HPI program.

Enhanced Customer Satisfaction

The objective was for ADET to be viewed by customers as the preferred solution provider for their clients. Based on 27 responses from the 54 key customers who received the survey, findings showed that customers perceived ADET as a training provider (versus a provider of solutions) and were somewhat satisfied with the current level of service. A follow-up survey would be administered approximately a year later to understand the extent to which the ASTD HPI Certificate Program had helped improve the customer satisfaction ratings.

Eight measures were defined that would satisfy the customer satisfaction objectives:

- *Perception of ADET:* Customers were asked to select a word or phrase from a list of five that best described the type of service they believed ADET provided. Seventy-four percent of those responding indicated that they perceived ADET to be a provider of training. Twenty-two percent perceived ADET to be a provider of educational programs. Only 7.4 percent of those responding perceived ADET as a provider of consulting. Seven percent of the respondents provided other descriptions of ADET.

- *Quality of services:* Quality of service was measured by the extent to which customers suggested changes. In the customer survey, customers were asked if there were any changes that could be made within ADET's services to better meet customer needs. Sixty-three percent of the respondents indicated there was room for change. Twenty-six percent indicated that no changes were necessary, and 11 percent responded that changes perhaps are needed. Supportive changes recommended by respondents included responding to customer needs by becoming a partner to help determine the training needs. This was an objective of the HPI program. Responsive changes suggested by respondents included that ADET could do a better job of responding to requests even if requests could not be taken care of at the time. Suggested changes with regard to flexibility included updating material and flexibility in timeline and classroom location. Other changes might be considered strategic in that customers suggested that programs be created and maintained with the mission purpose tied to the specific skills taught.

- *Implementation of consultant solutions:* Another measure of customer satisfaction was the extent to which customers implemented the solutions recommended by the ADET consultant. Forty-one percent of the responding customers indicated they implemented some of the recommendations made by ADET consultants. Nineteen percent indicated that no solutions were provided. Only 7.4 percent indicated that the recommendations made by the ADET consultants were not feasible.

• *Solution impact on customer needs (time, costs, quality, productivity):* The ultimate outcome of any intervention is saving time, cutting cost, improving quality, and increasing productivity for the customer. Customers were asked to select all areas in which ADET recommendations had an impact. As shown in figure 4-5, the most often selected area of the four defined measures was improved quality, with seven respondents selecting this measure. The least often selected area was cost. Most respondents identified some other measure on which ADET recommendations had an impact.

• *Confidence in ADET's ability to provide support:* Another measure of customer satisfaction is the confidence customers have in ADET's ability to support them. Customers were asked to rate ADET on a scale of 1 to 5 as to their level of confidence in ADET's ability to support them (1 = lowest level of confidence; 5 = completely confident). Overall, customers were somewhat confident in ADET's ability to support them. Only 7.4 percent of those responding indicated they were completely confident; however, 40.7 percent rated them a 4 or above on the 5-point scale. Twenty-two percent rated ADET a 2 or less on confidence.

• *Repeated use of ADET services:* Repeat business is a critical measure of customer satisfaction. Of those responding, 29.6 percent never used ADET services; 25.9 percent used ADET ser-

vices every year; 18.5 percent used ADET services on a quarterly basis. A second measure of repeat use includes the extent to which customers would use ADET's consulting services again. Customers were asked whether they would use ADET services again in the future: 60.8 percent of those responding answered yes to this question; only 4.3 percent answered no.

• *Overall satisfaction with ADET:* A final measure of customer satisfaction is the customers' overall satisfaction with ADET. Although not all the variables that define this measure are specific, this measure provided an overall metric by which future comparisons could be made. Table 4-7 shows that of those who responded 11.1 percent were completely satisfied; 29.6 percent were somewhat satisfied.

• *Improved ADET impact measures:* Along with customer baseline data, participants and supervisors were asked to identify specific customer

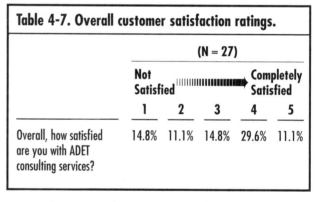

Table 4-7. Overall customer satisfaction ratings.

	(N = 27)				
	Not Satisfied				Completely Satisfied
	1	2	3	4	5
Overall, how satisfied are you with ADET consulting services?	14.8%	11.1%	14.8%	29.6%	11.1%

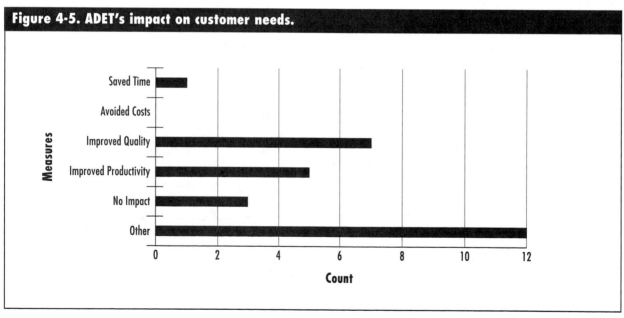

Figure 4-5. ADET's impact on customer needs.

outcomes they believed would occur as a result of their applying knowledge and skills learned during the HPI program. Unfortunately, only six participants and four supervisors provided input on the forecast questionnaires. It was understood by the management team that in reporting potential impact of the HPI program, the data reported would be applicable only to those who provided data; they would not be able to generalize the results to the entire group. Despite this limitation, it was decided to continue with the evaluation since the evaluation process itself was instrumental in driving needed changes in the HPI implementation strategy. Those responding identified impact with regard to productivity, quality, cost, and time as well as additional measures of success.

Based on the findings, customers perceived ADET to be a provider of training. This gave the HPI program opportunity to flourish. Customers recommended a number of changes categorized into four areas including supportive, responsive, flexible, and strategic. One concern based on the results, however, was that 55.5 percent of the 27 customers responding to the survey used ADET's services either on a yearly basis or not at all. This led to the question: To what extent should customers be using ADET services?

Productivity, Quality, Cost, and Time

Table 4-8 summarizes the improvements identified by participants and supervisors that could be categorized as productivity, quality, cost, and time. These measures have the potential of being converted to monetary value and applied to the ROI calculation.

Other Measures of Success

Along with measures of productivity, quality, cost, and time, participants and supervisors identified a number of other measures that could be improved as a result of the HPI program (table 4-9). These measures are considered intangible in that an attempt would not be made to convert these to monetary value. While they might not be included in the ROI calculation, they are important measures of success to the HPI program.

The final phase of the evaluation was to take measures identified by participants and supervisors, convert them to monetary value, and compare these values with the cost to calculate the forecast ROI.

Level 5

Although the forecasted ROI from the participant and supervisor perspectives was positive, a question of accuracy and credibility existed. Had a larger percentage of responses been obtained, a more credible value could have been calculated. But, for those who

Table 4-8. Measures of productivity, quality, cost, and time.

Participants (N = 6)	Supervisors (N = 4)
• Improved assessment and analysis	• Quality control of externally purchased programs
• Improved organization (management) of the HPI process	• Reduced redundancy of programs
• Costs savings in-house versus external product training video	• Reduced number of courses offered that do not advance customer goals
• Quality control of existing purchased programs	• Reduced course development time
• Ability to track dollars	• Increased number of courses meeting specific customer needs
• Increase proficiency in ROI evaluation process	• Translation of mission goals and performance objectives into a solution
	• Ability to track dollars

Table 4-9. Additional measures poised to improve after the course.

Participants	Supervisors
• Improved communication strategy	• A baseline level of instructor knowledge, better teaching delivery, and more relevant content
• Incorporation of evaluation concepts up-front, a beginning with the end in mind	• Better trained workforce that knows its job and duties
	• Development of evaluation strategy for new programs
	• Facilitation of discussion for articulating mission impact
	• Preferred solution for our customers

did respond, conservative steps were taken to ensure credibility of estimates.

Benefits Converted to Monetary Value

Using the forecast questionnaire, participants and supervisors were asked to identify one measure that would be most improved due to the ASTD HPI program. Respondents were then asked to place an annual monetary value on that improvement and adjust the error by placing their level of confidence on that value. To help them convert benefits to monetary value, the participants and supervisors were asked this set of questions:

1. As a result of applying the skills and knowledge learned in the ASTD HPI program, what specific measures, outcomes, or projects will improve (for example, reduction in time to develop a solution)?

2. Which one of the measures, outcomes, or projects identified in item 1 will most improve as a result of applying the skills and knowledge learned?

3. As a result of this improvement, what would you estimate in monetary terms to be the value of the benefits to your organization over a period of one year?

4. What is the basis of this estimate?

5. How confident, expressed as a percentage, are you in your estimate (0% = no confidence; 100% = certainty)?

The challenge in using this approach to data conversion is that respondents are often unfamiliar with the questions and the type of data being pursued. A successful approach to gathering monetary value using this series of questions includes introducing the questions to potential respondents at the outset of the program, reinforcing the need for these types of data throughout the process, then reminding potential respondents of the questions prior to administering the questionnaire. These steps were not completed for the HPI forecast evaluation.

Table 4-10 shows the results for the six participants responding to the questionnaire. Only three measures were converted to monetary value, resulting in a total projected monetary benefit of the HPI program of $270,157 as estimated by participants. As shown in the table, participants who estimated a value provided a basis for their estimate.

Supervisors were asked the same series of questions. Of the four supervisors responding to the forecast questionnaire, three provided estimated monetary values. Supervisors responding expected the monetary value of the HPI program to be $605,000. Table 4-11 summarizes the supervisors' forecasts. Again, the estimated values were supported by a basis.

ROI Calculation

At the outset of the evaluation, a 25 percent ROI was established as the target. Target ROI percentages depend on the organization. Some organizations set the target at the same level of other investments. Other organizations raise the bar on training ROI because of the expansive nature of programs. Still other organizations set the target at the rate the client expects. Finally, many organizations will accept a break-even ROI. For purposes of the HPI Certificate Program, a 25 percent ROI seemed reasonable. The effects of such a large investment and widespread culture change should reap high returns.

The equations used for the calculation were:

$$BCR = \frac{Benefits}{Costs}$$

$$ROI = \frac{Net\ Program\ Benefits}{Costs} \times 100$$

Based on the monetary benefits estimated by participants, the ROI forecast for the HPI program resulted in a 1.034:1 BCR and a 3.4 percent ROI. In other words, for every $1 invested in the HPI program, NSA gets 3.4 cents back after costs:

$$BCR = \frac{\$270,157}{\$261,235.54} = 1.034$$

$$ROI = \frac{(\$270,157 - \$261,235.54)}{\$261,235.54} \times 100 = 3.4\%$$

The supervisors were more optimistic. The ROI forecast based on the supervisors' responses resulted in a BCR of 2.32:1 and an ROI of 132 percent. This suggests that for every $1 invested in the HPI program, NSA gets $1.32 back after costs:

$$BCR = \frac{\$605,000}{\$261,235.54} = 2.32$$

$$ROI = \frac{(\$605,000 - \$261,235.54)}{\$261,235.54} \times 100 = 132\%$$

Given the limited amount of data and the lack of understanding of the evaluation process, these projections are not unreasonable. Although the participant

Table 4-10. Participants' estimates of monetary benefit of the HPI program.

Participant	Measure	Estimated Monetary Value	Basis	Confidence	Adjusted Value
1	Ability to track dollars	$500,000	Less redundancy	50%	$250,000
2	Increase proficiency in ROI process	$20,000	Less contractor support and more ROI conducted	0	0
3	Improved assessment and analysis	$7,488	$48 per hour × 3 hours saved per week (48 × 3) × 52 weeks per year	80%	$5,990
4	Increased use of technology	Not applicable	5% decrease in development time	25%	0
5	Not applicable	Not applicable	Not applicable	Not applicable	Not applicable
6	Reduced video retakes	$16,667	Time (salary and benefits)	85%	$14,167
	Total Forecasted Monetary Benefit Attributable to ASTD's HPI Certificate Program:				**$270,157**

Table 4-11. Supervisors' estimates of monetary benefit of the HPI program.

Supervisor	Measure	Estimated Monetary Value	Basis	Confidence	Adjusted Value
1	Facilitating discussion for articulating mission impact	$500,000	Reduced training time for participants and adjuncts	60%	$300,000
2	Ability to track dollars	$500,000	Less redundancy by reviewing the database and comparing usage of courses	50%	$250,000
3	Reduced number of courses offered that do not advance customer goals	Not applicable	Not applicable	Not applicable	Not applicable
4	Increased emulation of work environment	$220,000	Work-hours saved day to day (cost: hours spent learning and applying; benefit: 5% time savings × 40 teachers × salary)	25%	$55,000
	Total Forecasted Monetary Benefit Attributable to ASTD's HPI Certificate Program:				**$605,000**

forecast is less than the 25 percent target, the supervisors are optimistic the returns will far exceed the 25 percent target. To ensure a positive ROI, however, it will be necessary to further assist participants in the application of what they have learned as well as support them in providing data. Course 2 is a critical course in the transformation process. It is also the course that scored the lowest on most measures. Steps should be taken to ensure that participants understand what to do and how to apply the knowledge and skills in course 2.

The ultimate question asked in the ROI Methodology is this: *Do the monetary benefits meet or exceed the cost of the program?* Based on the participant and supervisor forecasts, the answer to this question is yes for those who provided data. The participant forecast did not meet the 25 percent ROI target, but positive returns are expected with a 3.4 percent ROI. Supervisors are optimistic with their forecasted 132 percent ROI.

Can a major funding decision be made based on these ROI calculations alone? Most likely not; however, in looking at the ROI in the context of other data provided, decisions can be made on how to improve the HPI implementation and the evaluation process within ADET.

Intangible Benefits

Only six measures were converted to monetary value for purposes of this study. Other measures identified for potential improvement are considered intangible—yet they are as critical as those used in the ROI calculation. Intangible measures identified by participants and supervisors included

- improved organization (management) of the HPI process

- reduced program costs
  - reduced redundancy of programs
  - reduced course development time
  - reduced costs of programs
  - quality control of externally purchased programs

- develop evaluation strategy for new programs
  - incorporation of evaluation concepts up front
  - beginning with the end in mind

- preferred solution for our customers
  - increased number of courses meeting specific customer needs

— translating mission goals and performance objectives into a solution.

These potential intangible benefits suggested that ASTD's HPI Certificate Program will prove valuable to ADET and the entire NSA organization. Opportunity to provide additional monetary benefits to the ROI equation lie in cost measures: reduced redundancy of programs, reduced course development time, reduced costs of programs, and quality control of externally purchased programs.

Communication Strategy

The primary researcher for this study was Patti Phillips, CEO of the Chelsea Group and president of the ROI Institute, who, in collaboration with the chief of evaluation, presented the findings of the ROI forecast to the ADET senior management team in a one-hour, face-to-face session. The chief of evaluation wanted to ensure there was perceived objectivity on the part of the evaluation staff, particularly relative to the HPI course 2 evaluation issues; therefore, it was important that Phillips address the senior managers about the lack of participant accountability for completing the evaluation questionnaires and action plans.

A formal report was provided a week before the briefing. Based on the positive ROI forecast results predicted by supervisors and the potential of the HPI program to improve the ADET value proposition, the ADET senior management team agreed to invest in a second offering of the ASTD HPI Certificate Program.

During the second implementation, Bernadette Schoukroun of the ADET evaluation organization (as well as a participant in the HPI program) coordinated the evaluation effort by serving as the ADET liaison and maintaining internal communications with the HPI program participants and supervisors. Throughout the evaluation period, Schoukroun and Phillips communicated with the participants by means of email exchanges, face-to-face dialog, focus groups, and one-on-one coaching. In addition, the chief of evaluation, as a member of the ADET senior management team, kicked off the HPI program with an overview of the importance of the HPI program and the ROI study and provided all participants and supervisors with a two-hour workshop on how to complete the ROI action plan.

One email was sent by the chief of ADET to all the participants and their supervisors as to the importance of the program. The email was coordinated with the chief of evaluation prior to release to ensure there was a consistent message of the importance of the HPI training program and the expected Level 4 objectives for implementing an HPI strategy.

Lessons Learned

The ASTD HPI Certificate Program has great potential to enhance ADET's capability to bring value to its customers. When mission-related measures are converted to monetary value and compared to the cost, the monetary benefits should outweigh the costs as long as participants see the value in the program, develop the intended skills, and apply those skills. The following lessons learned can be drawn from a analysis of the HPI program evaluation.

These lessons are grouped into three categories: the program, the HPI strategy implementation, and the evaluation strategy. Each of these areas was addressed in the second implementation of the ASTD HPI Certificate Program.

The Program

The program was somewhat of a success in that participants believed the courses were relevant to their job and for the most part they intended to use what they had learned in the courses back on the job, although no single course met the 80 percent high-rating target. As with any program of this magnitude, there is always room for improvement.

Acquiring evaluation data for course 2 was the biggest challenge. The evaluation data collected indicated there were serious issues with the course. Although it was one of the primary skill-building courses, course 2 received low ratings on all Level 1 measures except for frequency of use. Some participants who completed the PEAK questionnaire commented that there was too much information provided for the time allowed for the course. Others indicated that the facilitator was disorganized; yet, most recognized the importance of the course.

Although most participants responded to questionnaires for the other courses, 60 percent of the participants did not respond to survey questions for course 2. Why? When asked during a follow-up focus group, several of the participants who did not respond to the questionnaire claimed that the instructor was disorganized, did not respond to questions from the students, and rushed through the material. The students believed that they did not learn what was expected from the course. This finding served as the basis for changes to the second ASTD HPI program offering, particularly to course 2.

The ASTD HPI Program learning objectives were not written to address the intended Level 3 and Level 4 outcomes of ADET. In addition, the instructors were not prepared to provide ADET with formal learning assessments of how well the learners acquired new knowledge and skills. To maintain the chain of impact, the evaluator had to develop proxy measures of learning collected with a self-rated pre- and post-program assessment.

The HPI Strategy Implementation

Several issues surfaced during the evaluation: lack of understanding of the reasons for another change in direction, organizational management of the HPI process, and priorities relative to projects and tasking. As a result, ADET needs to articulate well-defined Level 4 objectives aligned with the organization's strategic drivers for change and communicate those objectives throughout the second offering of the HPI program.

Participants and supervisors identified several barriers that might have prevented the application of knowledge and skills learned. These barriers are categorized as culture, goals, and expectations. The most frequently cited comment was the need for ADET managers to establish a policy relative to management and implementation of an HPI process. The participants expressed a desire for supervisors to articulate how job performance expectations would change as a result of attending the HPI program.

Although learning and intent to use knowledge and skills were evident through the evaluation, they did not receive sufficient priority by the respondents. In addition, the participants' suggestions to make the ASTD HPI Certificate Program case studies more relevant to the participants' job focus indicate that the participants needed to have a clearer understanding of how the HPI process fits into the existing processes. This focus could be achieved through a well-thought-out communication strategy, additional coaching, follow-up training, and other interventions to further support the transfer of knowledge into practice.

Evaluation Strategy

Data collection was a challenge. A data collection administration strategy is important to ensure that the appropriate amount of data is provided. For the most part, participants returned their PEAK surveys at the end of each course (with the exception of course 2, in which only 40 percent of the participants returned surveys). ADET also encountered difficulties in getting completed participant and supervisor forecast questionnaires, thereby delaying the evaluation results. Still, the number of those who did provide data was minimal. Customer response was more positive; however, success was limited to 50 percent response rate out of 54 surveys distributed. Based on verbal feedback to the evaluation staff, limited response to the evaluation by all informants was partially due to a lack of understanding of the following:

- importance of the evaluation by participants and their supervisors
- evaluation process by participants and their supervisors
- ADET HPI strategy by customers.

Other than the Level 1 PEAK instrument, the ROI forecast and other aspects of a results-based evaluation strategy, such as a needs assessment, were not included in the initial planning stages of planning for purchasing and delivering the HPI program. Because of this, the students claimed they were overwhelmed by the various questionnaires and evaluation forms they had to complete. This may have led to "evaluation fatigue," which affected the quality of the evaluation data. ROI and evaluation must be considered during the needs assessment, design, and development stages of any major change initiative to enhance data collection, data accuracy, and results credibility.

Because this was an ROI forecast study, the estimated monetary values of the benefits could not be validated; however, ADET managers were satisfied with the projections as a basis for their decision to offer a second version of the HPI program. The ADET evaluation chief decided not to conduct a post-program evaluation; rather, an ROI study would be conducted for the second offering. The lessons learned and recommendations from this study would drive changes in the design and delivery of that iteration.

Conclusion

Based on the outcomes of the ROI forecast study, ADET implemented some significant changes to enhance the impact of the second offering of the HPI program. A new ADET organization was created to facilitate ADET's transition to a results-based learning organization. This new organization joined together ADET's requirements process, the new performance consulting line of business, needs assessment, evaluation, and faculty development. The integration of these key processes and functional areas into the Center for Learning Analytics and Strategies created a capability to strategically align the HPI process with the new direction of ADET. Consequently, the follow-on evaluation was systematically integrated into the HPI program at the outset.

The following actions were taken:

- The HPI program course instructors were informed and engaged in the ADET HPI program evaluation strategy.
- The Level 2 learning assessments were aligned with ADET's Level 3 performance and four mission objectives.
- Students and supervisors were engaged in the evaluation at the beginning of the program through a series of formal briefings to explain the program's purpose and establish accountability by defining roles and responsibilities of all informants in the evaluation process.
- Several customized workshops were designed to demonstrate the application of the HPI process at NSA, thus bridging the gap between theory and practice and providing context that participants can relate to.
- Certified performance improvement consultants were brought in to provide consultation, coaching, and mentoring on implementing the HPI process at NSA.
- The student selection process was modified to include a senior management review to ensure all students would have jobs requiring the application of new knowledge and skills gained in the program.
- A comprehensive communication strategy was implemented to include an HPI portal site.
- A special course offering of "What is HPI?" was offered to ADET supervisors, customers, and potential implementation partners of the strategy.
- Two key workshops, Action Planning, as a pre-program workshop, and ROI Certification, as a post-program workshop, were offered to the participants.

As ADET implements its performance consulting function, customers are beginning to appreciate the value of analyzing their problems in a more holistic way. The small successes are documented and communicated to help customers understand and embrace the HPI process. ADET has experienced an influx of customer requests for needs analysis, evaluation, and strategic guidance. Customers are returning for advice, support, and evaluation, and assessment projects have increased by 100 percent in the last year. ADET's response to customers at all levels of management has become "training will not solve all your problems," and the customers are starting to catch on.

 ## Questions for Discussion

1. How can a forecast ROI study and the resultant data be used to manage change and achieve greater value from an employee development initiative within public sector organizations?

2. Collecting valid and reliable data is a challenging task with any evaluation study. Although the number of respondents for this study is small, ADET senior managers used the results of the study to make significant changes. Was this an appropriate use of the study? Why or why not? Identify ways in which ADET could have improved its data collection efforts and increased the validity of the study.

3. Based on this study, was ADET ready to roll out a program of this magnitude? If not, what could it have done differently? What could it have done differently to improve learning transfer for its HPI program participants?

4. Were the appropriate key measures selected for the HPI program? What other measures might have been used to ensure that the program was aligned with ADET strategic direction?

5. Isolation techniques are considered an essential aspect of the ROI process. Isolation was not viewed as a critical step in this study. Do you agree with the decision not to isolate the impact of the changed behavior during a forecast study? Defend your answer.

About the Authors

Bernadette Schoukroun is an educational program evaluator and instructional technologist consultant for ADET. Schoukroun designs and conducts program evaluations as well as provides oversight for evaluations conducted by internal and external evaluators for HR reform initiatives. Her consulting services in instructional systems design methodologies facilitate the improvement of ADET HR programs. Her expertise is in innovative approaches to technology-based performance improvement initiatives including the groundbreaking Joint Intelligence Virtual University project, which received the National Intelligence Meritorious Unit Citation in 2002. She received a master's degree of arts in educational technology leadership from George Washington University. Evaluating and implementing effective educational technology interventions is at the forefront of her research. Schoukroun can be reached at bschouk @ nsa.gov.

Deborah Wharff is a senior manager with ADET. As the director of the Center for Learning Analytics and Strategies, she leads an organization with a diverse portfolio that includes strategic planning, HPI, research, requirements management, learning needs assessments, evaluation, organizational performance measures, and faculty development. Wharff has extensive experience in the field of adult development and learning, with an emphasis on leadership development. Her pioneering research of spiritual leadership in the public sector has been recognized by the Academy of Management and the Institute for Behavioral and Applied Management.

Wharff's accomplishments in measuring the impact of learning led her agency to achieve best-in-class status by the American Productivity and Quality Center. She is certified as an ROI professional by the ROI Institute and has conducted numerous ROI studies of key employee development programs, resulting in significant program improvements and cost avoidance to the taxpayers. Wharff holds a doctorate of management from the University of Maryland. She can be reached at dmwharf@nsa.gov.

Chapter 5

This case was prepared to serve as a basis for discussion rather than to illustrate either effective or ineffective administrative and management practices.

FORECASTING THE ROI OF SALES TRAINING
Wachovia Mortgage Corporation

Terri B. Burroughs

Senior leaders need information that is relevant to problems or issues they face that can assist them in making critical business decisions. This information must be supported by reliable and credible data, and presented in a concise, compelling, and timely manner. Wachovia's learning community acknowledges that evaluation is not the decision itself but, rather, the preparation for the decision. To that end, this case study demonstrates how the ROI Methodology was used to forecast the ROI of a major sales training initiative and helped inform the decision making of senior leaders that addressed performance issues well beyond training.

Background

Wachovia Mortgage Corporation (WMC) is a nationwide mortgage lender that offers a full array of first mortgage and home equity products and services for home purchase and refinance. WMC is the 17th largest retail mortgage lender and 23rd largest combined retail/wholesale mortgage lender in the United States and employs more than 2,300 people nationwide. The company addresses the unique needs of the low-to-moderate, middle market, and wealth-income segments through three origination channels: traditional retail lending; direct lending; and third-party lending, which originates loans via mortgage brokers and correspondents.

The residential mortgage lending business is production oriented and operates at its peak with a high

volume, continuous flow of loans being originated, marketed, and serviced (Mortgage Bankers Association of America, 1998). Like many industries, mortgage lending depends on supply and demand. Demand is driven by the prosperity of the consumers served by the residential mortgage lending industry. A good economy drives personal income and spending. Likewise, overall economic trends drive the demand for new and existing home financing. Consequently, the mortgage lending business is cyclical, and it is critical that companies investing in this line of business are able to capitalize on these cycles in order to remain profitable, especially when the demand for mortgage loans dries up.

This was the issue facing WMC. As a result of economic conditions and the end of the refinance boom, the industry anticipated a 53 percent decline in mortgage originations in 2004. To compound this issue, as part of a larger banking organization, WMC was tasked with doubling its current market share by 2006, regardless of market conditions. These issues challenged the mortgage corporation to find the answers to the following questions around the mortgage loan origination process:

- How can the organization build and retain a high-performing sales workforce?
- What are the critical components of high-performing sales organizations?
- What processes should sales leaders implement to sustain sales performance?
- How can the company maximize mortgage opportunities with existing bank customers?

Problem/Opportunity

Due to internal organizational changes and external mergers, by the end of 2002 WMC comprised mortgage operations from several organizations. The result was a lack of a companywide sales vision, process, and strategy. Not only did each legacy company use or have access to several sales training programs, many of them did not effectively address sales management and process needs. In addition, tactical learning needs for the salesforce were not being adequately addressed by channel. These issues, combined with the challenging economic

environment, were the catalysts for examining the WMC sales training and management processes.

Performance Improvement Process

The model in figure 5-1 depicts the process used by WMC for assessing performance issues in the organization. This is the foundation on which the ROI forecast presented in this case was based. The process begins with identification of the problem or opportunity and moves to a point where learning is prescribed and an evaluation strategy can be defined.

This performance-based approach has four important and very significant benefits (Wachovia Corporation, 2004):

- *More efficient use of resources:* This approach ensures that learning interventions are only undertaken if they are adding value and impacting important goals, strategies, and objectives of the business unit.
- *Improved business impact of all learning interventions:* Because the process is focused on important business unit needs, the success of learning opportunities will be enhanced to show improved business impact.
- *Increased client satisfaction:* Participants will clearly see the connection to business unit performance. Managers will have useful information to assist them as they coach and

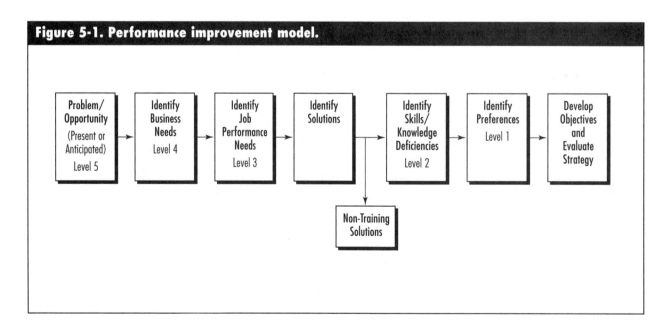

Figure 5-1. Performance improvement model.

inspect expected behavioral changes after training.

- *Increased support and commitment from senior management:* Quantifiable results of learning interventions and performance indicators will provide senior leaders with the hard and soft data required to assist them with measuring attainment of their business unit goals. Increased support of and commitment to the HR organization will follow.

This process drives the assessment, measurement, and evaluation (AME) work of WMC and requires effective partnership and collaboration between the human resources business partners (HRBPs), training teams, and the business leaders they support.

Business Needs

Integration efforts provided the perfect opportunity for the WMC training team to proactively identify and partner with their client to address the business and performance issues in the sales organization. In response to a routine question regarding a vendor invoice for sales training, the training team leader provided the information requested in addition to a summary of all the various sales programs currently deployed in the organization and their incumbent costs. The response from the training leader included a proposal that the training team be engaged to evaluate not only the existing sales programs, but more importantly the business and performance needs of the sales organization and the potential ROI of a proposed intervention.

The response closed with an offer to facilitate in-depth discussions around this issue. This overt request for inclusion, along with the focus on business and performance needs supported by business impact information versus just training, was a key driver in the collaborative nature of the relationship between the business unit and the training team on this initiative. As a result, training team members were at the table during strategic business discussions, and over the next several months the following business needs and opportunities surfaced:

- Double the market share from 1 percent to 2 percent by 2006.
- Design and retain a high-performance sales culture and workforce.

- Deepen customer relationships through cross-sell penetration by maximizing mortgage opportunities with the existing 13 million Wachovia households.
- Develop comprehensive sales and marketing plans for all business channels.

Job Performance Needs

As a first step in identifying the job performance needs, the training team conducted an assessment designed to identify performance issues and their causes. Although the leadership team began the process with training as the focal point, the performance analysis influenced them to think more broadly about what would be needed to attain the stated business objectives.

The WMC training team conducted a performance analysis that included written self-assessments and a focus group meeting with local and regional sales managers from all channels, account executives, mortgage consultants from all channels, and relationship managers. HRBPs participated in the meetings and collaborated in this performance assessment process. The analysis revealed the following skill/knowledge gaps for mortgage consultants and sales managers:

- identifying, understanding, and addressing customer needs
- applying sales skills effectively
- selling against the competition
- establishing and maintaining strategic relationships
- overcoming obstacles and objections
- developing business sales and marketing plans
- giving clear direction, setting goals, and establishing effective processes
- finding niche markets in the mortgage industry.

The analysis revealed the following environmental and resource gaps or issues:

- lack of a consistent coaching model/process
- poorly defined and communicated sales vision and culture
- no tools for measuring and reporting sales results

- lack of partnerships between sales and servi-center staff.

Last, but not least, feedback indicated that the learning environment should

- address the varied levels of experience and allow customization by channel as appropriate
- incorporate focus on customer service
- leverage industry expertise
- address product, process, and technology learning needs.

Solutions

As a result of this analysis, the WMC business unit implemented a sales initiative to address the skill, environmental, and resource gaps identified. This initiative has since evolved into the Market Share Initiative (MSI), which addresses five key focus areas for improving sales performance at WMC: sales vision and strategy, sales training, sales management, sales measurement and reporting, and motivational sales meetings.

In support of the training component of this initiative, the WMC training partners put together several recommendations for the WMC leadership team. The support, ongoing feedback, collaboration, and partnership were invaluable to the process and heavily influenced the development, credibility, and reception of the final proposal. The sales training proposal was designed to focus on three areas of skill development:

- *Generic/core sales skills:* The core sales skill-training program was to be developed and initially deployed by an external vendor. The leadership team had the opportunity to preview the program and offer input into the vendor selection process. The program was comprehensive in content and delivery options and addressed the majority of the common core skill needs identified by WMC. In addition, the delivery methods were customized to meet the needs of various audiences.
- *Mortgage-industry-specific sales skills:* In a blended design approach (self-study, leader-led conferences, Web-based training, classroom training, and so forth), applicable modules from a mortgage industry training leader

were offered in concert with the core skill training to enhance mortgage-specific skills.

- *WMC-specific/tactical skills:* The internal WMC training team was to continue to offer WMC specific sales skill training. Appropriate core and industry modules were integrated into these programs.

Objectives

Data collection plans were developed for each WMC delivery channel; figure 5-2 shows the one developed for the retail lending division. Learning and performance objectives were designed to target the following synopsized list of skills and behaviors:

- need-satisfaction selling
- professional selling skills and application
- selling against the competition
- professional sales negotiations
- winning account strategies
- professional sales coaching for managers
- specific mortgage-industry skills (for example, finding niche markets, marketing, selling to realtors and builders).

Evaluation Strategy

Because of the costs associated with the generic/core sales skills and the mortgage-industry-specific sales skills components of the proposal, the training team conducted an ROI forecast on the recommended program. This forecast, designed to estimate the potential success of the WMC sales training program, has several key objectives:

- to estimate the specific contribution of the training to the business
- to forecast the potential business impact to WMC
- to validate the proposal for WMC leaders.

Model for ROI Forecast

The ROI Methodology (Phillips, 1997) was applied to this business situation to forecast ROI. The training team developed the data collection plans in collaboration with WMC sales leaders and the HRBPs. These key stakeholders helped the team identify the important areas of data collection and analysis. Not only did this approach save the training team time

Figure 5-2. The data collection plan for the WMC sales training pilot, retail lending division.

Level	Objective(s)	Measures/Data	Data Collection Method	Data Sources	Timing	Responsibilities
1	**REACTION/SATISFACTION** • Positive reaction to content, relevance, importance, format, facilitation, materials, and intent to use skills learned	• 4 out of 5 on response scale • Completed action plans	• End-of-program questionnaire	• Participants (indirect sales staff)	• End of program	• Facilitator
2	**LEARNING** • Identify and act on sales opportunities • Increase chances of gaining customer commitment • Identify and respond to customer needs • Link solutions to customer needs and business challenges when approaching competitive sales situations • Establish and maintain relationship-enhancing strategies • Sell more competitively by establishing positive distinctive profiles for themselves and organization • Analyze competitive information • Overcome obstacles and objections • Identify, describe, and implement strategies for increasing mortgage sales • Learn strategies for acquiring and keeping new business • Identify, describe, and implement methods for reinforcing and coaching to performance	• Satisfactory score on self-assessment • Satisfactory performance on skill assessment • Satisfactory score on skill assessment	• End of program questionnaire (self-assessment for learning change)	• Participants	• End of program	• Facilitator
3	**APPLICATION/IMPLEMENTATION** • Utilize tools for increasing sales • Utilize tools for gaining customer commitment • Apply the skills gained for developing solid business relationships while improving sales performance • Increase effectiveness by applying skills for becoming knowledgeable business consultants • Apply skills for linking solutions to customer needs and business challenges • Utilize the skills for selling more competitively • Effectively and efficiently analyze competitive information when accessible • Demonstrate effective communication skills versus high-pressure sales tactics • Utilize coaching tools	• 4 out of 5 on response scale on questionnaire	• Follow-up questionnaire • Manager survey • Servicenter survey	• Participants • Manager • Servicenter reps	• 60–90 days post-program	• Evaluation team

(continued next page)

Figure 5-2. The data collection plan for the WMC sales training pilot, retail lending division *(continued)*.

Level	Objective(s)	Measures/Data	Data Collection Method	Data Sources	Timing	Responsibilities
4	**BUSINESS IMPACT**					
	• Increase customer satisfaction	• "Willingness to do business again" score on Gallup poll	• Business performance monitoring	• Customer satisfaction report	• 120 days post-program	• Evaluation team
	• Increase sales growth (volume/units) • Increase profit contribution	• Total increase (before/after comparison)	• Business performance monitoring	• Stack-ranking report	• 90–120 days post-program	
	• Reduce voluntary turnover	• Percent of employees leaving within 9 months • Percent of employees leaving overall	• Business performance monitoring	• Sales turnover report	• 9 months post-program	
	• Increase cross-sell percentages	• Change in percent by individual and region	• Business performance monitoring	• Cross-sell report	• 90–120 days post-program	
	• Enhance professional image of sales representative	• 4 out of 5 on response scale	• Questionnaire • Post-program focus group	• Participants • Managers	• 60–90 days post-program	
5	**ROI**					

Comments: Positive ROI expected.

when the program is deployed, but it also boosted the team's credibility when the ROI forecast data was presented.

Linking Training to Business Impact

One critical aspect of this study was to identify the linkage between the proposed training program and the stated business measures. To this end, WMC sales leaders were asked to identify the specific business measures that should be impacted by the proposed program. The sales leadership team identified the following business measures as the most likely to be influenced by the WMC sales training program:

- increased customer satisfaction
- increased sales growth
- increased revenue
- increased employee retention
- attainment of sales goals
- increased cross-sell percentages
- increased broker satisfaction
- increased correspondent satisfaction
- enhanced professional image of sales representatives.

The sales leaders were then asked to estimate the extent to which they felt these measures should be impacted by the training. Table 5-1 summarizes their responses.

Forecasting Business Impact

As stated previously, the training team employed the ROI Methodology to forecast the potential business impact of the proposed program on all WMC sales channels. This process required that the total benefit from the training program be calculated simply and conservatively. In keeping with this principle, the following adjustments were made to the benefits data:

- Only the first year's benefits were assumed.
- All known costs were fully loaded.
- Although the forecast return is based on first year's results only, the forecast data around subsequent year's ROI was included as a comparison point. This was important because costs associated with vendor facilitation and internal trainer certification would only occur in the first year.

- Because several factors usually influence performance data after training programs have been conducted, sales leaders were asked to estimate the amount of improvement directly related to the program.
- Confidence level percentages were used to acknowledge the subjective nature of these estimates. The benefit was adjusted downward to reflect the confidence levels.

The training leader made another critical decision that affected the credibility of the information presented. This decision involved reaching out to the WMC finance team to participate in the ROI forecasting process. Representatives of each WMC sales channel *and* from the WMC finance team provided volume forecast data. From a credibility perspective it was important to show the benefit and ROI calculations using the projections from both groups. The data from the finance team was much more conservative in that volume projections

Table 5-1. Linkage to business measures as perceived by WMC sales leaders.*		
Business Impact Measure	**Minimal Impact (% Responding)**	**Strong Impact (% Responding)**
Increased customer satisfaction	17	83
Increased sales growth	0	100
Improved revenue	8	92
Increased employee retention	42	58
Attainment of sales goals	17	83
Increased cross-sell percentages	17	83
Increased broker satisfaction	100	0
Increased correspondent satisfaction	100	0
Enhanced professional image of sales reps	17	83

* Total responses received = 12.

excluded referral, direct mail, and Internet business, nor did it include the expected lift from the MSI.

Via the questionnaire in figure 5-3, WMC sales leaders were asked to provide estimates to be used as the basis for the forecasts.

The questionnaire responses revealed that the unit of measure most directly impacted by the intended audience was sales volume. The sales leaders estimated that this measure (sales volume) could be expected to increase 10 to 15 percent after the training period; about 50 percent of this change could be attributable to the training itself. They were 50 percent confident in their estimates. Using these estimates, the WMC finance team calculated profitability (table 5-2).

Program Costs

The costs are important because they reflect the overall investment in this program. Costs were fully loaded to reflect the most conservative calculations, which again contributed to the credibility of the ROI

Figure 5-3. Questionnaire given to WMC sales channel leaders.

Projected Impact of Training

We expect that the application of the skills and knowledge learned in the WMC Sales Training Program will positively impact multiple key business measures within your division or line of business. Please reflect on the objectives of the training and respond to the questions listed below.

1. What is the unit(s) of measure most directly impacted by this training audience (sales)?

   _____

2. What is the value of one unit? $ _____

3. How did you arrive at this value? _____

   _____

   _____

4. How much do you expect this measure to change after the training process (monthly value)? _____

   _____

5. What percentage of the change above do you think will be influenced by the application of knowledge and skills gained from the sales training program?_____ % (0% = none, and 100% = all)

6. As a result of this program what do you estimate to be the increase in the personal effectiveness of participants, expressed as a percentage?
   _____ %

7. As a result of any changes in the thinking, new knowledge, or planned actions of participants and their managers, please estimate (in monetary value) the benefits to your organization (for example, increased customer satisfaction, reduced turnover, increased partner/broker/correspondent satisfaction, increased personal effectiveness, increased revenue) over a period of one year: $ _____

8. What is the basis of this estimate? _____

   _____

   _____

9. What level of confidence do you place on the above estimations? _____ % confidence (0% = no confidence, and 100% = certainty)

Table 5-2. Estimates of the training's impact.

2004 Base Volume (Units)*	Incremental Volume Change	Unit Change	Profitability ($/Unit)	Profitability ($)	Benefit After Isolation (50%)	Benefit After Confidence Adjustment (50%)
			WMC Sales Channel Estimates			
126,964	10%	12,696	$1,054	$13,382,006	$6,691,003	$3,345,501
126,964	12%	15,236	$1,054	$16,058,407	$8,029,203	$4,014,602
126,964	15%	19,045	$1,054	$20,073,008	$10,036,504	$5,018,252
			Finance Team Estimates			
34,168	10%	3,417	$1,054	$3,601,307	$1,800,654	$900,327
34,168	12%	4,100	$1,054	$4,321,569	$2,160,784	$1,080,392
34,168	15%	5,125	$1,054	$5,401,961	$2,700,980	$1,350,490

analysis. Trainer certification, vendor fees and expenses, and course customization costs were all fully loaded into the ROI calculation for this analysis even though these costs could be distributed over future deliveries of this program.

Based on a review of the program objectives, course descriptions, and desired impact, sales leaders defined ideal pilot scenarios. In setting the number of participants as well as potential rollout locations, they considered

- market conditions (for example, the anticipated decline in mortgage originations in 2004 with the end of the refinance boom)
- skill and experience levels of employees
- priority needs for the specific channel.

Consequently, several pilot options were developed, ranging from a full-scale pilot involving 440 sales team members to a reduced participant pilot targeting approximately 220 participants.

Forecasted ROI

Table 5-3 shows the various training pilot options and the corresponding ROI scenarios that were created and analyzed. The ROI forecast was calculated for each pilot option using the volume and benefit data provided by WMC. The standard ROI calculation was used.

Based on a review of the business unit priorities and program objectives, option 2B (the reduced impact pilot) was proposed. It should result in an ROI ranging from 4 percent (based on the finance team's volume estimates) to 285 percent (based on the WMC sales channels' volume estimates). This range was based on a 12 percent incremental volume change and represented the first and most conservative point at which the estimated change reflects a positive ROI using both finance and WMC volumes. The recommendation was based on the following:

- the ability to balance the need to increase sales skills while maintaining market coverage and profitability
- the need for capacity to focus on other key WMC priorities in 2004
- a smaller, more focused pilot enabling optimal testing with minimal investment.

Communications Process

The training team prepared and presented an executive summary of the findings to the WMC leadership

Table 5-3. ROI calculations for the various training pilot scenarios.

Option	Option Description	Option Cost	10% Incremental Volume Change	10% Benefit ROI	12% Incremental Volume Change	12% Benefit ROI	15% Incremental Volume Change	15% Benefit ROI
			ROI Forecasts Based on WMC Sales Channel Estimates					
1	Full-Scale Pilot (440 Participants)	$2,567,337	$3,345,501	30%	$4,014,602	56%	$5,018,252	95%
1B	Reduced Participant Pilot (224 Participants)	$1,444,664	$3,345,501	132%	$4,014,602	178%	$5,018,252	247%
2	Priority Course Pilot (440 Participants)	$1,849,692	$3,345,501	81%	$4,014,602	117%	$5,018,252	171%
2B	Priority Course Reduced Participant Pilot (224 Participants)	$1,040,450	$3,345,501	222%	$4,014,602	286%	$5,018,252	382%
	2005	$873,276	$3,345,501	283%	$4,014,602	360%	$5,018,252	475%
	2006 and beyond	$773,375	$3,345,501	333%	$4,014,602	419%	$5,018,252	549%
			ROI Forecasts Based on Finance Team Estimates					
1	Full-Scale Pilot (440 Participants)	$2,567,337	$900,327	−65%	$1,080,392	−58%	$1,350,490	−47%
1B	Reduced Participant Pilot (224 Participants)	$1,444,664	$900,327	−38%	$1,080,392	−25%	$1,350,490	−7%
2	Priority Course Pilot (440 Participants)	$1,849,692	$900,327	−51%	$1,080,392	−42%	$1,350,490	−27%
2B	Priority Course Reduced Participant Pilot (224 Participants)	$1,040,450	$900,327	−13%	$1,080,392	4%	$1,350,490	30%
	2005	$873,276	$900,327	3%	$1,080,392	24%	$1,350,490	55%
	2006 and beyond	$773,375	$900,327	16%	$1,080,392	40%	$1,350,490	75%

team. The executive summary was initially presented to the president and the director of strategic initiatives for WMC. Since then, the same report has been presented to several members of the WMC senior leadership team. These meetings have resulted in continued focus on the business goals as well as acknowledgement of the extent to which training could have an impact on performance improvement. The data from the report is also being used to support ongoing budget decisions in the various channels.

As a result of the careful and ongoing explanations to key leaders around the methodology used to collect and analyze the data and calculate the ROI, the leadership team was very receptive to the analysis. The president of WMC expressed his appreciation for the level of detail and the focus on the anticipated impact of this training on key performance indictors; he was especially impressed with the team's ability to link performance to potential business impact. Although the executives had always believed there was a connection between training and performance improvement, the leadership team had never personally experienced a process that defined and presented that link so clearly. The director of strategic initiatives summed up the positive feedback the training team has received around this work when she said: "Thank you for your time this morning. I have spoken with [several leaders in attendance] since then and they really appreciated the information and your commitment to quality and teamwork. [They] were very impressed that you spoke the *mortgage language*. It was a surprise they never expected! Thanks again. You make me proud to be your partner!"

Lessons Learned

The engagement of the business unit early in this project was critical to the ability to credibly forecast the ROI on this program. The forecast has proved to be a powerful tool that opened the door for deeper levels of collaboration between training and the clients served.

In WMC's quest for operational efficiency, performance management and improvement are critical. Providing leaders with data they can actually use to assist them as they lead their teams in this effort has been rewarding, and demonstrates the value HR partners can add in supporting the performance improvement efforts of the clients they serve.

Based upon this experience, here are a few key areas that the training time would address differently next time:

- Insist on a deeper level of engagement from the HRBPs throughout the performance improvement process.
- Survey exemplar performers as well as members of the leadership team on anticipated business impact.

 Questions for Discussion

1. To what extent does your relationship with your client enable you to participate in strategic discussions? What can you do to strengthen your relationship with your client in this area?

2. Do you have the processes, tools, and infrastructure in place to support this type of work? What can you do to put them in place?

3. Why is it important to engage the client and other HR partners in this work?

4. How important is it to identify all things that have an impact on performance?

5. What did you think about the strategies for isolating the impact of training?

6. How credible is the business impact and ROI data? Explain.

7. How might you have approached this impact study differently?

About the Author

Terri B. Burroughs is the learning manager for the general banking group credit products teams at Wachovia Corporation. She has 20 years' experience in the banking industry with the last four of those years focused on learning and development. She is an AME champion at Wachovia and consults with teams in the development and implementation of AME strategies. As she approaches performance improvement initiatives with a practical business management focus, she emphasizes the link between human performance and business results. Burroughs may be contacted at Terri.Burroughs@Wachovia.com.

Chapter 6

This case was prepared to serve as a basis for discussion rather than to illustrate either effective or ineffective administrative and management practices.

INSTRUCTIONAL DESIGN FOUNDATIONS COURSE

Bank of America

Scott Dade

This case study illustrates how Bank of America initiated a cultural change around training and development to help learning professionals focus on building solutions that accomplish business driven, observable, and measurable objectives. ASTD recognized the Instructional Design Foundations course and awarded it the 2003 ASTD excellence in practice citation. It was designed as a self-paced, blended learning solution that used the best of adult learning theory, e-learning technology, and evaluation techniques to provide associates with critical competencies in performance consulting, instructional design, and training evaluation. The evaluation strategy used Kirkpatrick's four levels of evaluation and Phillips's ROI Methodology (Level 5) to calculate a 115 percent return on the training investment.

Background

The goal of the Instructional Design Foundations course was to deliver a blended learning solution that provided the knowledge and skills necessary to design and develop curriculum throughout the bank using industry best practices. Bank associates responsible for developing learning solutions needed to be able to differentiate between a need for training and a need for some other performance intervention; create observable and measurable performance objectives; create valid, performance-based learning assessments; and demonstrate the ability to apply what they learned through work samples.

As a result of increased competencies, associates could create learning solutions that were aligned with the business needs of the bank. All new learning solutions would have performance-based objectives clearly defining what an associate will know or do differently as a result of the training and clearly state how success was to be measured. In addition, the implementation of a standard set of tools, templates, and examples reduced process variation and increased the quality of the learning solutions produced. A comprehensive evaluation strategy needed to be employed to justify the expense and validate the results of the solution. Never before had the bank applied an evaluation strategy of this magnitude.

The course was developed using the analysis, design, development, implementation, and evaluation (ADDIE) model of instructional design. The course rolled out on March 10, 2003, and had a goal of enrolling 300 associates within 12 months.

The course comprised five Web-based modules with pre- and posttests to assess learning and knowledge, comprehension, and application levels based on Benjamin Bloom's (1956) taxonomy. It also used an end-of-course questionnaire to capture reaction/satisfaction data and participant estimates of impact. The course's estimated shelf life was two to four years.

The course was implemented across all business units on the organization's intranet and was accessible by associates at home through authorized remote access and was an essential part of the development path for most bank associates involved with the ADDIE instructional design process.

Donald Kirkpatrick's (1994) Levels 1–4 and Jack Phillips's (1997) Level 5 ROI Methodology served as the basis for making changes and improvements to the course, as well as the means for determining the ROI for the course. Web-enabled pretraining assessments for the associates and the associates' managers in conjunction with posttraining assessments provided a basis for comparison and identified behavior change/application and business impacts.

Problem/Need Identification

The associates impacted by this course were located within separate learning groups supporting various lines of business within the bank. Associates operated with different tools, processes, and role definitions. Different levels of knowledge, skills, and abilities existed within the various lines of business in the bank. Many training professionals in the bank had little or no formal training in instructional design. This lack of consistency led to low associate satisfaction scores around individual and organizational performance on the annual associate survey.

The variation in processes and in knowledge and skill levels among the bank's training professionals led to many inappropriate and ineffective learning solutions that negatively affected business results. The use of focus groups, process improvements teams, and surveys drove a needs analysis to uncover ways to improve processes, reduce variation, and investigate ways to make learning solution development more responsive, efficient, and effective. A modified version of the Robinson and Robinson (1996) performance relationship map was used to identify knowledge and skill gaps around instructional design, performance needs assessment, and training needs analysis to develop performance-based objectives and determine the appropriate level of evaluation based on the business needs.

Several factors drove the decision to implement an e-learning solution:

- a large target audience of more 900 associates
- geographic distances between learners who were located around the globe
- existence of a business need to accelerate implementation of the program.

Collection, analysis, and reporting of evaluation data was accomplished through a combination of data-based query, automated assessment tools, and manual processing.

Design Values

The design team wanted the course to exemplify best practices of instructional design, adult learning theory, and evaluation methods. The team recognized that working adults need to learn when and where it is the most convenient and advantageous for them. The course used bank-relevant examples and case studies to capitalize on the "What's in it for me?" (WIIFM) style of adult learners. A blended learning approach leveraged technology, accessibility, and learning styles through the World Wide Web to address the learning needs of busy professionals. It allowed those with extensive experience in instructional design to advance through certain modules by passing a pretest given before each module.

The course had five Web-based modules with pre- and posttests to assess learning at the knowledge, comprehension, and application levels. The participants participated in threaded discussions located on a separate Web board. These threaded discussions encouraged interactivity through content-related questions and questions focusing on how they planned to use the new information and tools on the job. This activity also had the benefit of creating a community of practice within the organization where associates could network with colleagues and build relationships to enhance their career development. The use of posttraining deliverables further enhanced the learners' transfer of learning to the job by encouraging them to apply their learning to real-life projects. After successful completion, the associate could use the course and resource links as a form of performance support.

Aligned to Performance

To align this learning solution to critical performance requirements, the course focused on the knowledge and skill gaps identified during a needs analysis. The gaps were instructional design, performance needs assessment, training needs analysis, performance-based objectives, and evaluation strategies based on the specific business need. The goal was not only to be a learning solution but also a best practice for emulation. The development of the business goals, as well as performance and learning objectives for each of the five modules, enabled a strong correlation between the assessment items for each module, the posttraining deliverables, and on-the-job application of learning.

The Level 2 learning assessments were built using a table of specifications to link each assessment item to a specific objective, the number of items per objective, and the level of learning for each item measured. Tying learning objectives to performance objectives also enabled the development of the application level assessments of associates on the job. The instructions and templates for the associates to complete the posttraining deliverables were available through the Web board. To tie the threaded discussion to the Web-based modules, the access codes for the module pre- and posttests were embedded within threaded discussion questions. Initial evaluation results were favorable. The evaluation strategy called for the use of a training scorecard to reflect evaluation results, reporting the activity, reactions, learning, application/behavior change, business impact, and ROI.

The bank has been using Six Sigma tools and processes to become one of the world's most admired companies. The integration of the Six Sigma change process using the define, measure, analyze, improve, control (DMAIC) process and the ADDIE model of instructional design were main approaches to reduce variation in learning solution design, development, and evaluation. The course was also used as part of the education and communication plan for Six Sigma implementation and standardization of the training process within the bank.

Internal Partnering

The course designers partnered with representatives from different lines of business during the needs analysis and pilot-test phases of the course. This early partnership resulted in revisions and improvements to the course prior to its full rollout on March 10, 2003. Improvements included the addition of Note Taker software paralleling the course modules but not duplicating them, which enabled learners to take notes instead of printing each Webpage. It also encouraged more active learning and addressed the different learning styles of the participants. The inclusion of the line of business partners also resulted in getting buy-in and support from key business leaders. The support of these business leaders was critical to acceptance of the course and the evaluation strategy.

Evaluation Strategy

The evaluation strategy called for the use of all five evaluation levels to make course improvements and estimate the ROI. The course designers used Kirkpatrick's and Phillips's processes for evaluating training because they are recognized as industry best practices and because of the formal training and certifications offered in those methodologies. For example, the team leader completed the ROI Methodology certification using this project. To facilitate data collection, the course used Web-enabled pretraining assessments for both the associate and the associate's manager and posttraining assessments for comparison of application/behavior changes and observed business impact. It also had an end-of-course questionnaire used to capture reaction and participant estimates of impact.

The course was implemented across all lines of business on the bank's intranet and was also accessible by associates at home through remote access. The course was an essential part of the development path for any of the 900-plus associates involved with analysis, design, development, implementation, or evaluation of learning solutions in the bank. The course exceeded its first year target enrollment of 300 participants in just five months.

A review of the resources committed to implement this solution could be broken down into phases of the ADDIE process. On average, two full-time employees (FTEs) were assigned to complete the needs analysis. The time spent and costs involved were $3,470, based on average salary and benefits costs. The cost for design and development of the course, including the pilot, was $141,690, which included two full-time employees and three contractors for varying amounts of time throughout the project. The implementation costs were based on a target of 300 associates taking the course in the first year and any maintenance or facilitation costs.

Because it was a blended e-learning solution, facilitation costs were minimal and restricted to monitoring the threaded discussions and maintenance of the Websites by one FTE. Finally, the total evaluation costs were $8,096 performed by one FTE. All costs were fully loaded against the first year of the program. No costs were prorated over the expected two- to four-year life of the course. The fully loaded program cost for the instructional design course was $312,478.50.

Results

To comprehensively collect, analyze, and report the results from this course required the use of a training scorecard. The scorecard was built using the information first identified in the data collection and ROI analysis plans put in place during course development. These tools clearly identified the types of measures, levels of learning, data collection methods, data sources, and time and responsibilities of those completing the evaluation. The scorecard started with the traditional measures of activity and created a chain of impact leading to credible business results.

The collection of evaluation data at all five levels plus data on intangible benefits helped support a strong argument that this training had a business impact.

Level 1: Reaction/Satisfaction/ Expected Results

Data was collected using the Web-enabled end-of-course evaluation using a 1–5 Likert scale and business impact estimates. The responses to five to seven questions rolled up into each of the following key indicators:

- Content will be useful in my job: 4.5
- The course contained valuable information: 4.0
- This blended solution enhanced my learning experience: 4.0
- I would recommend this course to others: 4.2
- Is the course a good investment for the Bank? Fifty-seven percent of managers and 77 percent of associates responded affirmatively.

Level 2: Learning

Data collected from the Web-based pre- and posttraining assessments indicated that the average mod-ule pretest score was 65 percent, compared to the average posttraining score of 92 percent. This represents an average gain due to the course of 27 percent.

Level 3: Application/Behavior Change

Data collected using associate and manager pre- and posttraining assessments questionnaires revealed the following:

- Both managers and associates reported increases in the participants' levels of knowledge and skill on 10 key learning objectives from the course.
- Ninety percent of participants expected to use their new knowledge and skills on the job; in fact, 90 percent reported using their knowledge and skills within a week after completing the course.
- More than 76 percent of participants expected to coach other associates within a week; in actuality, more than 70 percent did coach associates within a week.
- Seventy-six percent expected to provide more effective solutions for partners within a week, and more than 70 percent reported actually doing so within a week.
- Before training, the greatest barriers to applying new skills were identified as a lack of knowledge and skill; after the training the greatest barriers were identified as a lack of time and management support.
- Both associates and managers reported an increase in their ability to apply the knowledge and skills learned from the course after training.

Level 4: Business Impact

The team collected associates' and managers' estimates on changes resulting from training. The managers' and associates' estimates of other factors contributing to the impacts versus training then reduced these estimates. To establish an even more conservative estimate, the managers and associates were also asked to rate their confidence in their own estimates of the business impacts. Both the isolation estimates and confidence estimates were then subtracted from the estimated benefits reported. Among the business impacts that were measured were the following:

- Associates' effectiveness to manage, develop, and implement training solutions increased 47 percent.

- Output increased 20 percent, quality increased 20 percent, and efficiency increased 20 percent.
- Costs were reduced by 20 percent, response time by 12 percent, and rework rates decreased 20 percent.
- The total business impact in dollars saved or generated as a result of the training, reduced by the managers' confidence rating and isolation of other factors, was $674,475.

Level 5: ROI

The ROI was based on the managers' estimates and adjusted for their confidence factor ratings and for the impact of other possible causes of benefits (isolation). The forecasted ROI was 61 percent, compared to the actual ROI of 115 percent calculated on August 21, 2003.

Intangible Benefits

The team used the associates' and managers' estimates, reduced by confidence ratings and isolation factors, to discern other benefits that were not converted to monetary value:

- increased use of standards, processes, and tools

- decreased absenteeism and reduced turnover among associates
- enhanced development of informal networks by associates, greater use of a common language around instructional design, and increased focus on performance needs assessment
- increased associate satisfaction and improved customer satisfaction.

Pretraining and Posttraining Data

The use of Web-enabled pre- and posttraining assessments assessed changes in the associates' knowledge, skills, and behaviors. Comparing the results helped identify key behaviors based on the objectives from the course determined during the needs analysis as being critical to quality knowledge and skills gaps. Both managers and associates reported increases in the participants' levels of knowledge and skill on 10 key learning objectives from the course.

Table 6-1 presents information taken from the associates' and managers' pretraining assessments of the associate.

The use of 90-day posttraining data collection revealed increases in both knowledge and skill

---

Table 6-1. Comparison of associates' and managers' pretraining assessments of associates.

Current Knowledge /Skills	Average Rating of Associates*	Average Rating of Managers*
Please rate current level of knowledge/skill on the following to:		
Explain how improvement processes such as ADDIE contribute to achieving business needs.	3.0	3.0
Determine an appropriate course of action using the performance improvement process.	2.9	3.0
Explain a training professional's role in addressing performance issues.	3.3	4.0
Determine the appropriate use of a training needs analysis.	3.1	3.0
Determine the information required to complete a training needs analysis.	2.9	3.0
Determine the appropriate use of performance-based objectives.	3.3	3.0
Indicate the risks of not using performance-based objectives when developing training.	3.2	3.0
Determine the appropriate use of training evaluation and learning assessment.	3.2	3.0
Describe the process of building assessments to evaluate learning outcomes.	3.1	3.0
Group Average	**3.1**	**3.1**

*Scale: 5 = Above Average, 4 = Average, 3 = Some, 2 = Little, 1 = None

(continued next page)

Table 6-1. Comparison of associates' and managers' pretraining assessments of associates (continued).

The pretraining assessments also captured the associates' and managers' expectations of when the associate should be using the new knowledge and skills learned from the course.

Expected Use of New Knowledge and Skills	Average Rating of Associates*	Average Rating of Managers*
Use the learned knowledge/skills in the workplace	4.5	4.0
Coach other associates	3.8	4.0
Provide more effective solutions for partners	4.4	4.0

*Scale: 5 = Immediately, 4 = Within a Week, 3 = Within a Month, 2 = Eventually, 1 = Never

Expected Use of New Knowledge and Skills	Average Rating of Associates*	Average Rating of Managers*
Percentage of time expected to work on tasks requiring the skills learned from the course	3.6	4.0

*Scale: 5 = 100%, 4 = 75%, 3 = 50%, 2 = 25%, 1 = 0%

The use of pretraining assessment questions also looked at expected barriers to implementation of the new knowledge and skills learned.

Barriers to Expected Use of New Knowledge and Skills	Average Rating of Associates*	Average Rating of Managers*
Lack of management support	1.9	2.0
Lack of partner acceptance	2.4	3.0
Lack of time	2.7	3.0
Lack of resources	2.5	3.0
Lack of knowledge and skills	2.7	3.0
Varying job responsibilities	2.8	3.0

*Scale: 5 = Always Inhibits, 4 = Usually or Often Inhibits, 3 = Occasionally Inhibits, 2 = Rarely Inhibits, 1 = Never Inhibits

reported by the associate and the associate's manager (table 6-2). The associates tended to self-report higher gains than their managers did.

Organizational Impacts

The impacts and changes as a result of the training can be summed up in a word—impressive! First, evaluation of a training course in the bank had never been done beyond Level 3. The bank had consistently used Level 1 evaluation of training, but Levels 2 and 3 were rarely used. Level 4 evaluation allowed an assessment of business impact and provided a basis for Level 5, ROI.

Second, the blended e-learning solution was the first of its kind used in the organization and showed

Table 6-2. Comparison of associates' and managers' posttraining assessments of associates.

Current Knowledge /Skills	Average Rating of Associates*	Average Rating of Managers*
Please rate current level of knowledge/skill on the following to:		
Explain how improvement processes such as ADDIE contribute to achieving business needs.	4.8	3.7
Determine an appropriate course of action using the performance improvement process.	4.7	3.9
Explain a training professional's role in addressing performance issues.	4.5	3.9
Determine the appropriate use of a training needs analysis.	4.9	4.0
Determine the information required to complete a training needs analysis.	4.9	3.7
Determine the appropriate use of performance-based objectives.	4.9	4.1
Indicate the risks of not using performance-based objectives when developing training.	4.7	4.3
Determine the appropriate use of training evaluation and learning assessment.	4.5	4.3
Describe the process of building assessments to evaluate learning outcomes.	4.7	4.4
Group Average	**4.7**	**4.0**

*Scale: 5 = Above Average, 4 = Average, 3 = Some, 2 = Little, 1 = None

The posttraining assessments also captured the associates' and managers' expectations of when the associate should be using the new knowledge and skills learned from the course.

Use of New Knowledge and Skills	Average Rating of Associates*	Average Rating of Managers*
Used the learned knowledge/skills in the workplace: *85% used immediately or within a week.*	4.9	4.3
Coached other associates: *70% used immediately or within a week after training.*	4.5	3.9
Provided more effective solutions for partners: *70% used immediately or within a week after training.*	4.9	4.0

*Scale: 5 = Immediately, 4 = Within a Week, 3 = Within a Month, 2 = Eventually, 1 = Never

Use of New Knowledge and Skills	Average Rating of Associates*	Average Rating of Managers*
Percentage of time working on tasks requiring the skills learned from the course: *70% or more of their time is spent on tasks requiring the knowledge and skills learned from the course.*	4.5	4.0

*Scale: 5 = 100%, 4 = 75%, 3 = 50%, 2 = 25%, 1 = 0%

(continued next page)

Table 6-2. Comparison of associates' and managers' posttraining assessments of associates *(continued).*

The use of posttraining assessment questions also looked at barriers to implementation of the new knowledge and skills learned.

Barriers to Use of New Knowledge and Skills	Average Rating of Associates*	Average Rating of Managers*
Lack of management support	4.5	4.3
Lack of partner acceptance	3.0	3.1
Lack of time	3.7	4.1
Lack of resources	2.3	3.0
Lack of knowledge and skills	2.1	2.7
Varying job responsibilities	3.2	3.6

*Scale: 5 = Always Inhibits, 4 = Usually or Often Inhibits, 3 = Occasionally Inhibits, 2 = Rarely Inhibits, 1 = Never Inhibits

Knowledge and Skills	Average Rating of Associates*	Average Rating of Managers*
Rate your/your associate's ability to apply the knowledge and skills, *before* training	3.7	3.0
Rate your/your associate's ability to apply the knowledge and skills, *after* training	4.5	4.0

*Scale: 5 = Always Inhibits, 4 = Usually or Often Inhibits, 3 = Occasionally Inhibits, 2 = Rarely Inhibits, 1 = Never Inhibits

the possibilities of using e-learning to accomplish professional development and continuing education for associates.

Business Impact

The use of posttraining surveys collected feedback from associates and their managers on business results. The results are illustrated in figures 6-1 and 6-2. The results were adjusted with isolation and confidence factors.

Intangible Benefits

Benefits that were attributed to the training but not converted to dollar savings or revenue are illustrated in figure 6-3.

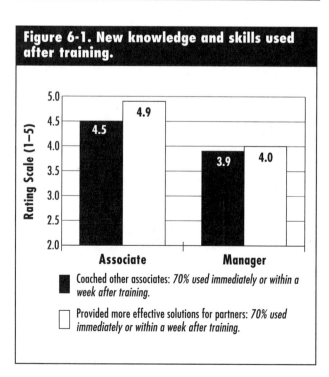

Figure 6-1. New knowledge and skills used after training.

■ Coached other associates: *70% used immediately or within a week after training.*

☐ Provided more effective solutions for partners: *70% used immediately or within a week after training.*

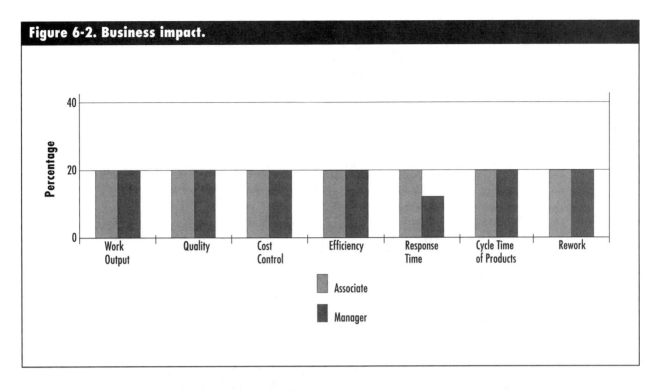

Figure 6-2. Business impact.

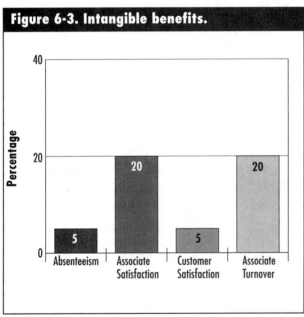

Figure 6-3. Intangible benefits.

Lessons Learned

The Bank of America's Instructional Design Foundations course is an ongoing, blended learning solution providing foundational knowledge and skills in the use of the ADDIE process of instructional design, performance needs assessment, training needs analysis, writing performance-based objectives, and the evaluation of training.

The lessons learned from this project ranged from gaining senior level support for learning solutions and evaluation strategies during the initial stages of development to the use of Web-enabled pre- and posttraining assessments to capture evaluation data as part of a comprehensive data collection and ROI analysis plan. In addition, the value of capturing customer feedback before, during, and after development cannot be stressed enough. There were many lessons learned from this project, a few of which are described in the paragraphs that follow.

The team used pilot testing to test the design and gain support from key stakeholders before rollout. Pilot testing involved representatives from the key stakeholders who possessed varying knowledge of and skill levels in the areas covered. The feedback from the bank's customers obtained from postpilot focus groups and reaction questionnaires contributed to the success of the course and the subsequent ROI impact study.

Using a formal project plan, data collection plan, and an ROI analysis plan ensured that the right information was collected, analyzed, and reported. The need for a disciplined approach to instructional design contributed to swift adoption by associates.

The use of business goals and performance-based objectives provided a direct link between the objectives of each module and the corresponding assessment items. Scores from the module tests showed consistent improvement as a result and validated the learning and evaluation approach taken. This answered the basic question of "Did they learn what they were supposed to learn?" The use of a pretest/test-out feature allowed associates with more experience to bypass certain Web-based portions while still requiring them to complete the posttraining deliverables for full credit in the bank's learning management system. This included the technology partners up front to determine capability and capacity before finalizing design reduced integration, distribution, and network bandwidth challenges.

The training of team members in the ROI Methodology enabled an internal team of associates to achieve breakthrough results in the field of training evaluation.

Questions for Discussion

1. Why use all levels of evaluation?

2. How can using a Level 1 ROI forecast help secure senior management support?

3. Why use the posttraining work deliverables with Web-based training?

4. How can you capture tangible benefits?

5. What is the benefit of capturing both the managers' and associates' feedback?

6. How can these techniques be used in your organization?

About the Author

Scott Dade is currently a vice president with Bank of America and is part of the learning and organizational effectiveness function. He has more than 15 years' experience in learning management, instructional systems design, facilitation, and evaluation of HRD and change initiatives.

Dade spent 20 years with the United States Air Force holding a variety of leadership positions before joining Bank of America. He specializes in creating blended learning solutions that drive measurable business results. Dade has presented at national conferences and written articles for publication. He holds a master's degree of science in adult education and is a certified performance technologist (CPT). He is certified in the ROI Methodology and is a national member of ASTD, the ROI Network, and Toastmasters International. He can be reached at scott.dade@bankofamerica.com.

Chapter 7

This case was prepared as a basis for discussion rather than to illustrate either effective or ineffective administrative and management practices. All names, dates, places, and organizations have been disguised at the request of the authors or organizations.

MEASURING THE ROI IN A COACHING PROGRAM

Nations Hotel Corporation

Jack J. Phillips

The learning and development team at the Nations Hotel Corporation was challenged to identify learning needs to help executives find ways to improve efficiency, customer satisfaction, and revenue growth in the company. A key component of the program was the development of a formal, structured coaching program called Coaching for Business Impact. The corporate executives were interested in seeing the actual ROI for the coaching project. This case study provides critical insights into how coaching creates value in an organization.

Background

Nations Hotel Corporation (NHC) is a large U.S.-based hotel firm with operations in 15 countries. The firm has maintained steady growth to include more than 300 hotels in cities all over the world. NHC enjoys one of the most recognized names in the global lodging industry, with 98 percent brand awareness worldwide and 72 percent overall guest satisfaction.

The hospitality industry is very competitive, cyclical, and subject to swings with the economy. Room rentals are price sensitive, and customer satisfaction is extremely important for NHC. Profits are squeezed if operating costs get out of hand. NHC top executives constantly seek ways to improve operational efficiency, customer satisfaction, revenue growth,

and retention of high-performing employees. Executives—particularly those in charge of individual properties—are under constant pressure to show improvement in these key measures.

The learning and development function, the Nations Hotel Learning Organization (NHLO), conducted a brief survey of executives to identify learning needs to help them meet some of their particular goals. NHLO was interested in developing customized learning processes including the possibility of individual coaching sessions. Most of the executives surveyed indicated that they would like to work with a qualified coach to assist them through a variety of challenges and issues. The executives believed that this would be an efficient way to learn, apply, and achieve results. Consequently, NHLO developed a formal, structured coaching program—

Coaching for Business Impact—and offered it to the executives at the vice president level and above.

As the program was conceived, the senior executive team became interested in showing the value of the coaching project. Although they supported coaching, they wanted to see the actual ROI. The goal was to evaluate 25 executives, randomly selected (if possible) from the participants in the coaching program.

The Program

Figure 7-1 shows the steps in the new coaching program from the beginning to the ultimate outcomes. This program involves 14 discrete elements and processes that together constitute a results-based initiative.

1. *Voluntary participation:* Executives had to volunteer to be part of this project. Voluntary commitment translates into a willing participant who is not only open to changing, improving, and applying what is being learned, but is also willing to provide the necessary data for evaluating the coaching process. The voluntary nature of the coaching program, however, meant that not all executives who needed coaching would be involved. When compared to mandatory

involvement, however, the volunteer effort appeared to be an important ingredient for success. It was envisioned that as improvements were realized and executives reflected on the positive perceptions of coaching that other executives would follow suit.

2. *The need for coaching:* An important part of the process was a dialog with the executive to determine if coaching was actually needed. In this step, NHLO staff used a checklist to review the issues, needs, and concerns about the coaching agreement. Along with establishing a need, the checklist revealed key areas where coaching could help. This step ensured that the assistance desired by the executive could actually be provided by the coach.

3. *Self-assessment:* As part of the process, a self-assessment was taken from the individual being coached, his or her immediate manager, and direct reports. This was a typical 360-degree assessment instrument that focused on areas of feedback, communication, openness, trust, and other competencies necessary for success in the competitive hospitality environment.

4. *Commitment for data:* As a precondition, executives had to agree to provide data

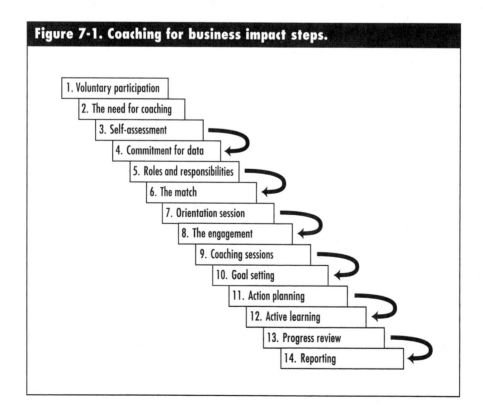

Figure 7-1. Coaching for business impact steps.

1. Voluntary participation
2. The need for coaching
3. Self-assessment
4. Commitment for data
5. Roles and responsibilities
6. The match
7. Orientation session
8. The engagement
9. Coaching sessions
10. Goal setting
11. Action planning
12. Active learning
13. Progress review
14. Reporting

during coaching and at appropriate times following the engagement. This up-front commitment ensured that data of sufficient quality and quantity could be obtained. The data made evaluation easier and helped executives see their progress and realize the value of coaching.

5. *Roles and responsibilities:* For both the coach and the executive, roles and responsibilities were clearly defined. It was important for the executive to understand that the coach was there to listen, provide feedback, and evaluate. The coach was not there to make decisions for the executive. This clear distinction was important for productive coaching sessions.

6. *The match:* Coaches were provided from a reputable business coaching firm where NHLO had developed a productive relationship. Coaching profiles were presented to executives, and a tentative selection was made on a priority listing. The respective coach was provided background information on the executive, and a match was made. After this match, the coaching process began.

7. *Orientation session:* The executive and coach formally met during an orientation session. Here, the NHLO staff explained the process, requirements, timetable, and other administrative issues. This was a very brief session typically conducted in a group; however, it could also be conducted individually.

8. *The engagement:* One of the most important aspects of the process involved making sure that the engagement was connected to a business need. Typical coaching engagements focused on behavioral issues (for example, an executive's inability to listen to employees), provided feedback, and set expectations. To connect to the business impact, the behavior change must link to a business consequence. In the initial engagement, the coach uncovered the business need by asking a series of questions to examine the consequences of behavior change. This process involved asking "so what?" and "what if?" as the desired behavior changes were described. After the business needs were identified—in the categories of productivity, revenue, efficiency, direct cost savings, employee retention, customer satisfaction, and other important measures—the engagement could be connected

to corresponding changes in one or more of those measures. Without elevating the engagement to a business need, it would have been difficult to evaluate coaching with this level of analysis.

9. *Coaching sessions:* Individual sessions were conducted at least once a month, usually lasting a minimum of one hour, sometimes more, depending on the need and issues at hand. The coach and executive met face to face, if possible. If not, coaching was conducted in a telephone conversation. Routine meetings were necessary to keep the process on track.

10. *Goal setting:* Although individuals could set goals in any area needing improvements, the senior executives chose five priority areas for targeting: sales growth, productivity/operational efficiency, direct cost reduction, retention of key staff members, and customer satisfaction. The executives selected one measure in at least three of these areas. Essentially, they would have three specific goals that would require three action plans, described next.

11. *Action planning:* To drive the desired improvement, the action planning process was utilized. Common in coaching engagements, this process provided an opportunity for the executive to detail specific action steps planned with the team. These steps were designed to drive a particular consequence that was a business impact measure. Figure 7-2 shows a typical action planning document used in this process. The executive was to complete the action plan during the first two to three coaching sessions, detailing step by step what he or she would accomplish to drive a particular improvement. At least three improvement measures were required out of the five areas targeted with the program. Consequently, at least three action plans had to be developed and implemented. The coaches distributed action plan packages that included instructions, blank forms, and completed examples. The coach explained the process in the second coaching session. The action plans could be revised as needed.

12. *Active learning:* After the executive developed the specific measures in question and the action plans, several development strategies were discussed and implemented with the

Figure 7-2. Action plan form.

ACTION PLAN: COACHING FOR BUSINESS IMPACT

Name: _____ Coach: _____ Date: _____

Impact Objective: _____ Evaluation Period: _____ to _____

Improvement Measure: _____ Current Performance: _____ Target Performance: _____

Action Steps

1. _____

2. _____

3. _____

4. _____

5. _____

6. _____

7. _____

8. _____

Intangible Benefits: _____

Analysis

A. What is the unit of measure? _____

B. What is the value (cost) of one unit? $ _____

C. How did you arrive at this value? _____
    _____
    _____
    _____

D. How much did the measure change during the evaluation period? (monthly value) _____

E. What other factors could have contributed to this improvement? _____
    _____

F. What percent of this change was actually caused by this program?
    _____ %

G. What level of confidence do you place on the above information? (100% = Certainty and 0% = No Confidence)
    _____ %

Comments: _____
_____
_____

help of the coach. The coach actually facilitated the efforts, utilizing any number of typical learning processes, such as reading assignments, self-assessment tools, skill practices, video feedback, journaling, and other techniques. In some cases, specific short courses, special projects, exercises, and other assignments were necessary to reveal areas where improvement was needed. Coaching is considered to be an active learning process where the executive experiments, applies, and reflects on the experience. The coach provides input, reaction, assessment, and evaluation.

13. *Progress review:* At monthly sessions, the coach and executive reviewed progress and revised the action plan, if necessary. The important issue was to continue to make adjustments to sustain the process.

14. *Reporting:* After six months in the coaching engagement, the executive reported improvement by completing other parts of the action plan. If the development efforts were quite involved and the measures driven were unlikely to change in the interim, a longer period of time was utilized. For most executives, six months was appropriate.

Objectives

An effective ROI study flows from the objectives of the particular project being evaluated. For coaching, it is important to clearly indicate the objectives at different levels. Figure 7-3 shows the detailed objectives associated with this project. The objectives reflect the four classic levels of evaluation plus a fifth level for ROI. Some of the levels, however, have been adjusted for the coaching environment. With these

---

Figure 7-3. Objectives of Coaching for Business Impact.

Level 1. Reaction
After participating in this coaching program, the executive will
1. perceive coaching to be relevant to the job
2. perceive coaching to be important to job success at the present time
3. perceive coaching to be value added in terms of time and funds invested
4. rate the coach as effective
5. recommend this program to other executives.

Level 2. Learning
After completing this coaching program, the executives should improve their understanding of or skills for each of the following:
1. uncovering individual strengths and weaknesses
2. translating feedback into action plans
3. involving team members in projects and goals
4. communicating effectively
5. collaborating with colleagues
6. improving personal effectiveness
7. enhancing leadership skills.

Level 3. Application
Six months after completing this coaching program, executives should
1. complete the action plan
2. adjust the plan accordingly as needed for changes in the environment

Level 3. Application (*continued*)
3. identify barriers and enablers
4. show improvements on the following items:
   a. uncovering individual strengths and weaknesses
   b. translating feedback into action plans
   c. involving team members in projects and goals
   d. communicating effectively
   e. collaborating with colleagues
   f. improving personal effectiveness
   g. enhancing leadership skills.

Level 4. Impact
After completing this coaching program, executives should improve at least three specific measures in the following areas:
1. sales growth
2. productivity/operational efficiency
3. direct cost reduction
4. retention of key staff members
5. customer satisfaction.

Level 5. ROI
The ROI value should be 25%.

---

objectives in mind, it becomes a relatively easy task to measure progress on these objectives.

Planning for Evaluation

Figure 7-4 shows the completed data collection plan for this project. The plan captures the following techniques and strategies used to collect data for this project:

1. *Objectives:* The objectives are listed as defined in figure 7-3 and are repeated only in general terms.

2. *Measures:* Additional definition is sometimes needed beyond the specific objectives. The measures used to gauge progress on the objective are defined.

3. *Methods:* This column indicates the specific method used for collecting data at different levels. In this case, action plans and questionnaires are the primary methods.

4. *Sources:* For each data group, sources are identified. In this case, sources are limited to the executive, coach, manager of the executive, and the individual/team reporting to the executive. Although the actual data provided by executives will usually come from the records of the organization, the executive will include the data in the action plan document. Thus, the action plan becomes a source of the data to NHLO.

5. *Timing:* The timing refers to the time for collecting specific data items from the beginning of the coaching engagement.

6. *Responsibility:* The responsibility refers to the individual(s) who will actually collect the data.

The data integration plan (figure 7-5) shows how the various types of data are collected and integrated to provide an overall evaluation of the program.

Figure 7-6 shows the completed plan for data analysis. This document addresses the key issues needed for a credible analysis of the data and includes the following:

1. *Data items:* The plan shows that a variety of data measurements will be collected from one of the five priority areas.

2. *Isolating the effects of coaching:* The method of isolating the effects of coaching on the data is estimation, where the executives allocate

the proportion of the improvement to the coaching process (more on the consequences of this later). Although there are more credible methods, such as control groups and trend analysis, they are not appropriate for this situation. Although the estimates are subjective, they are developed by those individuals who should know them best (the executives), and the results are adjusted for the error of the estimate.

3. *Converting data to monetary values:* Data is converted using a variety of methods. For most data items, standard values are available. When standard values are not available, the input of an in-house expert is pursued. This expert is typically an individual who collects and assimilates the data. If neither of these approaches is feasible, the executive estimates the value.

4. *Cost categories:* The standard cost categories included are the typical costs for a coaching assignment.

5. *Communication targets:* Several audiences are included for coaching results, representing the key stakeholder groups: the executive, the executive's immediate manager, the sponsor of the program, and the NHLO staff. Other influences and issues are also detailed in this plan.

Evaluation Results

The careful data collection planning allowed the coaching program to be evaluated at all five levels.

Figure 7-5. Data integration plan for evaluating the program.

Data Category	Executive Questionnaire	Senior Executive Questionnaire	Action Plan	Company Records
Reaction	×			
Learning	×	×		
Application	×	×	×	
Impact			×	
Costs				×

Figure 7-4. Completed data collection plan.

DATA COLLECTION PLAN

Purpose of This Evaluation: _____

Program/Project: Coaching for Business Impact   **Responsibility:** Jack Phillips   **Date:** _____

Level	Objective(s)	Measures/Data	Data Collection Method	Data Sources	Timing	Responsibilities
1	**REACTION/SATISFACTION** • Relevance to job • Importance to job success • Value added • Coach's effectiveness • Recommendation to others	• 4 out of 5 on a 1 to 5 rating scale	• Questionnaire	• Executives	• 6 months after engagement	• NHLO staff
2	**LEARNING** • Uncovering strengths/weaknesses • Translating feedback into action • Involving team members • Communicating effectively • Collaborating with colleagues • Improving personal effectiveness • Enhancing leadership skills	• 4 out of 5 on a 1 to 5 rating scale	• Questionnaire	• Executives • Coach	• 6 months after engagement	• NHLO staff
3	**APPLICATION/IMPLEMENTATION** • Complete and adjust action plan • Identify barriers and enablers • Show improvements and skills	• Checklist for action plan • 4 out of 5 on a 1 to 5 rating scale	• Action Plan • Questionnaire	• Executives • Coach	• 6 months after engagement	• NHLO staff
4	**BUSINESS IMPACT (3 of 5)** 1. Sales growth 2. Productivity/efficiency 3. Direct cost reduction 4. Retention of key staff members 5. Customer satisfaction	1. A change in monthly revenue 2. Varies with location 3. Direct monetary savings 4. Voluntary turnover 5. Customer satisfaction index	• Action Plan	• Executives	• 6 months after engagement	• NHLO staff
5	**ROI** • 25 percent					

Comments: Executives are committed to providing data. They fully understand all the data collection issues prior to engaging in the coaching assignment.

Figure 7-6. The ROI analysis plan for Coaching for Business Impact.

ROI ANALYSIS PLAN

Program: Coaching for Business Success   **Responsibility:** Jack Phillips   **Date:** _____

Data Items (Usually Level 4)	Methods for Isolating the Effects of the Program	Methods of Converting Data to Monetary Values	Cost Categories	Intangible Benefits	Communication Targets for Final Report	Other Influences / Issues During Application	Comments
• Sales growth	Estimates for executive	• Standard value • Expert input • Executive estimate	• Needs assessment • Coaching fees • Travel costs • Executive time • Administrative support	• Increased commitment • Reduced stress • Increased job satisfaction • Improved customer service • Enhanced recruiting image • Improved teamwork • Improved communication	• Executives • Senior executives • Sponsors • NHLO staff • Learning and Development Council • Prospective participants for Coaching for Business Impact	A variety of other initiatives will influence the impact measure including our Six Sigma process, service excellence program, and our efforts to become a great place to work.	It is extremely important to secure commitment from executives to provide accurate data in a timely manner.
• Productivity/ operational efficiency	(Method is the same for all data items.)	(Method is the same for all data items.)	• Administrative overhead • Telecommunication expenses • Facilities • Evaluation				
• Direct cost reduction							
• Retention of key staff members							
• Customer satisfaction							

Reaction

Reaction to the coaching program exceeded expectations of the NHLO staff. Comments received for Level 1 evaluation included these:

- "This program was very timely and practical."
- "My coach was very professional."

On a scale of 1 to 5 (1 = unacceptable and 5 = exceptional), the average rating of five items was 4.1, exceeding the objective of 4.0. Table 7-1 shows the items listed and their ratings.

Table 7-1. Executive reaction to coaching.

Level 1 Evaluation	Rating*
Relevance of coaching	4.6
Importance of coaching	4.1
Value of coaching	3.9
Effectiveness of coach	3.9
Recommendation to others	4.2

* Scale 1–5, where: 1 = Unacceptable
5 = Exceptional.

Learning

As with any process, the executives indicated enhancement of skills and knowledge in certain areas:

- "I gained much insight into my problems with my team."
- "This is exactly what I needed to get on track. My coach pointed out things I hadn't thought of and we came up with some terrific suggestions."

Table 7-2 shows seven items with inputs from both the executives and their coaches. For this level, it was considered appropriate to collect the data from both groups, indicating the degree of improvement. The most accurate, and probably most credible, is the input directly from the executive. The coach may not be fully aware of the extent of learning.

Application

For coaching to be successful, the executive had to implement the items on the action plans. The most important measure of application was the completion of the action plan steps. Eighty-three percent of the executives reported completion of all three plans. Another 11 percent completed one or two action plans.

Also, executives and the coach provided input on questions about changes in behavior from the use of skills. Here are some comments they offered on the questionnaires:

- "It was so helpful to get a fresh, unique point of view of my action plan. The coaching experience opened my eyes to significant things I was missing."
- "After spending a great deal of time trying to get my coach to understand my dilemma, I felt that more effort went into this than I expected."
- "We got stuck in a rut on one issue and I couldn't get out. My coach was somewhat distracted and I never felt we were on the same page."

The response rates for questionnaires were 92 percent and 80 percent for executives and coaches, respectively. Table 7-3 shows a listing of the skills and the rating, using a scale of 1 to 5 where 1 was "no change in the skill" and 5 was "exceptional increase."

Table 7-2. Learning from coaching.

Measures	Executive Rating*	Coach Rating*
Understanding strengths and weaknesses	3.9	4.2
Translating feedback into action plans	3.7	3.9
Involving team members in projects and goals	4.2	3.7
Communicating effectively	4.1	4.2
Collaborating with colleagues	4.0	4.1
Improving personal effectiveness	4.1	4.4
Enhancing leadership skills	4.2	4.3

* Program value scale 1–5.

Table 7-3. Application of coaching.		
Measures	Executive Rating*	Coach Rating*
Translating feedback into action plans	4.2	3.9
Involving team members in projects and goals	4.1	4.2
Communicating more effectively with the team	4.3	4.1
Collaborating more with the group and others	4.2	4.2
Applying effective leadership skills	4.1	3.9

* Program value scale 1–5, where: 1 = No change in skill
5 = Exceptional increase.

Barriers and Enablers

With any process, there are barriers and enablers to success. The executives were asked to indicate the specific barriers (obstacles) to the use of what was learned in the coaching sessions. Overall the barriers were weak, almost nonexistent. Also, they were asked to indicate what supported (enablers) the process. The enablers were very strong. Table 7-4 shows a list of the barriers and enablers.

Table 7-4. Barriers and enablers of the coaching process.	
Barriers	Enablers
• Not enough time	• Coach
• Not relevant	• Action plan
• Not effective when using the skill	• Structure of Coaching for Business Impact program
• Manager didn't support it	• Support of management

Impact

Specific business impact measures varied with the individual but, for the most part, were in the categories representing the five priority areas. Table 7-5

shows the listing of the actual data reported in the action plans. The table identifies the executive and the area of improvement, the monetary value, the basis of the improvement, the method of converting the monetary value, the contribution from coaching, the confidence estimate of the contribution, and the adjusted value.

Figure 7-7 shows a completed action plan from one participant, Caroline Dobson (executive #11). In this example, Caroline reduced annual turnover to 17 percent from 28 percent—an improvement of 11 percent. This represented four turnovers on an annual basis. Using a standard value of 1.3 times base salaries for the cost of one turnover and adding the total base salaries yields a total cost savings of $215,000.

As mentioned earlier, the estimates were used to isolate the benefits of coaching. After the estimates were obtained, the value was adjusted for the confidence of the estimate. Essentially, the executives were asked to list other factors that could have contributed to the improvement and allocate the amount (on a percentage basis) that was directly attributable to coaching. Then, using a scale of 0 percent (no confidence) to 100 percent (total certainty), executives provided the confidence levels for their estimates.

ROI

The costs were fully loaded and included both the direct and indirect costs of coaching. Estimates were used in some cases. Table 7-6 shows the costs of coaching for all 25 executives in the study.

Table 7-6. Costs of coaching 25 executives.	
Item	Cost
Needs Assessment/Development	$ 10,000
Coaching Fees	480,000
Travel Costs	53,000
Executive Time	9,200
Administrative Support	14,000
Administrative Overhead	2,000
Telecommunication Expenses	1,500
Facilities (Conference Room)	2,100
Evaluation	8,000
Total	**$ 579,800**

Table 7-5. Business impact from coaching (first measure).

Executive Number	Measurement Area	Total Annual Value	Basis	Method for Converting Data	Contribution Factor	Confidence Estimate	Adjusted Value
1	Revenue growth	$ 11,500	Profit margin	Standard value	33%	70%	$ 2,656
2	Retention	175,000	3 turnovers	Standard value	40%	70%	49,000
3	Retention	190,000	2 turnovers	Standard value	60%	80%	91,200
4	Direct cost savings	75,000	From cost statements	Participant estimate	100%	100%	75,000
5	Direct cost savings	21,000	Contract services	Standard value	75%	70%	11,025
6	Direct cost savings	65,000	Staffing costs	Standard value	70%	60%	27,300
7	Retention	150,000	2 turnovers	Standard value	50%	50%	37,500
8	Cost savings	70,000	Security	Standard value	60%	90%	37,800
9	Direct cost savings	9,443	Supply costs	Not applicable	70%	90%	5,949
10	Efficiency	39,000	Information technology costs	Participant estimate	70%	80%	21,840
11	Retention	215,000	4 turnovers	Standard value	75%	90%	145,125
12	Productivity	13,590	Overtime	Standard value	75%	80%	8,154
13	Retention	73,000	1 turnover	Standard value	50%	80%	29,200
14	Retention	120,000	2 annual turnovers	Standard value	60%	75%	54,000
15	Retention	182,000	4 turnovers	Standard value	40%	85%	61,880
16	Cost savings	25,900	Travel	Standard value	30%	90%	6,993
17	Cost savings	12,320	Administrative support	Standard value	75%	90%	8,316
18	Direct cost savings	18,950	Labor savings	Participant estimate	55%	60%	6,253
19	Revenue growth	103,100	Profit margin	Participant estimate	75%	90%	69,592
20	Revenue	19,500	Profit	Standard value	85%	75%	12,431
21	Revenue	21,230	Profit percent	Standard value	80%	70%	18,889
22	Revenue growth	105,780	Profit margin	Standard value	70%	50%	37,023
Totals		**$ 1,716,313**					**$ 817,126**

Figure 7-7. An example of an executive's completed action plan.

ACTION PLAN

Name: Caroline Dobson   **Coach:** Pamela Mills   **Follow-Up Date:** 1 September

Impact Objective: Improve retention for staff

Evaluation Period: January ____ to July

Improvement Measure: Voluntary turnover   **Current Performance:** 28% Annual   **Target Performance:** 15% Annual

Action Steps		Analysis
1. Meet with team to discuss reasons for turnover—using problem-solving skills.	31 January	A. What is the unit of measure? One voluntary turnover
2. Review exit interview data with HR—look for trends and patterns.	15 February	B. What is the value (cost) of one unit? $\frac{Salary \times 1.3}{\text{}}$
3. Counsel with "at-risk" employees to correct problems and explore opportunities for improvement.	1 March	C. How did you arrive at this value? Standard Value
4. Develop individual development plan for high-potential employees.	5 March	D. How much did the measure change during the evaluation period? (monthly value) 11% (annual %) (4 turnovers annually)
5. Provide recognition to employees with long tenure.	Routinely	E. What other factors could have contributed to this improvement? Growth opportunities, changes in job market
6. Schedule appreciation dinner for entire team.	31 May	F. What percent of this change was actually caused by this program? 75 %
7. Encourage team leaders to delegate more responsibilities.	31 May	G. What level of confidence do you place on the above information? (100% = Certainty and 0% = No confidence) 90 %
8. Follow-up with each discussion and discuss improvement or lack of improvement and plan other action.	Routinely	
9. Monitor improvement and provide recognition when appropriate.	11 May	

Intangible Benefits: Less stress on team, greater job satisfaction

Comments: Great Coach—He kept me on track with this issue.

Only a small amount of initial assessment cost was involved and the development cost was minor as well because the consulting firm had developed a similar coaching arrangement previously. The costs for sessions conducted on the phone were estimated, and sometimes a conference room was used instead of the executive offices.

Using the total monetary benefits and total cost of the program, two ROI calculations can be developed. The first is the benefit-cost ratio (BCR), which is the ratio of the monetary benefits divided by the costs:

$$BCR = \frac{\$1,861,158}{\$579,800} = 3.21$$

This value suggests that for every dollar invested, $3.21 was returned. The ROI formula for investments in training, coaching, or any human performance intervention is calculated in the same way as for other types of investments: earnings divided by investment. For this coaching solution, the ROI was calculated thus:

$$ROI\,(\%) = \frac{\$1,861,158 - \$579,800}{\$579,800} \times 100 = 221\%$$

In other words, for every dollar invested in the coaching program, the investment dollar was returned and another $1.21 was generated. In this case, the ROI exceeded the 25 percent target.

Intangibles

As with any project, there were many intangibles revealed by this analysis. Intangibles were collected on both the follow-up questionnaire and the action plan. Two questions were included on the questionnaire; one involved other benefits from this process and the other asked for comments about the program. Some individuals indicated intangibles when they listed the comments. Also, the action plan contained a place for comments and intangibles. The intangible benefits identified through these data sources included

- increased commitment
- improved teamwork
- increased job satisfaction
- improved customer service
- improved communication.

Note that this list includes only measures that were identified as being an intangible benefit by at least four of the 25 executives. In keeping with the conservative nature of the ROI Methodology, it was decided that intangibles identified by only a couple of executives would be considered extreme data items and not credible enough to list as an actual benefit of the program.

Credibility of the ROI Analysis

The critical issue in this study is the credibility of the data. The data was perceived to be very credible by the executives, their immediate managers, and the coaches. Credibility rests on eight major issues:

1. The information for the analysis was provided directly by the executives. They had no reason to be biased in their input.

2. The data was taken directly from the records and could be audited.

3. The data collection process was conservative, with the assumption that an unresponsive individual had realized no improvement. This concept—no data, no improvement—is ultraconservative in regard to data collection. Three executives did not return the completed action plans.

4. The executives did not assign complete credit to this program. Executives isolated only a portion of the data that should be credited directly to this program.

5. The data was adjusted for the potential error of the above estimate.

6. Only the first year's benefits were used in the analysis. Most of the improvements should result in second- and third-year benefits.

7. The costs of the program were fully loaded. All direct and indirect costs were included, including the time away from work for the executives.

8. The data revealed a balanced profile of success. Very favorable reaction, learning, and application data was presented along with business impact, ROI, and intangibles.

Collectively, these issues made a convincing case for the Coaching for Business Impact program.

Communication Strategy

To communicate appropriately with the target audiences outlined in the ROI analysis plan, three specific documents were produced. The first report was a detailed impact study showing the approach, assumptions, methodology, and results using all the data categories. In addition, barriers and enablers were included, along with conclusions and recommendations. The second report was an eight-page executive summary of the key points, including a one-page overview of the methodology. The third report was a brief, five-page summary of the process and results. These documents were presented to the different groups according to the plan in figure 7-8.

Because this was the first ROI study conducted in this organization, face-to-face meetings were conducted with the sponsor and other interested senior executives. The purpose was to ensure that executive sponsors had a clear understanding of the methodology, the conservative assumptions, and each level of data. The barriers, enablers, conclusions, and recommendations were an important part of the meeting. In the future, after two or three studies have been conducted, this group will receive only a one-page summary of key data items.

A similar meeting was conducted with the learning and development council. The council consisted of advisors to NHLO—usually middle level executives and managers. Finally, a face-to-face meeting was held

with the NHLO staff at which the complete impact study was described and used as a learning tool.

As a result of this communication, the senior executive decided to make only a few minor adjustments in the program and continued to offer the program to others on a volunteer basis. The executive sponsors were very pleased with the progress and were delighted to have data connecting coaching to the business impact.

Figure 7-8. NHLO's plan for communicating evaluation results.

Audience	Document
Executives	Brief summary
Managers of executive (senior executives)	Brief summary
Sponsor	Complete study, executive summary
NHLO staff	Complete study
Prospective participants	Brief summary

 Questions for Discussion

1. How would you critique the evaluation design and method of data collection?

2. What other strategies for isolating the impact of the coaching program could have been employed here?

3. Discuss the importance of credibility of data in an ROI study.

4. How can the outcomes of coaching be linked to your organization's business objectives?

About the Author

As a world-renowned expert on measurement and evaluation, **Jack J. Phillips** is chairman of the ROI Institute. Through the Institute, Phillips provides consulting services for *Fortune* 500 companies and workshops for major conference providers throughout the world.

Phillips is also the author or editor of more than 30 books—10 dedicated to measurement and evalu-

ation—and more than 100 articles. His most recent books include *The Leadership Scorecard* (Elsevier Science, 2004), *Proving the Value of HR: How and Why to Measure ROI* (SHRM, 2005), *Investing in Your Company's Human Capital: Strategies to Avoid Investing Too Little or Too Much* (AMACOM, 2005), *The Human Resources Scorecard: Measuring the Return on Investment* (Butterworth-Heinemann, 2001), *Managing Employee Retention* (Butterworth-Heinemann, 2003), *Retaining Your Best Employees* (ASTD Press, 2002), *Return on*

Investment in Training and Performance Improvement Projects, 2nd edition (Butterworth-Heinemann, 2003), *The Project Management Scorecard,* (Butterworth-Heinemann, 2002), *How to Measure Training Results* (McGraw-Hill, 2002), and *The Consultant's Scorecard* (McGraw-Hill, 2000).

His expertise in measurement and evaluation is based on extensive research and more than 27 years of corporate experience in five industries (aerospace, textiles, metals, construction materials, and banking). Phillips has served as training and development manager at two *Fortune* 500 firms, senior HR officer at two firms, president of a regional federal savings bank, and a professor of management at a major state university. Phillips can be reached at jack@roiinstitute.net.

Chapter 8

IN-COMPANY MANAGEMENT TRAINING PROGRAM

Ireland-Based Pharmaceutical Company

Gerry Doyle

This case study points out the difficulties of conducting a full ROI evaluation of a management training program in a pharmaceutical company some months after the program was completed. The evaluation was further hampered by a scarcity of adequate baseline data and a lack of an effective needs analysis.

Background

The company is a multinational corporation manufacturing active ingredients and final drug substances for a wide variety of products. The plant that implemented the training program employs 480 people and is situated within a cluster of pharmaceutical companies in southern Ireland. The key challenges facing the company are increasing its market share and maintaining competitiveness in a very tight marketplace. The Irish manufacturing plant faces increased competitive pressures from other plants owned by the corporation overseas.

Training Program

Senior company management had identified a number of areas where the performance of group leaders (GLs) could be improved. These GLs are first-line managers who play a key role in the effective opera-

tion of the plant by leading teams across all departments. All these GLs are promoted from the ranks. Although some GLs have long service with the company, the majority are in their late 20s or early 30s and have been promoted to GLs quite recently.

Management determined that the GLs needed to take more ownership of their jobs, exercise greater responsibility, make decisions instead of passing problems up the line, lead change rather than just responding to it, manage people better, and improve both their own and their teams' motivational levels.

The plant was under increasing pressure to improve quality, and management believed that an urgent response by way of training was necessary. Discussion at management level achieved a needs definition, and the HR department went about identifying a training provider to develop a program to respond to these needs. The company was assured by the selected training provider that the program offered would refine the GLs' needs at the individual and team levels and would serve as an effective training response to those needs. The training provider had a high level of credibility in providing this type of leadership program. The company decided to go ahead with the proposed training solution.

The program was attended by 32 GLs from different departments. The three-phase program was delivered as a package by the external trainer and covered a wide range of supervisor and team leader competencies. The initial classroom training was followed by one-to-one coaching sessions with some of the GLs.

The program outlined a range of skill levels it hoped the participants would achieve., There was, however, no structured system for monitoring the achievement of these targets apart from self-reporting by the participants and observation by the trainer during the follow-up one-to-one coaching sessions. In addition, the skills identified were generic, for example, "approaching things more proactively—looking ahead and outside my own area," rather than being linked to company-specific job performance or team performance targets. No business measures were identified that would be impacted by the program.

Evaluation Planning

The decision to undertake an evaluation of this program was made some time after the program had been completed. The catalyst for this decision came from Skillnets—an Irish government/industry–led body dedicated to increasing the range, scope, and quality of training in Irish enterprises. Skillnets had identified the need for better training evaluation among Irish companies and initiated a pilot project to test the ROI Methodology in Irish firms. It commissioned the Impact Measurement Centre (IMC) to deliver the pilot. Led by its managing partner, IMC identified 18 companies that would test the ROI Methodology. One of these was the subject of this case study.

Even though the training program had ended, the pharmaceutical company was keen to have it evaluated because of the following:

- It had entailed significant cost.
- It had been targeted at a crucial segment of the workforce.
- Its success should have had a major impact on the company's strategic objectives.

- It had high visibility in the plant and had become something of a talking point.
- The company was considering running similar programs in the future.

Evaluation Process

One of the major challenges of conducting evaluation *ex post facto* is the availability of credible baseline data. Also, a comprehensive needs analysis is a vital feature of any program that is intended to be evaluated to Level 5 (ROI). In this case, inadequate baseline data was available, and the needs analysis was practically nonexistent. Nonetheless, company management was eager to find out if this program had been worth the expense especially because other similar programs were contemplated. It was decided to try a full ROI evaluation.

Because no data had been collected at Level 1 or 2 during program delivery it was decided to issue a comprehensive anonymous questionnaire to all participants to collect data at Levels 1, 2 and 3, and 4 together. Considerable efforts were made by the company's training officer to gather the completed questionnaires, and he succeeded in getting 84 percent returned.

At Level 4, it was first decided to request senior management to identify the areas that might usefully be examined to determine a business impact resulting from the training. These included data on absenteeism and time lost due to accidents, turnover, unit productivity, and so forth. A focus group of managers was conducted to complete a detailed review of the program impact. Additionally, the trainees were asked certain questions relating to business results in the questionnaire.

Reaction

Obviously, it was difficult to assess reaction/satisfaction levels so long after the training. The evaluation staff decided to confine questions to four areas:

- Was the training at the right level for the skills and knowledge for the trainees?
- Was it delivered in a professional and competent manner?
- Were the objectives clear to the trainees beforehand?
- Overall, was the training considered by the trainees to have been beneficial?

The results showed that the training was delivered in a professional and competent manner, was at the right level for trainees, and, overall, the training was seen as being beneficial. However, there was a lack of clarity about the training objectives beforehand. This finding was to have important implications later.

Learning

Assessing learning after the event was equally challenging. Again, the staff decided to focus on two specific areas of the training curriculum and ask the trainees to rate the extent to which the training had helped them build self-esteem and develop a personal vision and goals. The ratings of 3.5 and 3.6, respectively, on a scale from 1 to 5 were not as high as might have been hoped for. An additional general statement, "I learned new knowledge and skills from the training," received an average rating of 4.0, which was sufficient to conclude that a reasonable level of learning had occurred.

Application on the Job

Assessment of application of the training on the job was carried out in three ways. First, the participants were asked to rate the following statements on a 1–5 scale (average results in brackets):

- I have been able to apply what I learned on the training to my job (3.9).
- I have been able to retain most of the skills/ knowledge that I learned on the course (3.8).
- I have been willing to use most of the skills/ knowledge that I learned on the course (4.4).

In addition, those who took advantage of the follow-up coaching and mentoring reported an average of 4.2 beneficial rating.

Second, the trainees were given a list of competencies that were extrapolated from the training program curriculum and asked to rate the extent to which they were using these skills since the training, again using a 1–5 scale (average rating in brackets):

- I am consistently achieving targets (3.9).
- I am better at anticipating and preventing problems (3.9).
- I approach things more proactively—looking ahead and outside my own area (4.2).
- The people I lead need less monitoring and direction (3.7).

- There is much more teamwork among supervisors/managers (3.1).
- I take more initiatives to improve performance in my area (4.0).
- I see our customers as being directly impacted by my performance (3.9).
- I have a strong sense of personal responsibility for making things happen and leading change/performance improvement (4.3).

The participants were also asked to estimate the percentage of new knowledge and skills learned from the training they directly applied to their job. The average result was 47 percent. Trainees reported a strong sense of personal responsibility and other improvements in their approach to the job as an effect of the training. Nevertheless, they reported a low level of improved teamwork. Less than half of what was learned was applied to the job. In answers to open-ended questions, the participants indicated that this lack of on-the-job application might be because the content was not all directly job related.

Third, the managers were asked in a focus group to estimate the percentage increase in knowledge/ skills resulting from the training; the managers gave an average estimate of 24 percent—half that estimated by the trainees.

Business Impact

The training officer then began the process of identifying financial data that could be used to arrive at a figure for ROI. Three data items were identified: lost time due to accidents, out-of-specification (OOS) data, and out-of-expectation data. Because there was only an indirect correlation between accidents and the training, this data item was not considered.

During complex manufacturing operations involving production of regulated products, such as in the case of pharmaceuticals, there are occasional deviations from the validated process. These "variances" can influence the quality and composition of product test samples sent to the quality control laboratory, resulting in sample failures or OOS incidents. Thus, variance and OOS are closely related phenomena that must be reported, documented in detail, and archived for audits per regulations of the U.S. Food and Drug Administration.

This is an expensive process, and any reduction in OOS will result in major savings. In the 12-month period immediately following the training, the costs associated with OOS incidents dropped by €684,829. In the same period, costs associated with investigation of out-of-expectation incidents (a similar aberrant data result) reduced by €21,555. This reduction led to total savings during the period of €706,384.

Both the participants (by way of questionnaires) and the managers (through a focus group) were asked about how their job performance on variance and OOS had improved since the training. They were asked to estimate how much of the improvement directly resulted from the training. The participants' estimate was 11 percent, and the managers said that 17 percent was due to the training.

Both groups were asked to apply a level of confidence to their answers. The participants, on average, were 85 percent confident, but the managers were 60 percent confident in their estimates. These confidence estimates allowed the company to adjust the estimates of improvement as a direct result of the training to be 9 percent, according to the participants, or 10 percent, according to the managers.

In reaching their estimate of the impact of the training on increased productivity, the managers identified the following factors that influenced productivity changes during the same period:

- transparency achieved through feedback systems on performance levels
- site supervisor meetings
- better cohesion between departments/shifts
- focus on performance management
- additional support to supervisors
- personnel changes at department level
- competition in the quality assurance department
- increased production pressures.

After considering the impact of each of these factors, the managers were satisfied to remain with their original estimate of the impact of training.

ROI

The following is a list of the fully loaded costs of the training:

- trainer (external) = €100,000
- training room rental in hotel = €495
- equipment rental = €510
- lunch/coffee €1,940
- group leaders' fully loaded cost for three days = €6,272.

Therefore, the total cost for the training was €109,217. The company decided to accept the lowest average estimate of the net benefits attributable to the training (the participants' estimate) of 9 percent of €706,384, yielding an adjusted estimate of €63,575 for the benefits of training.

$$BCR = \frac{€63,575}{€109,217} = 0.58$$

$$ROI = \frac{€63,575 - €109,217}{€109,217} \times 100 = -42\%$$

Intangible Benefits

Despite the negative ROI, the evaluation process identified a number of areas where the training had a positive impact even though these were not converted to monetary values: increased morale, increased customer satisfaction, decreased production times, and increased productivity.

Furthermore, the participants gave an average rating of 4.1 to the statement that the training was a worthwhile investment in their career development. Eighty-six percent of the participants believed the training was a worthwhile investment for the company, and 76 percent of managers believed it had been worthwhile.

Communicating the Results

The evaluation study was initially presented to the head of the human relations department and later to all department heads. The challenges of conducting this study such a long time after the training delivery were known, but the company proceeded with the evaluation more as an exploration of what a comprehensive ROI analysis could reveal.

Conclusions

The negative ROI supported the general view within the company that the training had not realized its potential to bring about the expected change, but not for the reason supposed—that the training itself had been poorly delivered. By collecting data at all levels it was possible to find out why the training had not delivered on its promise.

The Level 1 and 2 data (though gathered some time after the training) pointed to a generally satisfactory training exercise in which the participants had learned new skills and knowledge. In addition, the follow-up coaching had been very beneficial to those who had availed of it. The Level 3 data showed that only between a quarter or less than half of what had been learned had been applied on the job. This seems to have resulted from a number of factors including poor linking of job-related needs to training, lack of support to implement new skills, and lack of opportunity to implement new skills. It was clear from the focus group of managers that they did not feel part of the process and they admitted that they had not been as supportive as they could have been in the implementation stage.

This information allowed management to proceed with implementing further leadership focused training for GLs. However, the process has now been strengthened following a managerial review based on this ROI analysis, and a number of improvements have been implemented at the design and delivery stage of future programs, including

- comprehensive needs analysis
- training linked to actual job situation

- better buy-in by trainees and their superiors
- support follow-up systems in place
- impact to be determined before training
- training to have clear and measurable ROI targets
- trainees to have personal performance targets linked to training
- managers to be involved at all stages of training design, implementation, and follow-up.

Despite the negative ROI, there was agreement that most trainees obtained benefit from their participation, that the training was well conducted, and that the coaching was particularly helpful for those who used it.

There were a number of important intangible benefits, the effects of which should not be underestimated.

 ## Questions for Discussion

1. Why was it difficult to conduct a full ROI without an effective needs assessment?

2. This study used self-reporting by the participants and observation by the trainer as the means for monitoring the achievement of goals. What would be some other methods to use in this situation?

3. No business measures were identified in this study. What are some specific business measures that could have impacted the program?

4. What was the effect of the absence of credible baseline data on the evaluation process?

About the Author

Gerry Doyle is managing partner of the Impact Measurement Centre in Ireland. He has many years of practical business expertise with Irish and multinational companies in a number of middle and senior management positions in Ireland, the Middle East, and the Far East. He is a former chief executive of South Dublin Chamber of Commerce and program manager of the Chambers of Commerce of Ireland.

In the past decade, Doyle has provided consultancy services to some of Ireland's top companies and has guided scores of small firms toward viability. He is a consultant to Skillnets (the Irish government/ employer–led training body) and is the ROI Institute partner in Ireland. He is leading a major initiative to assist Irish companies with implementing the ROI Methodology for measuring the impact and ROI of in-company training. He can be contacted at info@ impact-measurement-centre.com.

Chapter 9

This case was prepared to serve as a basis for discussion rather than to illustrate either effective or ineffective administrative and management practices. All names, dates, places, and organizations have been disguised at the request of the authors or organization.

EFFECTIVE MEETING SKILLS
TechnoTel Corporation

Patti P. Phillips and Jack J. Phillips

Everyone has experienced long, meaningless meetings—the ones that seem to have no purpose. This case study presents the benefits that can be achieved by reducing the length of meetings, the number of meetings, and the number of meeting participants. Pre-program data was collected using a meeting profile worksheet; post-program data was collected using a comprehensive questionnaire. Participant estimates were used to isolate the effects of the workshop on the measures. Standard values of time (salary and benefits) were used to convert data to monetary values. Fully loaded program costs were developed.

Background

TechnoTel Corporation is a maker of telecommunications equipment. Although the firm has 22 locations, this case study takes place in Frankfurt, Germany. A comprehensive needs assessment targeting managerial and supervisory competencies revealed a lack of effective meeting skills, including the ability to prepare, conduct, facilitate, participate in, and follow up on meetings. The corporate learning department developed a two-day, facilitator-led workshop with specific objectives to address these needs. The program was designed to ensure successful application of the skills.

Program Objectives

The Effective Meeting Skills workshop was made available to managers and project leaders who regularly conduct meetings in all TechnoTel divisions.

Program objectives suggest that upon completion of the workshop, participants would have

- the tools and techniques to prepare, conduct, and follow up on meetings
- an understanding of the human dynamics of meetings
- strategies for participating in or leading meetings more effectively.

In addition to these program outputs, participation in the program was expected to lead to shorter meetings, fewer meetings, and a smaller number of participants attending meetings.

Program Design

To meet the identified objectives, the two-day Effective Meeting Skills workshop included a variety of knowledge-based exercises as well as skill-based

---

Figure 9-1. Outline for the effective meetings program.

1. Meeting activity profile completed by participants
2. Definition for an effective meeting
3. Criteria for effective meetings
4. Causes behind ineffective meetings
5. Tips for conducting effective meetings
   a. Determine purpose
   b. Recognize the type of meeting
   c. Arrange seating appropriately
   d. Set the agenda
   e. Assemble a set of all appropriate attendees
   f. Establish ground rules
   g. Bring closure and plan follow-up
6. Skill practices

7. Key roles in meetings
8. Meeting tasks
9. The human function in meetings
10. Debriefing model
11. Brainstorming
12. Decision making
13. Encouraging participation
14. Handling group dynamics
15. Dealing with difficult participants
16. Providing feedback
17. Handling conflict
18. Meeting simulations/exercises
19. Action plan requirements

---

practices and tasks. Figure 9-1 presents the complete outline for the program.

To assist the transfer of skills to the job, a brief action plan was required so that participants could identify specific new and enhanced behaviors and track their progress as they conduct future meetings. Although an important part of the program, the action plan was used primarily to assist participants in their tracking actual use of knowledge and skills.

Along with the action plan, a meeting profile was designed into the program to capture the current level and cost of meetings. It also provided baseline data for comparing improvements resulting from the program. Figure 9-2 presents the meeting profile.

Figure 9-2. Meeting profile.

Current Meeting Activity (Month Before Program)

Number of meetings chaired each month	_____ (A)
Average number of individuals attending each meeting each month	_____ (B)
Average length of time for each meeting (in hours)	_____ (C)
Total time consumed in meetings $(A \times B \times C)$	_____ (D)
Average hourly compensation of attendees (salary plus benefits)	_____ (E)
Total meeting costs $(D \times E)$	_____ (F)

Evaluation Need

The president of one of TechnoTel's major business units was interested in conducting this program for his middle management group—a total of 150 managers. Six programs were offered to the group within a one-month time period. The nature of the business and the president's interest in accountability led the president to request a comprehensive evaluation of the program. Not only was he interested in whether or not the program resulted in reduced meetings and fewer participants, but also in whether the benefits of his putting his people through the program exceeded the costs.

The president's desire to ensure a positive return on his investment as well as the corporate learning department's desire to gather data to improve the program overall led the learning staff to plan a comprehensive evaluation. The results of the evaluation would report success from the participant's perspective, the system perspective, and the economic perspective. Given these requirements, the learning staff implemented the ROI Methodology in its entirety.

Evaluation Methodology

The ROI Methodology (Phillips, 2003) had been integrated into TechnoTel's corporate learning function two years prior to the launch of the Effective Meeting Skills program. TechnoTel has successfully sustained the use of this process because it:

Table 9-1. The evaluation framework.

Level	Measurement Focus
1. Reaction, Satisfaction, and Planned Action	Measures participant satisfaction with the program and captures planned action
2. Learning	Measures changes in knowledge, skills, and attitudes
3. Application and Implementation	Measures changes in on-the-job behavior
4. Impact	Measures changes in critical business measures
5. Return-on-Investment (ROI)	Compares the monetary benefits to the costs

- reports a balanced set of measures
- follows a methodical step-by-step process
- adheres to standards and philosophy of maintaining a conservative approach and credible outcomes.

The ROI Methodology categorizes evaluation data into five levels as shown in table 9-1. These five levels tell the complete story of program success. The five levels balance economic impact with measures that address individuals' perspectives of the program and that of the systems and processes that support the transfer of learning.

Level 1: Reaction, Satisfaction, and Planned Action

This initial level of evaluation is the most commonly used within the TechnoTel learning environment. Reaction and satisfaction data is collected using a standard end-of-course questionnaire. Planned actions are often collected using action plans; however, a question asking the participants' intent to use what they learned is included on the end-of-course questionnaire and suffices for the planned action measure when action plans are not used.

The TechnoTel learning environment is interested in a variety of measures at Level 1, some of which are relevant only to the learning staff and their efforts to improve the learning process. These measures

address course design and delivery as well as participant perception of the learning environment. Because management is interested in potential use of all programs, TechnoTel's Level 1 evaluation also answers five important questions:

1. Is the program relevant to participants' jobs?
2. Is the program important to participants' jobs?
3. Do participants intend to use what they learned in the program?
4. Did the program provide participants with new information?
5. Would participants recommend the programs to others?

An acceptable rating, using a 1–5 rating scale (1 = Unacceptable; 5 = Acceptable), for all TechnoTel courses is 4.0 or above. Any measures that fall below these ratings are flagged and actions are taken to improve them in future courses.

Level 2: Learning

Participants' understanding of the knowledge and skills taught in a program is imperative to their ability to change behavior. Learning measurement at TechnoTel takes place during the program through a variety of techniques such as tests, facilitator assessment, peer assessment, self-assessment, observation, and reflective thinking with documentation. The questions that TechnoTel strives to answer when measuring learning are these:

1. Do participants understand what they are supposed to do and how to do it?
2. Are participants confident to apply their newly acquired knowledge and skills when they leave the classroom?

Level 3: Application and Implementation

For many programs, TechnoTel's supervisors and managers are interested in what participants do with what they learn. When this is the case, programs are evaluated at Level 3 using a variety of techniques including self-administered questionnaires, 360 degree-feedback, observations, focus groups, and interviews. Because there is more to learning transfer than just attending the program or course, it is important to TechnoTel to gather data related to how the organizational system (management, technology, and so forth) supports the transfer of training. With these considerations, three basic questions were answered at Level 3 for the Effective Meeting Skills workshop:

1. How much have participants changed their approach to planning and conducting meetings?

2. If they are applying their knowledge and skills, what is supporting their effort?

3. If they are not applying their knowledge and skills, why not?

Level 4: Impact

For many programs, TechnoTel is interested in impact on revenue, productivity, quality, cost, and time—measures of efficiency. The organization wants to know how programs influence customer satisfaction and employee satisfaction—measures that are critical to organizational success but not monetized. The ultimate question answered at Level 4 is: *So what?*

Level 5: ROI

This final measure of success answers the question: Do the monetary benefits of the program exceed the costs?

For some programs, the organization is not interested in calculating ROI. But, for programs that are costly or high profile, that drive business impact, or that are of particular interest to management, ROI is important. A standard ROI target of 25 percent is set for programs being evaluated to this level. This represents a slightly higher ROI than the ROI being achieved by other investments made by TechnoTel.

The balanced set of measures that is yielded by answering the key questions posed at each level of evaluation provides TechnoTel's corporate learning department a complete story of program success. Through this story, the department not only improves the immediate learning process, but also enhances how the system as a whole works to ensure successful transfer of learning and the achievement of desired outcomes. TechnoTel uses all of this information in combination with the ROI metric to determine if a program is a wise investment—either alone or in comparison to alternative programs that may yield similar outcomes.

Step-By-Step Process

The 10 steps in the ROI Methodology constitute a methodical process to evaluation. As shown in figure 9-3, the evaluation process begins with identifying program objectives and evaluation planning. From

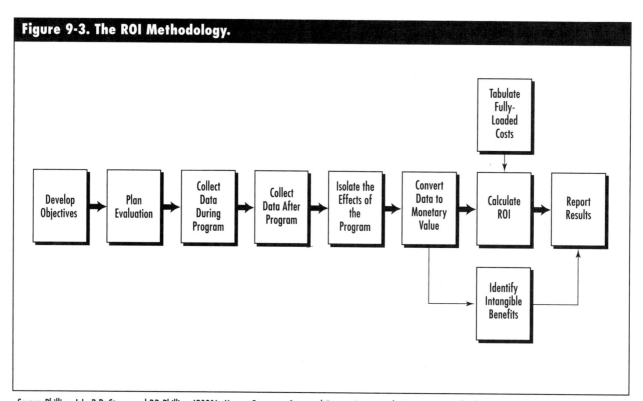

Figure 9-3. The ROI Methodology.

SOURCE: Phillips, J.J., R.D. Stone, and P.P. Phillips. (2001). *Human Resources Scorecard.* Boston: Butterworth-Heinemann. Used with permission.

there, execution requires that data be collected and analyzed before developing a final report.

Data Collection Procedures

A pragmatic approach to data collection was taken for the evaluation of the Effective Meeting Skills program. Because the cost of the program (as will be described in a later section) was not excessive, the corporate learning department staff determined that the prudent approach for this particular evaluation would be to keep the cost low while ensuring credible results. The data collection process began with a review of the objectives and measures of success, identification of the appropriate data collection methods and the most credible sources of data, and a determination of the timing of data collection.

Program Objectives and Measures

The needs assessment identified the skill deficiencies that kept managers from conducting effective meetings. Through the needs assessment process and the design of the Effective Meeting Skills program, specific outputs were defined as well as specific impact measures that would result if participants applied their newly acquired knowledge and skills. Measures of success at Level 1 are standard (4.0 out of 5.0), as is the measure of success at Level 5 (25 percent); measures of success for the other levels of evaluation were dependent on the program or the client expectations. In this case, the president of the division implementing the workshop was interested in improvement in the impact measures; even though he did not specify what improvement he was looking for, he did indicate by his request that the benefits should exceed the cost of the program. Therefore, the improvement in business impact measures must be such that when converted to monetary value a positive ROI was achieved. Table 9-2 summarizes the program's objectives and the measures used to determine success.

Data Collection Methods

Data was collected for this evaluation using multiple methods: end-of-course questionnaire, action plans, meeting profile, written test, skills practice observation, and a follow-up questionnaire. The successful meeting profile was designed into the program (see figure 9-2). It was used at the beginning of the program to capture the current level and costs of meetings. When completed, this exercise showed partici-

pants how much time they spent in meetings and the overall cost of meetings. These data served as baseline for comparing improvements identified in the follow-up questionnaire. The written test measured the improvements in knowledge of basic issues and meeting dynamics, and skill practices measured success in ability to use effective meeting skills.

The action plan was an important part of understanding how participants applied what they learned when they returned to the job; however, the follow-up questionnaire was the primary data collection method for Level 3 and Level 4 follow-up data. Figure 9-4 presents the complete follow-up questionnaire.

Because of their desire to limit the cost of the evaluation, the corporate learning department staff decided on the most feasible methods for data collection. Cost data was developed using company records, and table 9-3 summarizes the other data collection methods.

Data Sources

Data source selection is a critical step in data collection in that the source drives the credibility and validity of the study. Who knows best about the measures being taken? The primary source of data for the Effective Meeting Skills evaluation was the participants. The managers and project leaders participating in the workshop know the extent to which they apply their knowledge and skills; they are the people who plan and lead the meetings; they are the people who recognize the cost of too many unproductive meetings (they are the ones calling the meetings). Although it may have been valuable to administer surveys to the professional staff participating in the meetings, this step would have added additional cost to the data collection process. The information they would have provided would have been valuable, but the perceived value of their input did not appear to outweigh the time and cost involved in collecting and analyzing the additional data. It was decided that the participants would serve as the source of data for this evaluation.

The program was rolled out to the entire 150 middle managers of the Frankfurt division; the managers divided up into six groups. It was agreed with the division president that the target group for this evaluation would include only three of the six groups participating in the program. This limitation would save cost and time of evaluation and would provide the president the data he needed to make a fair

Table 9-2. Objectives and measures of success for the effective meeting skills program.

	Broad Objectives	Measures
Satisfaction Objectives	Positive reaction and planned action with the knowledge and skills presented in the course	Ranking of 4 out of 5 on • Relevance • Importance • Intent to use • New information • Recommendation to others
	Planned action	Three defined actions to be taken when returning to the job from each participant
Learning Objectives	Ability to identify the extent and cost of meetings	Given cost guidelines, determine the cost of last three meetings
	Ability to identify positives, negatives, and implications of basic meeting issues and dynamics	From a list of 30 positive and negative meeting behaviors, correctly identify the implications of each behavior
	Acquisition of effective meeting behaviors	Demonstrate appropriate responses to eight of 10 active role-play scenarios
Application Objectives	Use of effective meeting behaviors	Reported changes in behavior toward planning and conducting meetings
	Barriers to application	Number and variety of barriers identified
	Enablers to application	Number and variety of enablers identified
Impact Objectives	Shorter meetings	Reported time savings
	Fewer meetings	Reported time savings
	Fewer meeting participants	Reported time savings
ROI	25 percent	

Figure 9-4. Effective Meeting Skills follow-up impact questionnaire.

Are you currently in a people management role/capacity?

Yes ❏   No ❏

1. Listed below are the objectives of the Effective Meetings Skills workshop. After reflecting on this program, please indicate the degree of success in meeting the objectives:

As a result of this program, participants will have:	Failed	Limited Success	Generally Successful	Completely Successful
A. the tools and techniques to prepare for, conduct, and follow up on meetings	❏	❏	❏	❏
B. an understanding of the human dynamics of meetings	❏	❏	❏	❏
C. strategies to participate in and lead or chair meetings more effectively	❏	❏	❏	❏

2. Did you develop and implement an on-the-job action plan for Effective Meeting Skills?

Yes ❏   No ❏

If yes, please describe the nature and outcome of the plan. If you did not develop or implement an action plan, please explain why.

_____

_____

_____

_____

3. Please rate, on a scale of 1–5, the relevance of each of the program elements to your job (1 = No relevance; 5 = Very relevant).

	1	2	3	4	5
Interactive Activities	❏	❏	❏	❏	❏
Group Discussions	❏	❏	❏	❏	❏
Networking Opportunities	❏	❏	❏	❏	❏
Reading Materials/Video	❏	❏	❏	❏	❏
Program Content	❏	❏	❏	❏	❏

4. Have you used the written materials since you participated in the program?

Yes ❏   No ❏

Please explain. _____

_____

_____

(continued next page)

Figure 9-4. Effective Meeting Skills follow-up impact questionnaire (continued).

5. Please indicate the degree to which you have changed the use of the following items/actions/behaviors as a result of your participation in the Effective Meeting Skills workshop:

	No Change	Little Change	Some Change	Significant Change	Very Much Change	No Opportunity To Use Skill
A. Participating effectively in meetings	❏	❏	❏	❏	❏	❏
B. Avoiding meetings unless they are necessary	❏	❏	❏	❏	❏	❏
C. Minimizing the number of participants attending meetings	❏	❏	❏	❏	❏	❏
D. Setting objectives for meetings	❏	❏	❏	❏	❏	❏
E. Developing an agenda for each meeting	❏	❏	❏	❏	❏	❏
F. Controlling time of meetings	❏	❏	❏	❏	❏	❏
G. Enhancing participant satisfaction in meetings	❏	❏	❏	❏	❏	❏
H. Arranging the meeting site for maximum effectiveness	❏	❏	❏	❏	❏	❏
I. Scheduling an optimal time for meetings	❏	❏	❏	❏	❏	❏
J. Communicating the ground rules for meetings	❏	❏	❏	❏	❏	❏
K. Assigning appropriate roles for meeting participants	❏	❏	❏	❏	❏	❏
L. Reaching consensus in meetings when appropriate	❏	❏	❏	❏	❏	❏
M. Listening actively to meeting participants	❏	❏	❏	❏	❏	❏
N. Encouraging participation in meetings	❏	❏	❏	❏	❏	❏
O. Using brainstorming in meetings when appropriate	❏	❏	❏	❏	❏	❏
P. Dealing with difficult meeting participants	❏	❏	❏	❏	❏	❏
Q. Providing feedback to meeting participants	❏	❏	❏	❏	❏	❏
R. Handling conflict in meeting	❏	❏	❏	❏	❏	❏
S. Keeping the meeting on focus	❏	❏	❏	❏	❏	❏
T. Accomplishing meeting objectives	❏	❏	❏	❏	❏	❏
U. Evaluating the meeting process	❏	❏	❏	❏	❏	❏
V. Implementing action plans	❏	❏	❏	❏	❏	❏
W. Planning a follow-up activity	❏	❏	❏	❏	❏	❏

6. List the five (5) effective meeting behaviors or skills you have used most frequently as a result of the program.

_____

_____

_____

_____

7. What has changed about your meeting activity profile as a result of this program (for example, fewer meetings, fewer participants, shorter meetings)?

_____

_____

_____

8. Please estimate the following monthly time-saving measures. Use the most recent month compared to the month before attending this program. Provide only improvements directly related to this program and only when the time saved is used productively.

Number of meetings avoided each month with improved planning and analysis   _____

Average time saved per meeting per month (in hours)   _____

Average number of participants reduced per meeting per month   _____

9. What level of confidence do you place on the above estimations? (0% = No confidence, 100% = Certainty) _____%

10. Please identify any specific accomplishments/improvements that you can link to this program (for example, on-time schedules, project completion, response times, better decisions, more ideas from group):

_____

_____

_____

11. What specific value in U.S. dollars can be attributed to the above accomplishments/improvements? Use the first year's values only. Although this is a difficult question, try to think of specific ways in which the above improvements can be converted to monetary units. Along with the monetary value, please indicate the basis of your calculation: $_____

Basis _____

_____

_____

_____

12. Other factors often influence improvements in performance. Please indicate the percent of the above improvement that is related directly to this program. _____%

Please explain. _____

_____

13. What level of confidence do you place on the above estimations? (0% = No confidence, 100% = Certainty) _____%

(continued next page)

Figure 9-4. Effective Meeting Skills follow-up impact questionnaire *(continued)*.

14. Do you think the Effective Meeting Skills workshop represented a good investment for TechnoTel?

Yes ❑   **No** ❑

Please explain. _____

_____

Was it a good investment of your time?

Yes ❑   **No** ❑

Please explain. _____

_____

15. Indicate the extent to which you think the Effective Meeting Skills workshop has influenced each of these measures in your work unit, department, or business unit:

	No Influence	Some Influence	Moderate Influence	Significant Influence	Very Much Influence
A. Productivity	❑	❑	❑	❑	❑
B. Customer response time	❑	❑	❑	❑	❑
C. Cost control	❑	❑	❑	❑	❑
D. Employee satisfaction	❑	❑	❑	❑	❑
E. Customer satisfaction	❑	❑	❑	❑	❑
F. Quality	❑	❑	❑	❑	❑
G. Other	❑	❑	❑	❑	❑

16. What barriers, if any, have you encountered that have prevented you from using skills or knowledge gained in this program. Please explain, if possible.

_____

_____

_____

17. What enablers, if any, are present to help you use the skills or knowledge gained from this program? Please explain.

_____

_____

_____

18. What additional benefits have been derived from this program?

_____
_____
_____

19. What specific suggestions do you have for improving this program?

_____
_____
_____

20. Other comments:

_____
_____
_____
_____
_____

Table 9-3. Data collection methods.

	Level 1	Level 2	Level 3	Barriers/ Enablers	Level 4	Costs
End-of-Course Questionnaire	×					
Meeting Profile		×				
Written Test		×				
Skill Practice Observation		×				
Action Plan	×		×			
Questionnaire			×	×	×	
Company Records						×

assessment of the success of the program. Given this, a total of 72 managers participated in the evaluation process.

Data Collection Timing

When conducting a comprehensive evaluation such as that completed for the Effective Meeting Skills workshop, data is collected at two different time-frames: Levels 1 and 2 data is collected during the program, and Levels 3 and 4 data is collected after participants have had time to apply knowledge and skills on a routine basis. It was determined that given the type of skills being developed in the Effective Meeting Skills program and the numerous opportunities managers have to apply the skills, that three months would be ample time for the acquired skills to be internalized and produce results. Therefore, three months after completing the program, participants would receive the follow-up questionnaire.

Figure 9-5 presents the complete data collection plan. The corporate learning staff presented the data collection plan and the ROI analysis plan (described in the next section) to the division president for concurrence prior to execution.

Success With Data Collection

A data collection administration strategy is important for ensuring that the appropriate amount of data is provided. In the case of the Effective Meeting Skills workshop, the administrative strategy consisted of four primary actions:

1. The evaluation strategy was presented at the beginning of the program.

2. The facilitators reinforced the need for participants to respond to the follow-up questionnaire at the end of the program.

3. The division president signed a letter that was distributed three days prior to the questionnaires being mailed.

4. The questionnaire did not require that participants include their name or other demographic information; therefore, respondents remained anonymous.

All participants responded to the Level 1 and 2 evaluations; the follow-up for Levels 3 and 4 proved to be challenging, however. The overall response rate was 67 percent (48 respondents), which was satisfactory to the evaluation team and the division president. Unfortunately, only 43 percent (31 respondents) of the participants provided useable data on questions 7, 8, and 9 (see figure 9-4). These three questions were directly related to follow-up on the impact measures. With the understanding that the results would reflect only that which occurred for those responding, the division president was satisfied with the response rate.

Data Analysis Procedures

Data analysis comprises five key steps, each of which was carefully considered during the evaluation of this workshop:

1. isolating the effects of the program
2. converting data to monetary value
3. tabulating fully loaded costs
4. identifying intangible benefits
5. comparing the monetary benefits to the costs.

Isolating the Effects of the Program

This step of the ROI Methodology answers the question, "How do you know it was your program that influenced the measures?" Isolating the effects of the program considers all other variables that may have influenced improvement in specific measures of success for a program. Four of the 10 potential techniques were considered for the Effective Meeting Skills workshop: control group, trend-line analysis, forecasting, and participant estimations.

Because only three of the six groups were being evaluated, it was first suggested that a control group arrangement could be used to isolate the effects of the program. The thought was that the groups not participating in the evaluation process could serve as the control group. After much deliberation, however, it was agreed that it would be difficult to maintain the integrity of the experiment and it would be disruptive.

Participants completed a meeting profile during the program to determine the time, frequency, and participation of meetings along with the costs. To collect similar data from the control group, its members would have to complete meeting profiles as well. This would not only contribute to the contamination of the experiment, but would require additional work for the control group members. It was important to the division president to keep the evaluation low key by not requiring too much additional work and by not disrupting the organization. For

Figure 9-5. Data collection plan for the Effective Meeting Skills program.

DATA COLLECTION PLAN

Program/Project: Effective meetings

Purpose of This Evaluation: _____

Responsibility: _____

Date: _____

Level	Broad Program Objective(s)	Measures	Data Collection Method/Instruments	Data Sources	Timing	Responsibilities
1	**REACTION/SATISFACTION AND PLANNED ACTION** • Positive reaction • Planned actions	• Average rating of at least 4.0 on 5.0 scale on quality, usefulness, and achievement of program objectives • 100 percent submit planned actions	• End-of-course questionnaire • Completed action plans	• Participants	• End of course	• Facilitator
2	**LEARNING** • Identify the extent and cost of meetings • Identify positives, negatives, and implications of basic meeting issues and dynamics • Acquisition of Effective Meeting Behaviors	• Given cost guidelines, identify the cost of the last three meetings • From a list of 30 positive and negative meeting behaviors, correctly identify the implications of each behavior • Demonstrate appropriate response to eight of 10 active role-play scenarios	• Meeting profile • Written text • Skill practice observation	• Participants	• At the beginning of the program (pre) and at the end of the program (post) • During the program	• Facilitator
3	**APPLICATION/IMPLEMENTATION** • Use of Effective Meeting Behaviors • Barriers • Enablers	• Reported change in behavior to planning and conducting meetings • Number and variety of barriers • Number and variety of enablers	• Action Plan • Questionnaire (for 3 groups)	• Participants	• 3 months	• Program owner
4	**BUSINESS IMPACT** • Time savings from fewer meetings, shorter meetings, and fewer participants (hours savings per month) • Variety of business impact measures from more successful meetings	• Time savings • Time savings, cost savings, output improvement, quality improvement, project turnaround, as reported	• Questionnaire (for 3 groups)	• Participants	• 3 months	• Program owner
5	**ROI** • Target ROI at least 25 percent					

Comments: _____

these reasons, the control group arrangement was eliminated as an option.

Historical data was not available for the primary measure (time savings), so trend-line analysis and forecasting were inappropriate as well. The only remaining option was the use of participant estimations for isolating the effects of the workshop on the three impact measures: shorter meetings, reduced number of meetings, and fewer participants attending meetings.

Converting Data to Monetary Value

When moving from Level 4 to Level 5 evaluation, this step is the most critical because it determines the numerator (monetary benefits) in the ROI equation. Ten techniques to convert data to monetary value are possible. For this evaluation, however, the technique was apparent. As the outcome measures were all time related, the standard value of hourly compensation (salary plus benefits) for the participant chairing the meeting as well as those attending the meeting was used.

Tabulating Fully Loaded Costs

To calculate ROI, it is imperative to use the fully loaded costs of the program. Costs categories for the Effective Meeting Skills workshop were

- program fee (facilitator costs, materials, program design and development)
- travel, lodging, and meals
- facilities
- participants' salaries and benefits for their time in the classroom
- evaluation costs.

Identifying Intangible Benefits

Intangible benefits are any unplanned benefits derived from the program or any benefits not converted to monetary value. There were many intangible benefits of the Effective Meeting Skills workshop, which will be listed in the Results section that follows.

Calculating ROI

The ROI equation compares net benefits (earnings) to the program costs (investment). It can be reported as a BCR by comparing the benefits to the program costs. ROI is well used within the TechnoTel organization. Managers and professionals alike recognize

the acronym for what it is; therefore, to ensure that the corporate learning department speaks the same language as the business, the following equation is used to report ROI:

$$BCR = \frac{Benefits}{Costs}$$

$$ROI = \frac{Net\ Program\ Benefits}{Costs} \times 100$$

A 25 percent ROI target is standard for most programs being evaluated at this level. Because of the nature of the program, the evaluation team and the division president believed this to be a conservative target.

Figure 9-6 presents the completed ROI analysis plan. As in the case of the data collection plan, the ROI analysis plan was presented to the division president prior to implementing the evaluation. The division president concurred with the plan.

The ROI Methodology used for evaluating the Effective Meeting Skills program adhered to a set of operating standards or guiding principles as elaborated in table 1-5. These guiding principles were established to keep the process consistent and conservative.

Results

The results of the study indicated that the program was successful. Participants enjoyed the workshop, but, even more important, they saw it as relevant and useful. Participants quickly grasped the ability to define meeting costs and began implementing the new knowledge and skills. Although there were some barriers to application, they were minimal. From the perspective of the division president, however, the impact on time spent in meetings was significant; the investment returned positive results.

Level 1: Reaction, Satisfaction, and Planned Action

Level 1 objectives included reaction and satisfaction measures important to improving facilitation, content, and materials. The key measures of interest, however, addressed issues indicating intent to use, including three defined actions to be taken upon return to the job. The measure of success was a minimum score of 4.0 out of 5.0. Results were successful in regard to relevance, importance, intent to use, and willingness to recommend the workshop to others. Only one measure (new information) fell

Figure 9-6. Completed ROI analysis plan for the Effective Meeting Skills program.

ROI ANALYSIS PLAN

Program: Effective Meetings   **Responsibility:** _____   **Date:** _____

Data Items (Usually Level 4)	Methods for Isolating the Effects of the Program/Process	Methods of Converting Data to Monetary Values	Cost Categories	Intangible Benefits	Communication Targets on Final Report	Other Influences/Issues During Application	Comments
1. Time savings	1. Participants' estimates	1. Hourly wage and benefits	• Program fee per participant (facilitator costs, materials, design, and development)	• Improvement in individual productivity not captured elsewhere	• Business unit president		• Participants must see need for providing measurement
2. Miscellaneous business measures	2. Participants' estimates	2. Participants' estimates (using standard values when available)	• Travel/lodging/meals	• Stress reduction	• Senior managers		• Follow-up process will be explained to participants during program
			• Facilities	• Improved planning and scheduling	• Managers of participants		• Participants will identify specific improvements as a result of meetings being conducted more effectively
			• Participants' salaries plus benefits	• Greater participation in meetings	• Participants		
			• Evaluation costs		• Training and development staff		• Three groups will be measured

below the 4.0 target. This was anticipated in that most of the concepts were familiar, but the packaging and tools provided a new perspective on the familiar topics.

The participants listed three defined actions they planned to take when returning to the job. The most noted action was implementing the meeting activity profile as a routine tool when reflecting on meetings each month. Also participants indicated they would follow the seven steps to conducting an effective meeting as listed in the program outline (see figure 9-1).

Level 2: Learning

Level 2 objectives suggested that participants should be able to:

- identify the extent and cost of meetings
- identify positives, negatives, and implications of basic meeting issues and dynamics
- acquire effective meeting behaviors.

The meeting profile identifying costs of meetings was successfully completed by participants. They felt comfortable with the tool and indicated the ability to complete similar items during the follow-up. A simple multiple-choice test was administered to ensure that participants understood the basic issue of meetings. The average score on the test was a 92 out of a possible 100.

Exercises and skill practice indicated that participants were equipped with the knowledge and skills to successfully conduct meetings while reducing the cost of meetings by conducting shorter meetings, fewer meetings, and including fewer meeting participants.

Level 3: Application and Implementation

The follow-up evaluation (see figure 9-4) took place three months after the workshop. Questions 4, 5, 6, 16, and 17 related to application of knowledge and skills. The fundamental question with regard to application was question 5, which assessed how much participants had changed their approach to planning and conducting meetings using the knowledge and skills they learned from the workshop. Table 9-4 summarizes the degree of change in behavior that occurred. For the most part, participants did change their meeting practices; 10 out of the 23 measures, however, indicated that change did not occur for some people. Enhancing participant satisfaction in

meetings (item G), providing feedback to meeting participants (item Q), evaluating the meeting process (item U), and planning a follow-up activity (item W) appeared to be the least used skills.

Examining the barriers (question 16) to the use of the knowledge and skills learned in the workshop shed some light on the reasons why there was less change in some areas than in others. The most often cited barrier was time. Some participant indicated they did no have the time to evaluate the success of the meeting or follow-up with meeting participants; however, others indicated that both of these actions were a valuable part of the meeting process.

Enabling factors (question 17) supported the use of meeting skills learned in the workshop. The most often cited enabling factors were the job aids and materials participants took with them from the course. The workbook was cited as being the most valuable tool. Some participants indicated that senior management's interest in the tools and the workshop encouraged them to take the application of what they learned seriously.

Level 4: Impact

The intended outcomes of the Effective Meeting Skills workshop were shorter meetings, fewer meetings, and fewer meeting participants. By applying the knowledge and skills learned in the workshop, improvement in these three time-related measures occurred. Table 9-5 presents a comparison of the original meeting profile data obtained from participants during the program to the average post-program data. The average amounts taken from question 8 are subtracted from the average pre-program data to get the average post-program data. Only 31 participants (43 percent) responded to questions 8 and 9; the average confidence in the estimates for the group responding was 81 percent. The table shows that the intended outcomes (reduction in the number of meetings, less time spent in meetings, and fewer participants attending meetings) were achieved as a result of the program.

Other measures improved as a result of the program as well. Respondents indicated improvement in overall productivity and quality of the meetings, and six managers placed monetary values on these measures. However, the monetary payoff of the program is based on the time savings from the above measures. The other measures were reported as "other benefits" because they were not as credible as the time savings.

Table 9-4. Level 3 evaluation responses.

	No Change	Little Change	Some Change	Significant Change	Very Much Change	No Opportunity to Use Skill
A. Participating effectively in meetings	0	0	25%	44%	31%	0
B. Avoiding meetings unless they are necessary	0	0	19%	46%	35%	0
C. Minimizing the number of participants attending meetings	0	0	19%	50%	31%	0
D. Setting objectives for meetings	0	0	25%	42%	33%	0
E. Developing an agenda for each meeting	0	4%	27%	44%	25%	0
F. Controlling time of meetings	0	0	6%	44%	50%	0
G. Enhancing participant satisfaction in meetings	0	10%	31%	44%	15%	0
H. Arranging the meeting site for maximum effectiveness	0	0	4%	65%	31%	0
I. Scheduling the optimum time for meetings	0	0	25%	42%	33%	0
J. Communicating the ground rules for meetings	0	4%	27%	44%	25%	0
K. Assigning appropriate roles for meeting participants	0	0	6%	44%	50%	0
L. Reaching consensus in meetings when appropriate	0	0	13%	52%	35%	0
M. Listening actively to meeting participants	0	0	4%	65%	31%	0
N. Encouraging participation in meetings	0	0	25%	42%	33%	0
O. Using brainstorming in meetings when appropriate	0	4%	27%	44%	25%	0
P. Dealing with difficult meeting participants	0	0	6%	44%	50%	0
Q. Providing feedback to meeting participants	0	19%	56%	25%	0	0
R. Handling conflict in meeting	0	4%	31%	50%	15%	0
S. Keeping the meeting on focus	0	0	25%	42%	33%	0
T. Accomplishing meeting objectives	0	4%	27%	44%	25%	0
U. Evaluating the meeting process	0	10%	38%	38%	15%	0
V. Implementing action plans	0	2%	33%	46%	19%	0
W. Planning a follow-up activity	0	6%	42%	35%	17%	0

Table 9-5. Improvement in time spent on meetings.[*]

Current Meeting Activity[†]	Average, Pre-Program Data	Average, Post-Program Data (Question 8)[‡]	
Number of meetings chaired each month	6.5	5.2	(A)
Average number of individuals attending each meeting each month	7.2	5.1	(B)
Average length of time for each meeting (in hours)	2.6	1.7	(C)
Total time consumed in meetings (A × B × C)	121.68	45.1	(D)

	Pre- and Post-Program Difference
Meetings Avoided	
Estimate of the number of meetings avoided each month	1.3
Shorter Meetings	
Estimate of the average time saved per meeting (in hours)	0.9
Reduced Participants in Meetings	
Estimate of the number of participants reduced for each meeting	2.1

[*] Number completing programs   = 72 (3 groups)
Number of questionnaires returned   = 48 (67 percent)
Number of questionnaires with usable data for questions 8 and 9   = 31 (43 percent)
Average value of confidence level from question 9   = 81 percent.
[†] One month pre-program and the first three months post-program.
[‡] Level 3/4 Evaluation Follow-Up Questionnaire.

Level 5: ROI

The ROI for the Effective Meeting Skills workshop was calculated based on time savings. To calculate the ROI, improvement in time savings due to shorter meetings, fewer meetings, and fewer meeting participants was converted to monetary value and then compared to the costs of the program.

Monetary Benefits

The data conversion technique used was a standard value of time, which equates to average hourly compensation of attendees plus the benefits factor of 32 percent. The average hourly cost of an attendee was calculated to be $31. As shown in table 9-6, an average monthly savings in meeting costs based on the three measures was $2,373.98. This figure represents the average value at the three-month point when the follow-up data was collected. The ROI is an annual value, and the division president wanted to see a payoff within one year; the savings were annualized using this monthly average, yielding a monetary benefit of $28,487.76 for one participant.

To calculate the full benefits of the program, the monthly value was multiplied by the number of participants who provided useable data (31); the error adjustment was also considered (81 percent). The full value of the Effective Meeting Skills workshop was:

$$(\$28,487.76 \times 31) \times 0.81 = \$715,327.65$$

Fully Loaded Costs

Program costs included the program fee, which incorporated materials and facilitator costs; travel, lodging, and meals for participants; facilities; partic-

Table 9-6. Monetary benefits of time savings.

Current Meeting Activity	Average, Pre-Program Data	Average, Post-Program Data (Question 8)	
Number of meetings chaired each month	6.5	5.2	(A)
Average number of individuals attending each meeting each month	7.2	5.1	(B)
Average length of time for each meeting (in hours)	2.6	1.7	(C)
Total time consumed in meetings (A × B × C)	121.68	45.1	(D)
Average hourly compensation of attendees (salary plus benefits)	$ 31.00	$ 31.00	(E)
Total Meeting Costs (D × E)	**$ 3,772.08**	**$ 1,398.10**	(F)

	Pre- and Post-Program Difference	
Meetings Avoided		
Estimate of the number of meetings avoided each month	1.3	(G)
Shorter Meetings		
Estimate of the average time saved per meeting (in hours)	0.9	(H)
Reduced Participants in Meetings		
Estimate of the number of participants reduced for each meeting	2.1	(I)

Total Savings

Monthly meeting savings $\left(F_{\text{Pre-Program}} - F_{\text{Post-Program}}\right)$	$ 2,373.98	(J)
Annual Savings (J × 12)	$ 28,487.76	(K)

ipants' time in the workshop (salaries and benefits); and evaluation costs. Even though the benefits were calculated only for those responding, program costs accounted for all participant costs. The fully loaded costs of the Effective Meeting Skills workshop are shown in table 9-7.

The return on investing in the Effective Meeting Skills workshop was 482 percent as shown by the calculation below.

$$BCR = \frac{\$715,327.65}{\$123,008} = 5.81:1$$

$$ROI = \frac{\$715,327.65 - \$123,008}{\$123,008} \times 100 = 482\%$$

The ROI told the division president that for every dollar spent on the workshop, TechnoTel received $4.82 after costs. On the surface, the ROI seemed high in comparison to other investments. But, because the division president knew the value of time and knew how much time had been wasted in meetings in the past, the ROI calculation was believable. The evaluation team had been diligent in advising the division president of the evaluation

Table 9-7. Costs used in the ROI calculation for the Effective Meeting Skills workshop.

Item	Calculation	Cost
Program Fee	$800 per participant × 72	$ 57,600
Travel, Lodging, Meals	$245 × 72	17,640
Facilities	$190 × 6*	1,140
Participant Time	$219 per day × 1.32 × 2 × 72†	41,628
Evaluation Costs		5,000
Total Costs		**$123,008**

* Facilities cost $190 per day; the workshop required two days and was offered to three groups.

† Participant time includes average salaries of $219 per day multiplied by the benefits factor of 32 percent. Each participant was in the workshop for two days; the cost accounts for all 72 participants.

process and keeping him abreast of the findings, thereby enhancing the credibility of the ROI process.

Intangible Benefits

The financial impact to TechnoTel was an important outcome of the evaluation; however, other important outcomes occurred as well. Along with improvement in overall productivity and quality of meetings, employees and their supervisors in TechnoTel were becoming happier in the work setting due to the reduction in wasteful meetings. The groups who had attended the Effective Meeting Skills workshop took the process seriously and had a keen desire to improve their meeting process; therefore, tools were being implemented. This also helped improve customer satisfaction—both external and internal customers. Respondents to the evaluation reported being more accessible and more focused on customer concerns.

An interesting unexpected benefit of the program was that the division president began using the meeting profile worksheet as a tool to manage the cost of his own meetings. He asked that his senior leaders do

the same. The tool has become a time management tool throughout this division of TechnoTel.

Communication Strategy

The success of the ROI study at TechnoTel can be attributed to the continuous communication throughout the process. From the outset, the division president was kept informed of the progress with the study. He was involved in the planning stage and data collection. As results at Levels 3 and 4 began rolling in, the evaluation team kept him informed. Once the study was completed and the division president was aware of the results, the senior management team participated in a one-hour briefing. Because there were several new senior managers who were unfamiliar with the evaluation practice at TechnoTel, a full presentation was conducted. The presentation topics included

- need for effective meetings
- program design
- need for evaluation
- evaluation methodology
- evaluation results.

At the end of the presentation, each person received a copy of the complete report as well as a summary copy.

Based on the questions and the response to the presentation, the senior management saw the evaluation process as credible. Even more important, they saw the value of the Effective Meeting Skills workshop and asked that the program be implemented in other areas of TechnoTel.

Lessons Learned

Regardless of the number of evaluation studies conducted, there are always lessons to learn. Because the evaluation team thought there was an understanding of the evaluation process, they did not spend time explaining questions 7, 8, and 9; had they done a better job covering those questions on the questionnaire, they might have achieved a greater response rate.

Because evaluation is routine at TechnoTel, the questionnaire administration strategy seemed appropriate; however, with only a 67 percent response rate, there was room for improvement.

Questions for Discussion

1. What steps could have been taken to ensure a higher response rate, especially for questions 7, 8, and 9 on the questionnaire?

2. How credible is the time savings data?

3. How credible is the study?

4. How credible is the analysis of the study?

5. How would you have approached the evaluation strategy for the Effective Meeting Skills workshop?

About the Authors

Jack J. Phillips, a world-renowned expert on measurement and evaluation, is chairman of the ROI Institute. Through the Institute, Phillips provides consulting services for *Fortune* 500 companies and workshops for major conference providers throughout the world. Phillips is also the author or editor of more than 30 books and 100 articles.

His expertise in measurement and evaluation is based on 27-plus years of corporate experience in five industries (aerospace, textiles, metals, construction materials, and banking). Phillips has served as training and development manager at two *Fortune* 500 firms, senior HR officer at two firms, president of a regional federal savings bank, and management professor at a major state university.

His background in training and HR led Phillips to develop the ROI Methodology—a revolutionary process that provides bottom-line figures and accountability for all types of training, performance improvement, human resources, and technology programs.

Patti P. Phillips is an internationally recognized author, consultant, and researcher. She is president and CEO of the ROI Institute, the leading source of ROI evaluation education, research, and networking. She is a chairman of the Chelsea Group, an international consulting organization supporting organizations and their efforts to build accountability into their training, human resources, and performance improvement programs. She helps organizations implement the ROI Methodology in countries around the world including South Africa, Singapore, Japan, New Zealand, Australia, Italy, Turkey, France, Germany, Canada, and the United States.

Phillips's academic accomplishments include a doctorate in international development and a master of arts degree in public and private management. She is certified in ROI evaluation and has been awarded the designation of certified performance technologist. She has published several books and articles, serves as adjunct faculty teaching training evaluation, and speaks on the subject at conferences including ASTD's International Conference and Exposition and the ISPI International Conference. She can be reached a patti@roiinstitute.net.

Chapter 10

This case was prepared to serve as a basis for discussion rather than to illustrate either effective or ineffective administrative and management practices.

MEASURING ROI FOR A LEADERSHIP MASTERY PROGRAM

BMW Manufacturing Company

Michelle Wentz and Toni Hodges

The Leadership Mastery Program was first delivered at BMW Manufacturing Company. The program includes a three-day training program, the BMW 360-degree leadership inventory, and posttraining individual coaching sessions. An ROI impact study was commissioned to evaluate the program's effectiveness and financial benefit to BMW Manufacturing Company. The program realized a 19.9 percent ROI. When collecting ROI data, the Leadership Mastery participants were not expected nor prepared to list Leadership Mastery Program business benefits or assign monetary values to such benefits. Although many were able to list intangible benefits, they were unable to assign monetary values to them. Assuming that more of those surveyed would be able to provide monetary estimates if prepared or trained to, the ROI assessment is conservative. The analysis also adhered to principles that demand a conservative approach be taken. The conclusion is that the Leadership Mastery Program is successfully leading BMW toward leadership while realizing a modest return on its investment. The evaluation revealed several ways in which the program can be enhanced to ensure improved effectiveness and even greater future financial return.

Organizational Background

BMW Manufacturing Company is located in upstate South Carolina where it manufactures the Z4 roadster and X5 Sports Activity Vehicle for worldwide distribution. The company employs approximately 4,700 associates and is the only BMW plant located in the United States.

Program Background

BMW recognized the need to continue leaders' professional development after the BMW LIFE program, an introductory five-day management training program. Subsequently, BMW conducted a task analysis to determine the skills to be taught in the new program. The task analysis culminated in a three-day performance improvement program called Leadership Mastery.

Originally, the target audience for the program included coordinators and managers who manage supervisors and individual contributors. The audience also includes individual contributors who are responsible for an entire functional area of the company. The goal and subsequent performance objectives of Leadership Mastery are the BMW leadership competencies with an emphasis on business competencies, as well as the continued reinforcement of various communication skills, the DiSC (dominance, influence, steadiness, conscientiousness) style-adapting model, and conflict resolution.

In mid-2002, the training and associate development function embarked on an effort to evaluate the effectiveness of the Leadership Mastery Program to include the training, a 360-degree leadership inventory, and eight hours of subsequent coaching sessions. Additionally, the business impact was assessed to determine the ROI achieved from the program.

Evaluation Methodology

The process used for data collection and analysis was adapted from the widely accepted ROI Methodology (Phillips, 2003). This process embodies many principles considered imperative for training program evaluations to be considered credible and useful. These guiding principles include the following:

- When analyzing data, select the most conservative alternative for calculations.
- At least one method must be used to isolate the effects of the solution.
- If no improvement data is available for a population or from a specific source, it is assumed that little or no improvement occurred.
- Estimates of improvements should be adjusted for the potential error of the estimate.
- Extreme data items and unsupported claims should not be used in ROI calculations.
- Costs of a solution, project, or program should be fully loaded for ROI analysis.

Reaction Data

Reaction data was collected to determine the extent to which the program participants believed the pro-

gram was beneficial. The BMW reaction form was used as the data collection instrument. The following questions from the form were the most critical to this impact study:

- How would you rate your ability to apply new skills/knowledge back on the job?
- How would you rate the overall value of the program?

Learning Data

Learning data was collected at the end of the program as part of the reaction questionnaire.

Job Application Data

Performance or job application data was collected by using the BMW 360-degree Leadership Inventory. The inventory is given before each Leadership Mastery Program to participants, their supervisors, peers, and direct reports. These raters evaluate the participants' level of performance of 18 leadership competencies (the performance objectives for leadership mastery). For the impact study, an inventory was used to compare pretraining performance to post-training performance.

Business Data

The task analysis for the Leadership Mastery Program did not attempt to look at the expected business objectives for the program. To provide the link between the performance objectives and potential business objectives, a focus group was conducted with representatives from the participant audience, selected for their knowledge of their business areas.

In addition, 170 participants completed a survey to determine the extent to which the participants believed the program had an impact on business and performance objectives. This survey also asked for their estimates of the value of the training portion of the program versus the coaching portion. The objective of this survey was to isolate the impact of the training and the coaching on the business impact data.

ROI Data

The Leadership Mastery team compiled program cost data. They collected information on tangible and intangible benefits using a survey, which asked participants to estimate the tangible monetary value of the Leadership Mastery Program. As determined by the focus group, the potential business areas of feasible impact were listed on the survey for considera-

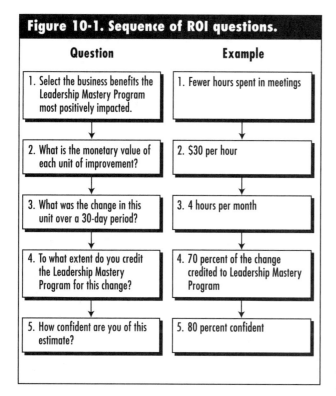

Figure 10-1. Sequence of ROI questions.

Question	Example
1. Select the business benefits the Leadership Mastery Program most positively impacted.	1. Fewer hours spent in meetings
2. What is the monetary value of each unit of improvement?	2. $30 per hour
3. What was the change in this unit over a 30-day period?	3. 4 hours per month
4. To what extent do you credit the Leadership Mastery Program for this change?	4. 70 percent of the change credited to Leadership Mastery Program
5. How confident are you of this estimate?	5. 80 percent confident

tion. Figure 10-1 depicts the sequence of the questions and provides an example of possible answers.

Question 4 asked the participant to isolate the impact of the Leadership Mastery Program from all other contributing factors, and question 5 asked the participant to adjust the estimate for the potential error of the estimate.

Determining the monetary benefits of a program using participant estimates is a method that is gaining widespread acceptance in organizations in the United States, Canada, and Europe. When participant estimates are compared to data collected from a "control versus experimental group" design, the estimates actually come in lower, thus providing conservative figures. In addition to this practical acceptance, recent research conducted as part of doctoral dissertations is validating participant estimates as a method of determining monetary benefits.

Often, as was the case for the Leadership Mastery Program, no other method is available to provide a good assessment of the value of the program. The only alternatives would be to:

1. Claim that the Leadership Mastery Program is responsible for *all* positive changes that occurred since the program implementation.

2. Claim that the Leadership Mastery Program cannot take *any* credit for positive changes that occurred.

Neither of these alternatives was acceptable. No one is in a better position to provide an estimate of the specific value he or she has seen as a result of the program than the participants who have experienced the value of utilizing new skills and knowledge. And, when adjusted for error, their estimates are credible.

Conclusion and Recommendations

Once the results from the data collection described in the results section of this case study were compiled, a task force was convened to discuss potential conclusions and recommendations that could be made from the result data. The task force included representatives from the impact study analysis team, the design and development team, former participants, and the facilitation/coaching group. An initial logic map (Hodges, 2002) was developed from this task force to draw conclusions from the results and determine potential recommendations based on those conclusions. The impact study analysis team then reviewed these findings and revised the map as needed.

Communication Strategy

It was decided that an impact study report would be prepared and the results presented to senior management. Senior management had asked in a quarterly review session with the training manager, "What are we getting for our training dollars?" thus triggering the need for the impact study.

Evaluation Results

Evaluation was conducted at all five levels.

Level 1: Reaction

One hundred fifty-eight surveys were collected from 16 groups. Figure 10-2 provides the results of the data for reaction and learning data. On a rating scale of 1.0 (low) to 5.0 (high), the respondents' responses ranged from 3.8 to 5.0 for question number 5 ("How would you rate the overall value of the program?").

Level 2: Learning

On question number 3 ("How would you rate your ability to apply new skills/knowledge back on the job?"), the scores ranged between 3.9 to 4.7. There was little variability in these ranges, and the scores were high.

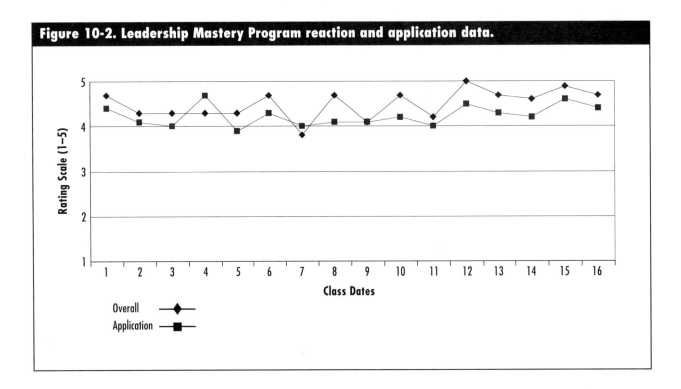

Figure 10-2. Leadership Mastery Program reaction and application data.

Level 3: Job Application

Tables 10-1 and 10-2 provide the results of the BMW 360-degree leadership inventory. The tables provide ratings for competency levels before and after the participants participated in the program. The differences were tested for significance to indicate where the differences showed 90 or 95 percent confidence. The shaded rows are those differences that are significant either negatively or positively. Table 10-1 provides the ratings the participants gave for themselves.

There was an improvement in 13 of the 18 competencies; four of the 13 were significantly different and in order of highest impact are

1. Communicates with impact
2. Fresh thinking
3. Decision making
4. Positive disposition.

Table 10-2 provides the results of the ratings of the participants' managers, peers, and direct reports.

There was an improvement in 16 of the 18 competencies. Overall, participants were rated the highest in the business knowledge competency category. The four most significant competencies in order are

1. Process development
2. Takes ownership

3. Drives change
4. Planning and organizing.

These results should be considered cautiously because approximately 50 percent of the raters were not the same as the original raters because of staff and assignment changes. It is interesting to note that both participants (self) and others rated decision making as having a significant positive difference.

Level 4: Business Impact

The focus group determined that the Leadership Mastery Program could potentially impact the following business areas:

• reduced time to full productivity
• fewer hours spent in meetings
• reduced overtime
• reduced minutes spent in rework
• reduced number of issues reported
• improved vehicle quality measures
• improved customer satisfaction
• fewer associate complaints
• reduced turnover.

These potential business impact areas were used in the development of the ROI survey and the Leadership Mastery Program review survey.

Table 10-1. Self-ratings for 360-degree leadership inventory competencies.*

Competencies	Self-Ratings							
	Before Program		After Program			Difference		
	Mean	Number	Mean	Number	Mean	Difference	Significance
Leadership Effectiveness							
Develops a team(s)	2.30	11	2.35	11	0.05	0.5586	0.7115
Takes ownership	2.33	12	2.32	13	−0.01	−0.1034	0.4589
Guides the development of associates	2.15	12	2.21	12	0.06	0.6587	0.7448
Drives change	2.18	13	2.28	13	0.10	0.9415	0.8263
Overall category	2.23	12	2.29	12	0.06	1.1405	0.8728
Business Knowledge							
Business knowledge	1.98	12	2.10	12	0.12	0.8380	0.7984
Planning and organizing	2.36	12	2.30	12	−0.06	−0.5052	0.3070
Decision making	2.32	13	2.50	13	0.18	1.8508	0.9674
Priority management	2.27	13	2.46	13	0.19	1.5076	0.9330
Process development	2.11	13	1.98	12	−0.12	−1.0219	0.1539
Overall category	2.22	12	2.28	12	0.06	1.1564	0.8761

(continued next page)

* Gray shading indicates pre- and posttraining differences that are significant at a confidence level of at least 95 percent.

Table 10-1. Self-ratings for 360-degree leadership inventory competencies *(continued)*.

Competencies	Self-Ratings							
	Before Program		After Program			Difference		
	Mean	Number	Mean	Number	Mean		Difference	Significance
Interpersonal Effectiveness								
Builds trust	2.44	13	2.58	13	0.14		1.4576	0.9268
Builds business partnership	2.38	13	2.44	13	0.06		0.5161	0.6967
Interpersonal influence	2.28	13	2.22	13	−0.06		−0.6693	0.2519
Communicates with impact	2.20	13	2.51	13	0.31		3.1923	0.9992
Overall category	2.33	13	2.43	13	0.11		2.0946	0.9818
Personal Attributes								
Values diversity	2.16	12	2.24	12	0.08		0.5729	0.7162
Positive disposition	2.22	13	2.43	13	0.22		1.9096	0.9712
Fresh thinking	1.81	13	2.10	13	0.29		2.1310	0.9828
Quality orientation	2.39	12	2.44	13	0.04		0.3436	0.6341
Safety and environmentally aware	2.51	10	2.47	11	−0.04		−0.3437	0.3657
Overall category	2.21	12	2.34	12	0.13		2.2499	0.9876

Table 10-2. Others' ratings for 360-degree leadership inventory competencies.*

Competencies	Ratings of Managers, Peers, and Direct Reports					
	Before Program		After Program		Difference	
	Mean	Number	Mean	Number	Mean	Difference	Significance

Competencies	Before Program Mean	Before Program Number	After Program Mean	After Program Number	Difference Mean	Difference Difference	Significance
Leadership Effectiveness							
Develops a team(s)	2.11	72	2.19	68	0.08	1.9650	0.9752
Takes ownership	2.10	81	2.20	77	0.10	2.0333	0.9789
Guides the development of associates	2.02	68	2.09	66	0.07	1.6126	0.9465
Drives change	2.07	89	2.19	82	0.12	2.8634	0.9979
Overall category	2.07	77	2.16	73	0.09	4.2400	1.0000
Business Knowledge							
Business knowledge	2.10	78	2.17	72	0.07	1.3169	0.9059
Planning and organizing	2.14	91	2.22	84	0.08	1.8569	0.9683
Decision making	2.16	91	2.22	84	0.07	1.7824	0.9626
Priority management	2.12	85	2.25	85	0.13	2.6812	0.9963
Process development	1.92	82	2.14	76	0.21	4.7233	1.0000
Overall category	2.09	86	2.20	80	0.11	5.5051	1.0000

(continued next page)

* Gray shading indicates pre- and posttraining differences that are significant at a confidence level of at least 95 percent.

Table 10-2. Others' ratings for 360-degree leadership inventory competencies *(continued)*.

Competencies	Ratings of Managers, Peers, and Direct Reports							
	Before Program		After Program			Difference		
	Mean	Number	Mean	Number	Mean	Difference	Significance
Interpersonal Effectiveness							
Builds trust	2.33	95	2.35	85	0.02	0.5716	0.7162
Builds business partnership	2.19	93	2.29	86	0.10	2.0833	0.9813
Interpersonal influence	2.06	89	2.12	83	0.06	1.4990	0.9330
Communicates with impact	2.27	95	2.26	86	0.00	-0.0762	0.4696
Overall category	2.21	93	2.25	85	0.04	1.8797	0.9699
Personal Attributes							
Values diversity	2.13	51	2.23	54	0.10	1.6168	0.9469
Positive disposition	2.29	94	2.20	86	-0.09	-2.1835	0.0145
Fresh thinking	2.00	87	2.13	79	0.12	2.5025	0.9938
Quality orientation	2.21	86	2.25	81	0.04	0.7527	0.7741
Safety and environmentally aware	2.28	65	2.34	58	0.06	1.4138	0.9212
Overall category	2.19	76	2.22	71	0.03	1.4614	0.9280

The Leadership Mastery Program review survey results are depicted in figures 10-3 and 10-4 and table 10-3. Figure 10-3 provides participants' ratings of the degree that training and coaching impacted the performance and business objectives. A 10-point scale was used providing the following anchors: 1 = Not at all (0 percent), 5 = Somewhat (50 percent), and 10 = To a great extent (100 percent).

Training has a slight lead in terms of impact, with approximately 81 percent falling into the first five groups (ratings between 6.0 and 10.0) and only 14 percent falling in the second five groups (ratings between 0 and 5.9). Coaching had approximately 73 percent falling in the first five groups and 31 percent falling in the second five groups. Figure 10-4 provides the results of the participants' ratings in terms of recommending either the training or the coaching to colleagues.

More participants were likely to recommend the training portion of the program than the coaching portion, although both had high scores. The percentage for participants (very likely or somewhat likely) to recommend training was 89 percent and those recommending coaching was 76 percent. Survey results were analyzed to determine if there were relationships between these results and other factors.

Table 10-3 provides the results of how the number of coaching sessions the participants received influenced their perception of the impact of coaching on performance and how highly they would recommend the coaching to their colleagues.

Ratings were much higher for the perceived impact on business objectives for associates who had attended more coaching sessions. In fact, perceived impact increased more than threefold for those attending more than five coaching sessions. In addition,

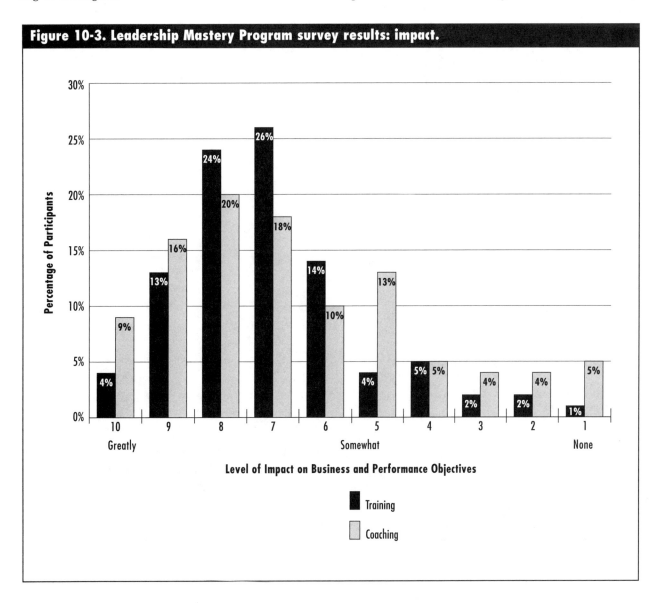

Figure 10-3. Leadership Mastery Program survey results: impact.

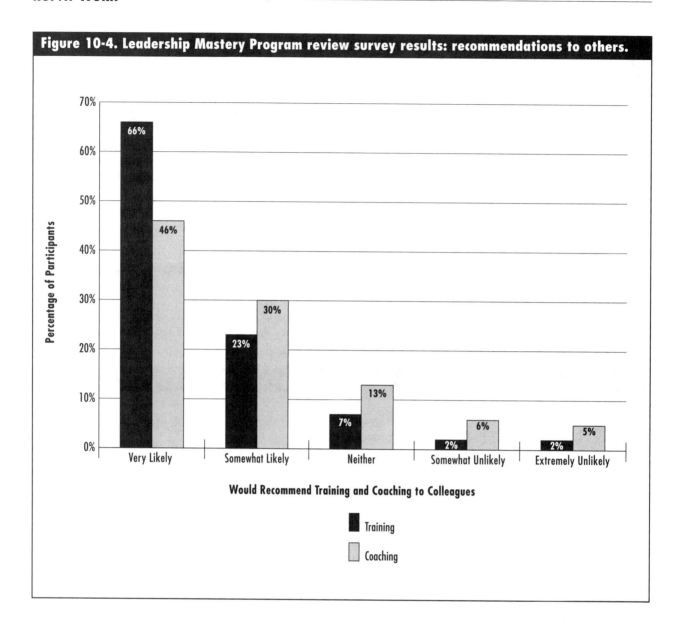

Figure 10-4. Leadership Mastery Program review survey results: recommendations to others.

Would Recommend Training and Coaching to Colleagues

- Training
- Coaching

Table 10-3. Leadership Mastery review survey results: relationship between number of coaching sessions and impact or recommendation.

Number of Coaching Sessions Attended	Perceived Impact	Recommendation to Colleagues
1–2 sessions	20%	27%
3–4 sessions	36%	40%
5 + sessions	68%	71%

ratings were higher for recommending coaching to colleagues for associates who had attended more coaching sessions.

Verbatim comments were also offered on the Leadership Mastery review survey. Several themes ran throughout the comments as to various components of the program. Here are some of the comments regarding training improvements:

- Twelve of 16 comments asked for training time to be extended because participants felt rushed or believed that the content was "crammed" into three days.

- Some participants suggested using more role playing or practice-type teaching methods.

- Others suggested using videotaping as a learning/teaching method.
- Eight of nine comments suggested that the simulation be based on a real BMW situation or example instead of the fictitious one.
- Six of eight comments requested more attendance by managers at the higher levels of the organization to ensure understanding and reinforcement.
- Some participants suggested offering some type of follow-up to the Leadership Mastery Program, such as a one-day follow-up session or a reading list or newsletter to reinforce skills learned.

In terms of coaching improvements, the following comments were reflected on the review survey:

- Most comments (13) emphasized a need to gear the coaching sessions to real-work situations instead of being a "feel good" or "vent" session. Comments expressed need for more focus, greater personalization, more structure, and greater emphasis on specific ideas for improvement.
- Many comments reflected concern about how the coaching is scheduled and a desire for more flexibility or consistency. Some wanted more time with their coach, to have the coaching period extended, or to have more frequent interaction with their coaches.
- Several participants raised questions and concerns about the number of coaching sessions allowed, needed, and required.
- Many expressed the desire that allotted coaching sessions be able to carry over from one year to the next instead of being based on the calendar year.
- Some suggested that the coaches should have manufacturing experience or "been there and done that." Some asked that coaches be internal to BMW.
- Others opined that supervisors should be involved in some manner to provide accountability or reinforcement.

Overall, both the training and coaching sessions were perceived as having impact, with training receiving a somewhat higher rating. The quantifiable data showed little or no relationship between these perceptions and the time since training or receiving the coaching. Those who participated in more coaching provided higher ratings on coaching positively impacting business and performance objectives. They also recommended coaching to colleagues more. Verbatim comments indicate a need for more focused, relevant training and coaching, and more flexibility in the number of coaching sessions allowed and flexibility in scheduling.

Level 5: ROI

Thirty-six participants were sent the Leadership Mastery ROI survey. They were selected based upon when they had completed the program. They had at least five months but no longer than 11 months to realize the benefits of the program. Twenty-four associates responded, providing a 67 percent response rate.

Table 10-4 provides a breakout of the monetary values assigned to each business benefit after adjusting for isolating the effects of training and the subsequent confidence adjustment.

Although more respondents listed "fewer hours spent in meetings" as a tangible benefit of the Leadership Mastery Program, "reduced number of issues" was credited with the largest monetary value from the program. Table 10-5 enumerates the benefits and costs used as a basis for calculating the BCR and ROI. The BCR was calculated thus:

$$BCR = \frac{\$124,008 \text{ (benefits attributed to training)}}{\$103,392 \text{ (training costs)}} = 1.20 = 1.20:1$$

Then, ROI was calculated:

$$ROI = \frac{\begin{array}{c}\$124,008 \text{ (benefits attributable to training)} \\ - \$103,392 \text{ (training costs)}\end{array}}{\$103,392 \text{ (training costs)}}$$

$$= 0.199 \times 100 = 19.9\%$$

The Leadership Mastery Program realized a 19.9 percent ROI, which means that for every $1 invested in the program there was a return of almost $.20 in net benefits, after costs are covered. The BCR is 1:1.20, which means for every $1 invested, $1.20 was returned. These calculations were based on the following considerations and management decisions:

- The estimates are based on 24 respondents only (36 surveyed).
- The costs do not include evaluation costs.
- The benefits are adjusted down from actual reported values based on extreme data.

Table 10-4. Monetary values assigned to business benefit categories.

Business Benefit Category	Monetary Value Assigned	Percent of Total (Rounded)	Number of Responses
1. Reduced number of issues reported	$ 50,284	41%	4
2. Fewer hours spent in meetings	27,446	22%	8
3. Reduced time to full productivity	14,275	12%	4
4. Reduced turnover	13,970	11%	3
5. Fewer associate complaints	9,714	8%	4
6. Reduced overtime	4,644	4%	2
7. Improved customer satisfaction	3,200	2%	1
8. Reduced minutes spent in rework	300	0%	1
9. Improved vehicle quality measures	175	0%	1
Total	**$ 124,008**	**100%**	**28**

Table 10-5. ROI and BCR calculations for the Leadership Mastery Program.

Benefits

(Perceived annual monetary value from 24 participants, adjusted for isolation and confidence)

Reduced number of issues reported	$ 50,284
Fewer hours spent in meeting	27,446
Reduced time to full productivity	14,275
Reduced turnover	13,970
Fewer associate complaints	9,174
Reduced overtime	4,644
Improved customer satisfaction	3,200
Reduced minutes in rework	300
Improved vehicle quality measures	175
Benefit Attributable to Training	**$ 124,008**

Costs

(Actual costs for 24 participants)

Design and Development:
($190.80 cost per participant × 24 participants) $ 4,579

Leadership Mastery Delivery Costs:
Facilities + Instructor + Materials
($1,924 × 24 associates)   46,176

Associate Participation Costs:
(Fully loaded hourly labor rates)
[$57.48/hr. (Level IV rate) × 24 hrs. × 4 associates
+ $53.01/hr. (Level V rate) × 24 hrs. × 9 associates
+ $34.02/hr. (Level VI rate) × 24 hrs.
× 11 associates]   26,910

Report:
$150/report × 24 associates   3,600

Coaching:
$250/hr. × 75 coaching hours (coach)   18,750
$45.02/hr. × 75 coaching hours (participant time)   3,377

Total Training Costs $ 103,392

- This calculation does not include reported intangible benefits.
- This calculation does not include tangible benefits that participants were unable to convert to monetary values.

Intangible Benefits

Table 10-6 provides a list of the intangible benefits (those benefits to which a monetary value could not be assigned) provided from the Leadership Mastery Program ROI survey.

Improved teamwork, reduced conflict, and improved clarity of roles and responsibilities were indicated by more than half of the respondents as intangible benefits of the Leadership Mastery Program.

Program Enablers and Barriers

Table 10-7 provides the factors that the respondents believed assist them in applying the skills they learned from the Leadership Mastery Program.

Table 10-8 lists issues that the participants believed interfere with their ability to apply the skills they learned in the Leadership Mastery Program.

Table 10-6. Leadership Mastery Program intangible benefits.

Intangible Benefit	Percentage Selecting
Improved Teamwork	83%
Reduced Conflict	74%
Improved Clarity of Roles and Responsibilities	61%
Improved Associate Job Satisfaction	39%
Improved Associate Development Plans	35%
Increased Cross-Functionality	30%
Additional Intangibles Noted	
Improved Customer Satisfaction	4 responses
Improved Organizing Skills	1 response
Improved Communication	2 responses

It is clear that many of the respondents were interpreting "enablers" as "benefits." Those that appear as benefits support the other results of this study.

Conclusions and Recommendations

Management support and the ability of one's co-workers to use the Leadership Mastery Program skills appear to concern some participants. Refer to the logic map (table 10-9) for the results listed about the program enablers and barriers and for additional results.

Communication

The communication strategy was set up to describe the results from this study to the BMW Manufacturing Company senior management, including the BMW executive team; the president; and vice presidents of communications, procurement, and manufacturing operations. The reactions were interesting:

- One vice president was concerned that by putting so much emphasis on the ROI, they might lose sight of the value of the intangible benefits that were uncovered.
- The president understood the importance of this program.
- Overall, the executive team was impressed that the training organization saw itself as part of the business.

In addition to the positive reaction from the BMW executive team, an auditor conducting an internal ISO matrix certification gave the ROI impact study an honorable mention as a best practice taking place within the organization.

Lessons Learned

This was the first ROI impact study BMW has conducted so there were many lessons that were learned. Key ones include the following:

- Although it was recommended that the financial part of the organization be consulted prior to the study conduct, it was not envisioned that the study would receive the type of attention that would warrant it. Including the senior management and the financial department before a study would ensure the analysis would include financial requirements that they would want to see.

Table 10-7. Work environment enablers for performance transfer.

Improvements/Results Experienced

1. Dealing with my peers more effectively has gained me additional respect from them and confidence in myself.
2. Since attending the Leadership Mastery Program, I have been able to develop better relationships with my customers. They provided me with the tools needed to better understand and deal with the different styles of the individuals that I interact with daily.
3. Interactions with other departments have been improved.
4. I can perform strategy planning more effectively.
5. I've learned about working with people and understanding how to communicate more effectively.
6. I'm better equipped to handle conflict and work in a team environment.

Address Work Problems

1. I have an increased awareness of the need to communicate well and listen to the ideas of others.
2. I'm more aware of the changing demands of the business.
3. I understand better what's behind constant conflict and the need to overcome it in order to continue working here.
4. The training can help me deal better with my workload.
5. It can help me overcome the feeling that as the newest of department, I don't have a clear direction.

Teamwork/Communication

1. I can use my knowledge each day with associates working together to complete the job that needs to be done.
2. Open communication is facilitated.
3. I'm better equipped to deal with project responsibilities, department/team communication.
4. Teamwork, tasking skills, and role responsibility are all improved.

Coaching

1. The one-on-one sessions, 360-degree evaluation were the most valuable.
2. Coaching provided by Leadership Mastery Program was useful.
3. I'd like more flexibility to spend time with coach.

Management Support

1. Cooperative management is necessary.
2. I have a manager who supports me 100%!

Motivation/Drive

1. My personal drive helps me to apply the things I have learned.
2. Associates who have had this type of training and do want to improve and utilize their skills can help motivate me.

Table 10-8. Work environment barriers to performance transfer.

Management Support

1. Management. They are in need of this training as well. Though I see this training as a grass-roots attempt to change the work environment, unless there is follow-up support on a regular basis, it can be easy to lose focus and this all could fade away like all the other attempts to change the corporate workplace.
2. Favoritism by immediate supervisor, secrecy of favoritism.
3. Management's philosophy/expectations.
4. The openness of management to consider our words and actions thus decreasing the class and training's effectiveness.

Peer Support/Knowledge

1. Some people who don't take the new tools seriously enough.
2. Others who have not had the benefit of this type of training.
3. Working with associates who have not attended the Leadership Mastery Program.

Workload

1. Schedules being driven by production requirements to get the cars out the door.
2. "Fighting fires" tends to drive one back to not using tools.
3. Workload—this program is not a top priority.

Role/Shift

1. My current role is out of the realm of involvement in the big decisions that are made with respect to a new model launch and, therefore, some of the training is less likely to be tapped into in the near future. The training, with respect to teamwork, tasking skills, and role-responsibility training, are invaluable tools learned for future opportunities and growth.
2. My position on night shift prevents me from utilizing these skills at this time. I do, however, feel I will utilize some of the skills and techniques in the future. B shift is almost void of meeting or projects that affect more than daily occurrences or incidents.

Time

1. Time and application of tools.

Diversity

1. Cultural diversity.

Table 10-9. Leadership Mastery Program impact study logic map.

Results	Conclusions	Recommendations
Reaction and Learning Data The *overall* reaction to the Leadership Mastery Program immediately following training ranged from 3.8 to 5.0 on a 5-point scale. Participants rated *the ability to apply on* the job between 3.9 and 4.7.	Participants were satisfied with the Leadership Mastery Program and believed they would be able to apply the skills they learned on the job.	
Job Application Data *Self-Ratings:* Participants believed there was an improvement in 13 of 18 competencies, four of which were significant (Decision Making, Communicates With Impact, Positive Disposition, and Fresh Thinking). Two categories showed overall significant improvement: Interpersonal Competencies and Personal Attributes.	The competency categories of Interpersonal and Personal Attributes improved after participating in the Leadership Mastery Program especially with respect to Communicates with Impact, Positive Disposition, and Fresh Thinking.	Refine and clarify the business objectives of the Leadership Mastery Program to determine which of the 18 competencies should be targets and enhanced within the program. The competencies categories include Leadership Effectiveness, Business Knowledge, Interpersonal Competencies, and Personal Attributes.
Business Data *Training and Coaching Effectiveness:* Participants believed both the training and coaching had a positive impact on meeting business and performance objectives, with training having a slightly larger impact at 81 percent and coaching at 73 percent. Eighty-nine percent recommend the training, and 76 percent recommend the coaching to their colleagues. Those who participated in more coaching sessions provided higher ratings on coaching positively impacting business and performance objectives. They also recommended coaching to colleagues more. Verbatim comments indicate a need for more focused, relevant training and coaching and more flexibility in the coaching session timeframe and flexibility in scheduling. Comments also indicate a general level of confusion surrounding coaching requirements and expectations.	The Leadership Mastery Program training and coaching have a positive impact on participants' performance. The more coaching the participant receives, the more positive the impact on performance. Training and coaching may be improved with more realistic and relevant work-related focus.	Investigate adding more coaching sessions, extending the length of coaching sessions, or changing coaching time period from calendar year to a 12-month time period. Investigate replacing fictitious classroom scenario with a BMW-based situation. Gear coaching sessions to work-relevant focus. Provide more communication around expectations and requirements of coaching.

(continued next page)

Table 10-9. Leadership Mastery Program impact study logic map *(continued)*.

Results	Conclusions	Recommendations
Business Data		
ROI survey: Fourteen out of 24 respondents were able to provide monetary estimates.	The number of participants not providing monetary estimates may be due to the fact that they did not expect nor were they trained to provide this type of estimate. This conclusion is supported by the number of incomplete responses where efforts were made to isolate and provide confidence ratings even though they were unable to provide a monetary estimate.	A higher ROI for future implementations of the Leadership Mastery Program can be potentially realized with the following program enhancements:
The "reduced number of issues reported" received the highest estimated monetary benefit of $50,284. Participants selected the "Fewer hours spent in meetings" as the business benefit most often noted from the Leadership Mastery Program.		1. Incorporate a module in the training program to explain how the learning objectives will result in meeting the job application objectives and how meeting those objectives will meet BMW's business objectives for the program.
The Leadership Mastery Program received a 19.9 percent ROI and a 1.20:1 BCR.		2. Incorporate action planning as a component of the program. Train designers, facilitators, and coaches to implement action planning. This will provide the following benefits:
The highest rated intangible benefits of the Leadership Mastery Program were: Improved teamwork (83 percent) Reduced conflict (74 percent) Improved clarity of roles and responsibilities (61 percent).	The Leadership Mastery Program is leading BMW employees toward leadership with a financial return.	— It will demonstrate to the participants the ways in which they can be accountable for what they learn and apply on the job and will make them much more active learners. — It will provide clear job performance direction upon training completion. — It will provide a tool to assist coaching. — It will allow for quick and accurate future evaluations of program impact, including ROI studies.
Business Data		
Enablers: Coaching and management support were listed as environmental factors that enable the participants to use the Leadership Mastery Program skills.	A better understanding by management of how the participants are attempting to use Leadership Mastery program skills and the expected value of their using the skills would be beneficial.	Investigate ways to actively involve Leadership Mastery Program participants' management.
Barriers: Lack of management and associates' knowledge of and involvement with the Leadership Mastery Program were seen as barriers to participants being able to successfully use the skills. Heavy workload and scheduling were also noted.		Evaluate the Leadership Mastery Program 1 year after suggested ROI impact study program enhancements have been incorporated.

- Learning objectives are not enough. In this case, we had to derive the business objectives from the focus groups. All programs should be initiated with business objectives.

- Participants should be prepared for accountability, especially when the data collected is using participant estimates.

- Instructors, training designers, and learners should document and track tangible benefits.

- Utilize a field perspective whenever possible by using focus groups and taskforces.

 ## Questions for Discussion

1. Would it have been fair to have prepared the participants to answer the ROI survey questions prior to their receiving the survey?

2. Were the conclusions drawn supported by the results of the study?

3. What other strategies for isolating the impact of the Leadership Mastery Program could have been used?

4. Were the estimates used conservative enough?

5. Was the ROI large enough for this program?

About the Authors

Michelle Wentz is the assistant manager of training and associate development at BMW Manufacturing Company. She has more than 12 years of broad-based training and development experience working in the manufacturing and financial services industries. Currently, Wentz is responsible for learning technologies, computer application training, and training measurement at BMW. She earned a bachelor's degree of business administration in management and a master's degree of science in adult education from the University of Wisconsin.

Toni Hodges consults with public and private organizations providing evaluation services. Prior to becoming a consultant, Hodges managed an award-winning evaluation group at Verizon Communications and Bell Atlantic. She was selected as ROI practitioner of the year by the ASTD ROI Network and featured in *T&D* as one of training's new guard. In addition to conducting impact studies, she designs strategic evaluation programs that establish learning and development as a partner to the business. Her publications include *Linking Learning and Performance* (Butterworth-Heinemann, 2002), *In Action: Measuring Learning and Performance* (edited with Jack J. Phillips, ASTD Press, 1999), and *Make Evaluation Work* with Jack J. Phillips and Patricia Pulliam Phillips (ASTD Press, 2004). She may be reached at TH & Company, 1011 Shore Drive, Edgewater, MD 21037 or via telephone at 410.956.0475 or email at tonihodges@mindspring.com.

Chapter 11

This case was prepared as a basis for discussion rather than to illustrate either effective or ineffective administrative and management practices. Names of places, organizations, or people have been disguised at the request of the author or organization.

AN ROI IMPACT STUDY ON LEADERSHIP DEVELOPMENT

Gobal Car Rental

Jack J. Phillips and Patti P. Phillips

This case describes how one organization—a leading car rental corporation—implemented a program to improve profitability and efficiency by developing leadership competencies for first-level managers. The learning and development team was asked to identify measures influenced by this program and link these competencies to job performance and business impact. However, the team was faced with a difficult challenge because it was not given the time, resources, or encouragement to conduct a comprehensive analysis to link the need for leadership development to business needs. Could the participants themselves help with this task?

Background

Global Car Rental (GCR) operates in 27 countries with 27,000 employees. The U.S. division has 13,000 employees and operates in most major cities in the United States. The auto rental business is very competitive, and several major firms have been forced into bankruptcy in the last few years. The industry is price sensitive, and customer service is critical. Operating costs must be managed carefully to remain profitable. Senior executives were exploring a variety of ways to improve GCR, and they perceived that developing leadership competencies for first-level managers would be an excellent way to achieve profitable growth and efficiency.

The Need

A recent needs assessment for all functional areas conducted by the learning and development (L&D) staff determined that several leadership competencies were needed for first-level managers. The needs included typical competencies such as problem solving, counseling, motivation, communication, goal setting, and feedback. In addition to developing these competencies, the L&D staff attempted to link the competencies to job performance needs and business needs.

The senior management team, however, did not want the L&D staff to visit all locations to discuss business needs and job performance issues. The senior executives were convinced that leadership skills are needed and that these skills should drive a variety of business measures when applied in the work units. The L&D team was challenged to identify the measures influenced by this particular program. Additionally, top executives were interested in knowing the impact and even ROI for a group of U.S. participants in this program.

This challenge created a dilemma. The L&D staff members realized that for a positive ROI study to be generated, the program should be linked to business needs. They knew, though, that they did not have the time, resources, or the encouragement to conduct a comprehensive analysis linking the need for the leadership development to business needs. The team was faced with the challenge of connecting this program to business impact. They thought that perhaps the participants themselves could help with this task.

Attempting to address the needs, the L&D staff developed a new program, the Leadership Challenge, designed for team leaders, supervisors, and managers who are responsible for those who actually do the work (the first level of management). Program participants were located in rental offices, service centers, call centers, regional offices, and headquarters. Most functional areas were represented, including operations, customer service, service and support, sales, administration, finance and accounting, and information technology. Essentially, this was to be a cross-functional program in the organization.

The Leadership Challenge involved four days of off-site learning with input from the immediate manager who served as a coach for some of the learning processes. Before attending, the program participants had to complete an online pretraining instrument and read a short book. Because few senior executives at GCR had challenged the L&D staff to show the business impact of the program, two groups were evaluated with 36 participants total (that is, 18 in one group and 18 in the other).

Business Alignment

To link the program to business and job performance needs, prior to attending the program, each manager was asked to identify at least two business measures in the work unit that represent an opportunity for improvement. The measures were available in operating reports, cost statements, or scorecards. The selected measures had to meet an additional two-part test:

1. They had to be under the control of the team when improvements were to be considered.

2. They had to have the potential to be influenced by team members whose managers used the competencies in the program. A description of the program was provided in advance, including a list of objectives and skill sets.

A needs assessment appeared appropriate for the situation, even though there was some concern about whether it could be thorough. The initial needs assessment on competencies uncovered a variety of deficiencies across all the functional units and provided the information necessary for job descriptions, assignments, and key responsibility areas. Although basic, the additional steps taken to connect the program to business impact were appropriate for a business needs analysis and a job performance needs analysis.

Identifying two measures in need of improvement was a simple business needs analysis for the work unit. Restricting the selected measures to only those that could be influenced by the team with the leader using the skills from the program essentially defines a job performance need. (In essence, the individual leader is identifying something that is not currently being done in the work unit that could be done to enhance the business need.) Although more refinement and detail would be preferred, the results of this assessment process should have sufficed for this project.

Objectives

The L&D staff developed the following objectives for the program:

1. Participants will rate the program as relevant to their jobs.

2. Participants will rate the program as important to their job success.

3. Participants must demonstrate acceptable performance on each major competency.

4. Participants will use the competencies with team members on a routine basis.

5. Participants and team members will drive improvements in at least two business measures.

ROI Appropriateness

With the business and job performance needs analyses complete, this program became a good candidate for the ROI. Without these two steps, it would have been difficult to conduct a successful ROI study. A consideration for conducting the ROI study was identifying the drivers for ROI analyses. In this case, the senior team was challenging the value of leadership development. An ROI study should provide convincing evidence about a major program. Also, this was a highly visible program that merited evaluation at this level because it was strategic and expensive. Consequently, the L&D staff pursued the ROI study, and an ROI objective of 20 percent was established.

ROI Planning

Data Collection Plan

Figure 11-1 shows the completed data collection plan. Although several data collection methods were possible, the team decided to use a detailed follow-up questionnaire to reflect the progress made with the program. Focus groups, interviews, and observations were considered too expensive or inappropriate. The L&D team explored the possibility of using the 360-degree feedback process to obtain input from team members but elected to wait until the 360-degree program was fully implemented in all units in the organization. Therefore, the questionnaire was deemed the least expensive and least disruptive method.

The questionnaire was sent directly to the participant three months after program completion. At the same time, a shorter questionnaire was sent to the participants' immediate manager. Initially, a six-month follow-up was considered instead of the three-month follow-up shown on the data collection plan. However, the L&D staff thought that six months was too long to wait for results and too long for managers to make the connection between the program and the results.

Questionnaire Topics

Figure 11-2 shows the email questionnaire used with this group. Important areas explored included application of skills, impact analysis, barriers to application, and enablers. A similar questionnaire that explored the role of the manager in the coaching process was sent to the next level managers without the questions on the impact data.

To achieve a response rate of 81 percent, the L&D team used 12 different techniques:

1. Provide advance communication about the questionnaire.
2. Clearly communicate the reason for the questionnaire.
3. Indicate who will see the results of the questionnaire.
4. Show how the data will be integrated with other data.
5. Communicate the time limit for submitting responses.
6. Review the questionnaire at the end of the formal session.
7. Allow for responses to be anonymous or at least confidential.
8. Provide two follow-up reminders, using a different medium each time.
9. Have the introduction letter signed by a top executive.
10. Enclose a giveaway item with the questionnaire (pen, money, and so forth).
11. Send a summary of results to the target audience.
12. Have a third party collect and analyze the data.

Another important technique was to review the questionnaire with participants—question by question—at the end of the four-day workshop to clarify issues, create expectations, and gain commitment to provide data. Third-party collection was achieved by using automated external data collection. Essentially, the data was sent by email to the data collector's server.

ROI Analysis Plan

The completed ROI analysis plan is shown in figure 11-3 on page 152. This plan details the specific issues that must be addressed and the particular techniques selected to complete the ROI analysis.

Method of Isolation

The method the L&D team used to isolate the effects of the program proved to be a challenge. Because the managers represented different functional areas, there was no finite set of measures that could be linked to the program for each participant. Essentially, each manager could have a different set of measures as he or she focused on specific business needs in the work unit. Consequently, the use of a control group was

Figure 11-1. Data collection plan for the Leadership Challenge program.

DATA COLLECTION PLAN

Program/Project: _____

Purpose of This Evaluation: _____

Responsibility: _____   Date: _____

Level	Objective(s)	Measures/Data	Data Collection Method	Data Sources	Timing	Responsibilities
1	**REACTION/SATISFACTION** • Participants rate the program as relevant to their jobs • Participants rate the program as important to their job success	• 4 out of 5 on a 5-point scale	• Questionnaire	• Participants	• End of program	• Facilitator
2	**LEARNING** • Participants demonstrate acceptable performance on each major competency	• 2 out of 3 on a 3-point scale	• Observation of skill practices • Self-assessment via questionnaire	• Facilitator • Participants	• End of program • End of program	• Facilitator • Facilitator
3	**APPLICATION/IMPLEMENTATION** • Participants utilize the competencies with team members routinely	• Various measures (ratings, open-ended items, and so forth)	• Questionnaire • Questionnaire	• Participants • Participants' managers	• 3 months	• L&D staff
4	**BUSINESS IMPACT** • Participants and team members drive improvements in at least two business measures	• Various work unit measures	• Questionnaire	• Participants	• 3 months	• L&D staff
5	**ROI** • Achieve a 20 percent ROI					

Comments: _____

Figure 11-2. Questionnaire for leaders.

FOLLOW-UP QUESTIONNAIRE

Program Name_____ **End Date of Program**_____

Our records indicate that you participated in the above program. Your participation in this follow-up survey is important to continuously improve this program. Completion of this survey may take 45 to 60 minutes. Thank you in advance for your input.

Currency

1. This survey requires some information to be completed in monetary value. Please indicate the currency you will use to complete the questions requiring monetary value._____

Program Completion

2. Did you: complete ❑   partially complete ❑   not complete ❑   the program? If you did not complete, go to the final question.

Reaction

	Strongly Disagree				Strongly Agree	Not Applicable
	1	2	3	4	5	
3. I recommended the program to others.	❑	❑	❑	❑	❑	❑
4. The program was a worthwhile investment for my organization.	❑	❑	❑	❑	❑	❑
5. The program was a good use of my time.	❑	❑	❑	❑	❑	❑
6. The program was relevant to my work.	❑	❑	❑	❑	❑	❑
7. The program was important to my work.	❑	❑	❑	❑	❑	❑
8. The program provided me with new information.	❑	❑	❑	❑	❑	❑

Learning

	Strongly Disagree				Strongly Agree	Not Applicable
	1	2	3	4	5	
9. I learned new knowledge/skills from this program.	❑	❑	❑	❑	❑	❑
10. I am confident in my ability to apply the knowledge/skills learned in this program.	❑	❑	❑	❑	❑	❑

11. Rate your level of improvement in skill or knowledge derived from the program content.
(0% = no improvement; 100% = significant improvement.) Check only one.

0%	10%	20%	30%	40%	50%	60%	70%	80%	90%	100%
❑	❑	❑	❑	❑	❑	❑	❑	❑	❑	❑

Application

	None				Very Much	Not Applicable
	1	2	3	4	5	
12. To what extent did you apply the knowledge/skills learned during the program?	❑	❑	❑	❑	❑	❑

(continued next page)

Figure 11-2. Questionnaire for leaders (continued).

Application (continued)

	Infrequently (unacceptable) ⟶ Frequently (exceptional)					Not Applicable
	1	2	3	4	5	
13. How frequently did you apply the knowledge/skills learned during the program?	❑	❑	❑	❑	❑	❑

	Low ⟶ High					Not Applicable
	1	2	3	4	5	
14. What is your level of effectiveness with the knowledge/skills learned during the program?	❑	❑	❑	❑	❑	❑
15. Rate the effectiveness of the coach.	❑	❑	❑	❑	❑	❑

	Not Critical ⟶ Very Critical					Not Applicable
	1	2	3	4	5	
16. How critical is applying the content of this program to your job success?	❑	❑	❑	❑	❑	❑

	Not Well ⟶ Very Well					Not Applicable
	1	2	3	4	5	
17. To what extent did you stay on schedule with your planned actions?	❑	❑	❑	❑	❑	❑

18. What percent of your total work time did you spend on tasks that require the knowledge/skills presented in this program? Check only one.

0%	10%	20%	30%	40%	50%	60%	70%	80%	90%	100%
❑	❑	❑	❑	❑	❑	❑	❑	❑	❑	❑

Barriers/Enablers to Application

19. Which of the following deterred or prevented you from applying the knowledge/skills learned in the program? (Check all that apply.)

No opportunity to use the skills	❑
Lack of management support	❑
Lack of support from colleagues and peers	❑
Insufficient knowledge and understanding	❑
Lack of confidence to apply knowledge/skills	❑
Systems and processes within organization will not support application of knowledge/skills	❑
Other	❑

20. If you selected "other" above, please describe here. _____

Barriers/Enablers to Application *(continued)*

21. Which of the following supported you in applying knowledge/skills learned in the program? (check all that apply)

Opportunity to use the skills ☐

Management support ☐

Support from colleagues and peers ☐

Sufficient knowledge and understanding ☐

Confidence to apply knowledge/skills ☐

Systems and processes within organization will
support application of knowledge/skills ☐

Other ☐

22. If you selected "other" above, please describe here. _____

Results – 1st Measure

23. Please define the first measure you selected and its unit for measurement. For example, if you selected "sales," your unit of measure may be "one closed sale."

_____

24. For this measure, what is the monetary value of improvement for one unit of this measure? For example, the value of a closed sale is sales value times the profit margin ($10,000 × 20% = $2,000). Although this step is difficult, please make every effort to estimate the value of a unit. Put the value in the currency you selected, round to nearest whole value, and enter numbers only (for example, $2,000.25 should be entered as $2,000).

_____

25. Please state your basis for the value of the unit of improvement you indicated above. In the closed sale example, a standard value, profit margin, is used, so "standard value" is entered here.

_____

26. For the measure listed as most directly linked to the program, how much has this measure improved in performance? If not readily available, please estimate. If you selected "sales," show the actual increase in sales (for example, four closed sales per month, enter the number 4 here). You can input a number with up to one decimal point. Indicate the frequency base for the measure.

_____ daily ☐ weekly ☐ monthly ☐ quarterly ☐

Return on Investment – 1st Measure

27. What is the annual value of improvement in the measure you selected above? Multiply the increase (question 29) by the frequency (question 26) times the unit of value (question 24). For example, if you selected "sales," multiply the sales increase by the frequency to arrive at the annum value (for example, four sales per month × 12 × $2,000 = $96,000). Although this step is difficult, please make every effort to estimate the value. Put the value in the currency you selected, round to nearest whole value, enter numbers only (for example, $96,000.50 should be entered as $96,000).

_____

28. List the other factors that could have influenced these results. _____

_____

(continued next page)

Figure 11-2. Questionnaire for leaders *(continued)*.

Return on Investment – 1st Measure *(continued)*

29. Recognizing that the other factors could have influenced this annual value of improvement, please estimate the percentage of improvement that is attributable to the program. Express as a percentage. For example, if only 60% of the sales increase is attributable to the program, enter 60 here.

    _____ %

30. What confidence do you place in the estimates you have provided in the questions above? 0% means no confidence, and 100% is certainty. Round to nearest whole value, and enter a number only (for example, 37.5% should be entered as 38).

    _____ %

Results – 2nd Measure

31. Please define the second measure you selected and its unit for measurement. For example, if you selected "sales," your unit of measure may be "one closed sale."

    _____

32. For this measure, what is the monetary value of improvement for one unit of this measure? For example, the value of a closed sale is sales value times the profit margin ($10,000 × 20% = $2,000). Although this step is difficult, please make every effort to estimate the value of a unit. Put the value in the currency you selected, round to nearest whole value, and enter numbers only (for example, $2,000.25 should be entered as $2,000).

    _____

33. Please state your basis for the value of the unit of improvement you indicated above. In the closed sale example, a standard value, profit margin, is used, so "standard value" is entered here.

    _____

34. For the measure listed as most directly linked to the program, how much has this measure improved in performance? If not readily available, please estimate. If you selected "sales," show the actual increase in sales (for example, four closed sales per month, enter the number 4 here). You can enter a number with up to one decimal point. Indicate the frequency base for the measure.

    _____   daily ☐   weekly ☐   monthly ☐   quarterly ☐

Return on Investment – 2nd Measure

35. What is the annual value of improvement in the measure you selected above? Multiply the increase (question 37) by the frequency (question 34) times the unit of value (question 32). For example, if you selected "sales," multiply the sales increase by the frequency to arrive at the annum value (for example, four sales per month × 12 × $2,000 = $96,000). Although this step is difficult, please make every effort to estimate the value. Put the value in the currency you selected, round to nearest whole value, and enter numbers only (for example, $96,000.25 should be entered as $96,000).

    _____

36. List the other factors that could have influenced these results. _____

    _____

37. Recognizing that the other factors could have influenced this annual value of improvement, please estimate the percentage of improvement that is attributable to the program. Express as a percentage. For example, if only 60% of the sales increase is attributable to the program, enter 60 here.

    _____ %

38. What confidence do you place in the estimates you have provided in the questions above? 0% means no confidence, and 100% is certainty. Round to the nearest whole value, and enter a number only (for example, 37.5% should be entered as 38%).

    _____ %

Return on Investment – 2nd Measure (continued)

39. What other benefits have been realized from this program? _____

_____

40. Please estimate your direct costs of travel and lodging for your participation in this program. Put the value in the currency you selected, round to nearest whole value, and enter numbers only (for example, $10,000.49 should be entered as $10,000).

_____

41. Please state your basis for the travel and lodging cost estimate above. _____

_____

Feedback

42. How can we improve the training to make it more relevant to your job? _____

_____

_____

_____

_____

Thank you for taking the time to complete this survey!

---

not feasible. In addition, the trend-line analysis and forecasting methods proved to be inappropriate for the same reason.

Therefore, the evaluation team had to collect estimations directly from participants on the questionnaire. Question 29 isolated the effects of this program using an estimate. Question 30 adjusted for the error of the estimate. The challenge was ensuring that participants understood this issue and were committed to provide data for the isolation.

Converting Data to Monetary Value

The participants provided estimates for converting their selected measures to monetary values. In the planning, the L&D team assumed that there were only a few feasible approaches for participants to place monetary value on measures. Because there was little agenda time to discuss this issue, the L&D staff had to rely on easy-to-obtain data using three options. The good news was that in GCR, as with many other organizations, standard values have been developed for the measures that matter and they were the first option. If a measure is something that the company wants to increase, such as productivity or sales, someone already will have placed

a value on that measure to show the contribution of the improvement. If it's a measure the company wants to reduce, such as turnover, accidents, or absenteeism, someone has more than likely placed a monetary value on that critical measure to show its impact. Consequently, the participants were asked to use standard values if they were available.

If these were not available, as a second option participants could call on an internal expert who knew more about that particular measure. In many cases, this person was an individual from the department furnishing a particular report because the data came directly from the operating reports. Essentially this was expert input. If no standard was available or experts identified, the last option was for the participants to estimate the value. Because this was a measure that mattered to the participant, he or she should have some perception about the value of improving it.

The actual amount was entered on question 24. Then, question 25 provided the basis for showing the details for how that value was developed. Question 25 is critical. If omitted, the business impact measure was removed from the analysis under the guiding principle of not using an unsupported claim

Figure 11-3. The ROI analysis plan.

ROI ANALYSIS PLAN

Program: _____   Responsibility: _____   Date: _____

Data Items (Usually Level 4)	Methods for Isolating the Effects of the Program/Process	Methods of Converting Data to Monetary Values	Cost Categories	Intangible Benefits	Communication Targets for Final Report	Other Influences/ Issues During Application	Comments
Varies, depending on measures selected	• Participant estimate	• Standard value • Expert value • Participant estimate	• Needs assessment (prorated) • Program development (prorated) • Facilitation fees • Promotional materials • Facilitation and coordination • Meals and refreshments • Facilities • Participants' salaries and benefits for time away from work • Managers' salaries and benefits for time involved in program • Cost of overhead • Evaluation costs	• Job satisfaction for first-level managers • Job satisfaction for team members • Improved teamwork • Improved communication	• Participants (first-level managers) • Participants' managers • Senior executives • L&D staff • Prospective participants • L&D council members	• Several process improvement initiatives are going on during this program implementation	• Must gain commitment to provide data • A high response rate is needed

in the analysis. Incidentally, the participants were informed about this principle as the questionnaire was reviewed with them at the end of the workshop.

Costs

The costs for the program were typical—analysis, design, development, and delivery components—and represented the fully loaded costs containing both direct and indirect categories.

Other Issues

The L&D team anticipated some intangible benefits and, consequently, added a question to identify improvements in these intangible benefits (question 39). To ensure that all the key stakeholders were identified, the evaluation team decided which groups should receive the information in the impact study. Six specific groups were targeted for communication. The remainder of the ROI analysis plan listed other issues about the study.

Results

Twenty-nine questionnaires were returned for an 81 percent response rate. Participants provided a rich database indicating success at each level of evaluation.

Reaction

Table 11-1 shows the reaction data obtained from the follow-up questionnaire. Although some initial reaction was collected at the end of the workshop using a standard reaction questionnaire, the team

Table 11-1. Reaction data from participants.

Issue	Rating*
Recommended to others	4.2
Worthwhile investment	4.1
Good use of time	4.6
Relevant to my work	4.3
Important to my work	4.1
Provided me with new information	3.9

*Rating scale: 1 = Strongly disagree;
5 = Strongly agree.

decided to collect and present to the senior team the reaction obtained in the follow-up. Each of the reaction measures exceeded the goal of a 4.0 rating, except for the issue about the amount of new information, which was slightly less than the desired level.

Learning

Although several skill practices and self-assessments were taken during the workshop to measure learning, the team decided to present the learning data directly from the follow-up questionnaire. As shown in table 11-2, the learning measures met or exceeded expectations in terms of the amount of new skills and knowledge and confidence in using them. Also, the average skill or knowledge improvement was 48 percent (question 11).

Table 11-2. Learning data from participants.

Issue	Rating*
Learned new knowledge/skills	4.3
Confident in my ability to apply new knowledge/skill	4.1

*Rating scale: 1 = Strongly disagree;
5 = Strongly agree.

Application

Table 11-3 shows application data obtained in the follow-up questionnaire. The applications exceeded expectations, and the effectiveness of the coach rating was a particular highlight. The percentage of time spent on tasks requiring the use of the acquired knowledge/skills averaged 43 percent (question 18). The participants' managers received the questionnaire primarily about the coaching component, and they reported success. They routinely coached the participants when requested and frequently reinforced the use of the skills.

Barriers and Enablers

Much to the surprise of the staff, the barriers were minimal and the enablers were strong. The program enjoyed good management support and was tailored to the job environment. Therefore, few barriers prevented the transfer of learning, and the enablers were built into the program. Table 11-4 shows the barriers and enablers.

Table 11-3. Application data from participants.

Issue	Rating*
Extent of use of knowledge/skills	4.3
Frequency of application of knowledge/skills	3.8
Effectiveness with using knowledge/skills	4.3
Effectiveness of coach	4.7
Criticalness to job	4.2

* Rating scale: 1 = Lowest;
             5 = Highest.

Table 11-4. Top five barriers and enablers identified by participants.

	Frequency
Barrier	
1. No opportunity to use skills	24%
2. Lack of support from colleagues and peers	17%
3. Insufficient knowledge and understanding	17%
4. Lack of management support	10%
5. Lack of confidence to apply learning	7%
Enabler	
1. Management support	55%
2. Opportunity to use skills	51%
3. Confidence to apply learning	38%
4. Support from colleagues and peers	34%
5. Sufficient knowledge and understanding	34%

Business Impact

Business impact data (Level 4) is shown in table 11-5. This table shows specific improvements identified directly from the questionnaire, by participant number, for the first 15 participants. To save space, the remaining 14 participants are included as a total. Usually, each participant provided improvements on two measures. The total for the second measure is shown at the bottom of table 11-5.

The top row of table 11-5 reveals the linkage between the questions on the questionnaire and the columns in this table. The total annual improvement

for each measure is reported first. Incidentally, the specific measure was identified and could be reported as well, but to reduce confusion only the measure categories were reported. The heading "Converting Data to Monetary Value" shows the extent to which the three options were used to convert data to monetary value. Most participants selected "Standard" because standard values were readily available. The column of "Other Factors" indicates the number of other factors that contributed to the results. In most cases, several factors were present. No more than four other factors were identified in any section. In a few cases, there were no other factors. In summary, the standard values were used 71 percent of the time, and other factors were identified 85 percent of the time.

ROI Analysis

The total cost of the program, using a fully loaded analysis, is shown in table 11-6. The needs assessment was prorated over four years, based upon the anticipated life cycle of the project. A thousand managers in the United States would attend this program in the four-year time period before another needs assessment was conducted. Program development was prorated over three years assuming that the delivery could change significantly in that timeframe. The remainder of the costs were directly charged and included the delivery expenses, the salaries for the participants (the first level managers), as well as their managers (second level). The training

Table 11-6. Summary of fully loaded costs.

Cost of Item	Cost
Needs assessment (prorated over 4 years)	$ 900
Program development (prorated over 3 years)	2,000
Program materials ($120/participant)	4,320
Travel, meals, and lodging ($1,600/participant)	57,600
Facilitation and coordination ($4,000/day)	32,000
Facilities and refreshments ($890/day)	7,120
Participants salaries (plus benefits) for time and program	37,218
Manager salaries (plus benefits) for time involved in program	12,096
Training and education overhead (allocated)	2,500
ROI evaluation costs	5,000
Total for 36 Participants	**$ 160,754**

Table 11-5. Business impact calculations.

Participant Number	Annual Improvement (Q27)*	Measure (Q23)*	Converting Data to Monetary Value (Q25)*	Contribution of Program (Q29)*	Other Factors (Q28)*	Confidence Estimate (Q30)*	Adjusted Value[†]
1	$ 13,100	Sales	Standard	60%	3	80%	$ 6,288
3	41,200	Productivity	Expert	75%	1	95%	29,355
4	5,300	Sales	Standard	80%	1	90%	3,816
6	7,210	Cost	Not Applicable	70%	2	70%	3,533
9	4,215	Efficiency	Standard	40%	3	75%	1,265
10	17,500	Quality	Expert	35%	4	60%	3,675
12	11,500	Time	Standard	60%	2	80%	5,520
14	3,948	Time	Standard	70%	1	80%	2,212
15	14,725	Sales	Standard	40%	3	70%	4,123
17	6,673	Efficiency	Estimate	50%	3	60%	2,002
18	12,140	Cost	Not Applicable	100%	0	100%	12,140
19	17,850	Sales	Standard	60%	2	70%	7,497
21	13,920	Sales	Standard	50%	3	80%	5,568
22	15,362	Cost	Not Applicable	40%	4	90%	5,530
23	18,923	Sales	Standard	60%	1	75%	8,515

Total for the items above		$ 101,039
Total for the next 14 items		$ 84,398
Total for 2nd measure		$ 143,764
Total Benefits		**$ 329,201**

* Question numbers in figure 11-2 questionnaire.

[†] Total Monetary Benefits = Q27 × Q29 × Q30.

and education overhead was allocated using a figure of $625 per day of training.

The BCR was calculated as follows:

$$BCR = \frac{\text{Total Benefits}}{\text{Total Costs}} = \frac{\$329,201}{\$160,754} = 2.05$$

The ROI was calculated as follows:

$$ROI = \frac{\text{Net Total Benefits}}{\text{Total Costs}}$$

$$= \frac{\$329,201 - \$160,754}{\$160,754} \times 100 = 105\%$$

Major Issues

The data was perceived to be credible by both the L&D staff and senior management group. Credibility rests on seven major issues:

1. The information for the analysis was provided directly from the new managers. The managers had no reason to be biased in their input.

2. The data was provided anonymously because no one had to provide his or her name on the questionnaire. Anonymity helped eliminate the possibility of bias.

3. The data collection process was conservative under the assumption that an unresponsive individual has realized no improvement. This concept—no data, no improvement—is an ultraconservative approach to data collection.

4. The L&D staff did not assign complete credit to this program. The participants isolated a portion of the data that should be credited directly to this program.

5. The data was adjusted for the potential error of the estimate. Estimates were used to isolate the effects of the program.

6. Only the first year of benefits was used in the analysis. Most of the improvement should result in second- and third-year benefits.

7. The costs of the program were fully loaded. All direct and indirect costs were included, including the time away from work for the participants and managers.

The data represents a balanced profile of success. Very favorable reaction, learning, and application data was presented along with business impact, ROI, and intangibles. Collectively, these issues made a convincing case for the program.

Communication Strategy

To communicate appropriately with the target audiences outlined in the ROI analysis plan, the L&D team produced three specific documents. The first report was a detailed impact study showing the approach, assumptions, methodology, and results using all six data categories. In addition, barriers and enablers were included in the study, along with conclusions and recommendations. The second report was an eight-page executive summary of the key points, including a one-page overview of the methodology.

Figure 11-4. Distribution plan for Leadership Challenge evaluation reports.

Audience	Document
Participants	Brief summary
Managers of participants	Brief summary
Senior executives	Complete study, executive summary
L&D staff	Complete study
L&D council	Complete study, executive summary
Prospective participants	Brief summary

The third report was a brief, five-page summary of the process and results. These documents were presented to the different groups according to the plan presented in figure 11-4.

Because this was the first ROI study conducted in this organization, face-to-face meetings were conducted with the executives. The purpose was to ensure that executives understood the methodology, the conservative assumptions, and each level of data. The barriers, enablers, conclusions, and recommendations were an important part of the meeting. In the future, after two or three studies have been conducted, this group will receive only a one-page summary of key data items. A similar meeting was conducted with the L&D council. The council members were advisors to the L&D department who are usually middle- and upper-level executives and managers. Finally, a face-to-face meeting was held with the learning and development staff where the complete impact study was described and used as a learning tool.

Lessons Learned

This case study shows how the evaluation process can be accomplished with minimal resources. The approach shifted much of the responsibility for evaluation to the participants as they collected data, isolated the effects of the program, and converted the data to monetary values—the three most critical steps in the ROI process. The results were easily communicated to various target groups through three specific documents. L&D staff and senior management perceived the data to be credible. The ROI was positive, and the program showed important connections with business results.

 ## Questions for Discussion

1. Is this approach credible? Explain.

2. Is the ROI value realistic?

3. What types of programs would be appropriate for this approach?

4. What additions or revisions could be made to the evaluation strategies provided?

5. What evaluation strategies other than the questionnaire could be used in this situation?

About the Authors

Jack J. Phillips, a world-renowned expert on measurement and evaluation, is chairman of the ROI Institute. Through the Institute, Phillips provides consulting services for *Fortune* 500 companies and workshops for major conference providers throughout the world. Phillips is also the author or editor of more than 30 books and 100 articles.

His expertise in measurement and evaluation is based on 27-plus years of corporate experience in five industries (aerospace, textiles, metals, construction materials, and banking). Phillips has served as training and development manager at two *Fortune* 500 firms, senior HR officer at two firms, president of a regional federal savings bank, and management professor at a major state university.

His background in training and HR led Phillips to develop the ROI Methodology—a revolutionary process that provides bottom-line figures and accountability for all types of training, performance improvement, human resources, and technology programs.

Patti P. Phillips is an internationally recognized author, consultant, and researcher. She is president and CEO of the ROI Institute, the leading source of ROI evaluation education, research, and networking. She is a chairman of the Chelsea Group, an international consulting organization supporting organizations and their efforts to build accountability into their training, human resources, and performance improvement programs. She helps organizations implement the ROI Methodology in countries around the world including South Africa, Singapore, Japan, New Zealand, Australia, Italy, Turkey, France, Germany, Canada, and the United States.

Phillips's academic accomplishments include a doctorate in international development and a master of arts degree in public and private management. She is certified in ROI evaluation and has been awarded the designation of certified performance technologist. She has published several books and articles, serves as adjunct faculty teaching training evaluation, and speaks on the subject at conferences including ASTD's International Conference and Exposition and the ISPI International Conference. She can be reached a patti@roiinstitute.net.

Chapter 12

MEASURING THE ROI OF AN E-LEARNING SALES PROGRAM
Financial Services Company

Lizette Zuniga

This case study is focused on the ROI of an e-learning sales intervention. There are several aspects that made this project one to share with others. This particular case focuses on competency modeling, competency assessment, and evaluation components for the sales academy at a large Midwestern financial services company that was undergoing a large merger integration process. The learning group enlisted the assistance of LCZ Integrated Solutions to provide consultation for the competency development and evaluation aspects. This study outlines the business need for the intervention, the e-learning program, and the evaluation plan, including how data was collected and analyzed. Finally, the study concludes with the results from implementing the e-learning program as well as lessons learned.

Description of the Performance and Business Needs

A large Midwestern company in the financial services industry implemented a revised sales program in its sales academy. There were three drivers for the revised program. First, the learning group identified the knowledge requirements and critical skills for their business and documented key competencies required to move the business forward. Not only did the content of the sales academy need to be revised to match the new competencies, but the time spent in training needed reviewing. Second, the former sales academy consumed three weeks of the new hires' time. A sig-nificant impetus for the e-learning version of the sales academy was the need to reduce the amount of time spent in training and, thus, enable sales associates to generate sales earlier in their tenure. Finally, the company was in the process of acquiring a large company and wanted to capitalize on cross-selling its products. This meant that sales associates needed to increase their knowledge of all products and develop new transactions with existing customers.

Two additional issues of consideration occurring simultaneously were a new product launch and the fact that the call center was undergoing customer service training, which could affect customer satisfaction. An audience analysis confirmed that e-learning was an appropriate medium for the sales associates. The analysis showed that there were 3,000 sales associates scattered throughout the United States and more than 200 countries around the world. Many of the sales associates were remote employees. As road warriors, these sales associates used laptop computers to access the company's intranet.

Description of the E-Learning Program

The learning group enlisted the assistance of LCZ Integrated Solutions to assist with competency modeling, competency assessment, and evaluation components of this project. Additional outsourcing assistance was obtained to develop Web-based training.

The sales e-learning program was designed to improve the skills in the following seven competencies: general sales skills, technical knowledge of the products, customer focus skills, prospecting, negotiating, managing resistance, and gaining business results. A basic sales skills segment permitted the sales associates to test their foundational skill level. Refresher content guided the learners through specific competencies before moving into the remaining sales topics.

The assessment provided immediate input on strengths and areas of improvement for each member of the sales team. This information was tracked in a database and triggered an automatic individual development plan to improve skills in the seven competencies. The skill-gap assessment coupled with the e-learning design allowed individual sales associates to customize their learning experience. If the sales associate already had strengths in negotiating skills, then the program allowed the learner to bypass negotiating skills and focus on specific areas needing improvement.

Evaluation Plan and Objectives

The learning management system (LMS) was the primary vehicle used to launch, score, and track the modules and the evaluations. At the close of each module, the learner was triggered to automatically complete a Level 1 evaluation. Figure 12-1 presents the full data collection plan.

The satisfaction goal (Level 1) was set for an average rating of 90 percent. Mastery learning checks

were embedded in the design of the e-learning modules. The learner was required to complete the mastery checks before completing the module. A goal of 85 percent correct was set for the mastery checks. Pre- and posttraining skill gap assessments (Level 3) were administered online to measure and track the level of sales competencies among the sales associates. A minimum score for the posttraining skill assessment, administered three months after training, was set for 80 percent. Other performance and business impact measures, which were tracked in an online sales workforce database, included the following:

- ability to contact 10 new prospects and conduct needs assessment on those prospects within a week after attending the sales academy
- number of sales proposals that the sales associates generated based on the assessments within 30 days
- number of new accounts opened
- weekly amount of dollars earned from sales in the first four weeks after sales academy
- monthly amount of dollars earned from sales thereafter
- number of customers retained out of total customer load
- dollar amount gained from new accounts
- reduction of time spent in training
- amount gained from cross-selling products (new initiative).

See figure 12-2 for the ROI analysis plan. To isolate the impact of the e-learning program, participants and their managers were asked to estimate the impact of the e-learning program on the business results. Confidence levels for estimates were used to adjust for any indecision (Phillips, 2003).

Cost of the E-Learning Program

The total cost of the former sales academy was $18,890,800. This included analysis, design, marketing, delivery, evaluation, and overhead costs. Each sales associate already owned an assigned personal laptop, and the company already had purchased an LMS; nevertheless, a proportionate amount of the hardware and software was allocated to this project. The costs of the program are illustrated in table 12-1.

Figure 12-1. Data collection plan.

DATA COLLECTION PLAN

Purpose of This Evaluation: To demonstrate monetary benefits from impact of sales academy on sales performance

Program/Project: Online Sales Academy

Responsibility: Consultant

Date: 03/03/03

Level	Broad Program Objective(s)	Measures	Data Collection Method/Instruments	Data Sources	Timing	Responsibilities
1	REACTION/SATISFACTION AND PLANNED ACTION	• Item #6 *I am generally satisfied with this course*	• Course evaluation hosted on online assessment Website • Distribution method: email to participant with hyperlink to Website with course evaluation	• Online assessment database	• Upon completion of course	• Facilitator
2	LEARNING	• 85% correct on mastery learning check	• Mastery learning checks hosted on online assessment Website	• LMS tracking system	• Before and after course	• Facilitator
3	APPLICATION/IMPLEMENTATION	• Increased skill assessment ratings on sales competencies	• Skill gap assessment launched through LMS • Automated through LMS	• LMS competency management system	• Before course and 90 days posttraining	• Monitored by consultant
4	BUSINESS IMPACT	• Increased new accounts • Increased dollars made from sells	• Database fields for number of new accounts and dollars from sales	• Sales workforce database	• 180 days posttraining	• Consultant
5	ROI					

Comments: Baseline Data:

- In 2002, 5,000 new accounts opened
- In 2002, $15,000,000 sold in those new accounts

Source: Adapted from Phillips, J.J. (1997). *Return on Investment in Training and Performance Improvement Programs.* Boston: Butterworth-Heinemann.

Figure 12-2. ROI analysis plan for the e-learning training.

ROI ANALYSIS PLAN

Program: E-Learning Sales Program

Responsibility: LCZ Integrated Solutions   **Date:** 4/25/04

Data Items (Usually Level 4)	Methods for Isolating the Effects of the Program/Process	Methods of Converting Data to Monetary Values	Cost Categories	Intangible Benefits	Communication Targets for Final Report	Other Influences/Issues During Application	Comments
• Number of new accounts generated	• Control group			• Customer satisfaction	• Senior vice president of sales	• New product launch	
• Dollars made from sales	• Control group	• Dollars made from sales in both groups pre- and posttraining; convert gross sales to net	• Net profit from sales		• Vice president of sales	• Call center undergoing customer service training, which could affect customer satisfaction	
			• Cost of online sales academy		• Vice president of sales academy		
					• Sales academy project work team		
			• Cost of lost productivity		• Company's online newsletter		
					• LMS (messaging for registrants)		

Source: Adapted from Phillips, J.J. (1997). *Return on Investment in Training and Performance Improvement Programs.* Boston: Butterworth-Heinemann.

Table 12-1. E-learning cost tabulation worksheet.

Item	Itemized Cost	Total Cost
Upfront Costs		
Servers (to accommodate learning technology)	$ 10,000	$ 10,000
Software	60,000	60,000
(authoring software, LMS, survey software, virtual classroom setup): Depreciation Rate per Year × Number of Years		
Hardware (PCs)	18,000	18,000
Total Upfront Costs		$ **88,000**
Recurring Technology Costs		
Annual software maintenance	$ 500	$ 500
Upgrades for software	300	300
Total Recurring Technology Costs		$ **800**
Analysis Costs		
Number of employees × average salary × benefits × number of hours on project	$ 6,500	$ 6,500
Meals, travel, and incidental expenses		
Office supplies and expenses		
Outside services	2,000	2,000
Equipment expense		
Other miscellaneous expenses		
Total Analysis Costs		$ **8,500**
Development Costs		
Number of employees × average salary × benefit rate × number of hours on project	$ 6,500	$ 6,500
Program materials and supplies		
CDs/diskettes		
Artwork/graphics		
Other		
Outsourced services	300,000	300,000
Internal services	7,500	7,500
(for example, information technology staff), including salaries and charge-backs for services: number of employees × average salary × benefit rate × number of hours on project OR amount billed by department		
Registration fees		
Other miscellaneous expenses	5,500	5,500
Testing (alpha and beta testing): # of testers × average salary × benefit rate × # of hours on project	5,500	5,500
Total Development Costs		$ **325,000**

(continued next page)

SOURCE: Adapted from J. Phillips (1997). *Return on Investment in Training and Performance Improvement Programs.* Boston: Butterworth-Heinemann.

Table 12-1. E-learning cost tabulation worksheet *(continued)*.

Item	Itemized Cost	Total Cost
Marketing Costs		
Marketing staff:	$ 1,000	$ 1,000
number of marketing employees × average salary × benefit rate × number of hours on project		
Meals, travel, and expenses		
Office supplies		
Printing and reproduction		
Outsourced services		
Internal services		
Equipment expense	150	150
Hardware expense	175	175
Software expense	175	175
Miscellaneous expenses		
Total Marketing Costs		$ 1,500
Delivery Costs		
Participants' time in training:	$ 4,557,000	$ 4,557,000
number of employees × average salary × benefit rate × number of hours of training time (tracked by either timestamp actual or average)		
Lost production (explain basis)		
Program materials and supplies, if required		
Instructor costs for synchronous learning		
Instructors' salaries and benefits		
Meals and travel expenses for synchronous learning, if applicable		
Outside services		
Facility/rental costs (synchronous, satellite studio, distance learning lab)		
Facilities expense allocation		
Hardware expense		
Software expense		
Miscellaneous expenses		
Total Delivery Costs		$ 4,557,000
Evaluation Costs		
Number of employees × average salary × benefit rate × number of hours on project	$ 6,800	$ 6,800
Meals, travel, and incidental expenses		
Participants' costs for interviews, focus groups, surveys, and so forth		
Office supplies and expenses		
Printing and reproduction		
Internal services		

Item	Itemized Cost	Total Cost
Evaluation Costs (continued)		
Outsourced services	$ 8,000	$ 8,000
Hardware expense	100	100
Software expense	100	100
Other miscellaneous expenses		
Total Evaluation Costs for Program/Project		$ 15,000
Total Program/Project Costs		**$ 4,995,800**

Results

Overall, the number of hours spent in training was cut from 105 hours to 49 hours per sales associate. Annual earnings showed a revenue increase of approximately 13 percent. One-year tracking showed the following: Within a week after attending the sales academy, sales associates were contacting 10 new prospects and conducting needs assessment 80 percent of the time; the number of sales proposals that the sales associates generated based on those analyses within 30 days increased 22 percent; the number of new accounts open increased 32 percent; and the number of customers retained increased 8 percent.

Intangible results included customer satisfaction and retention. There was also a notable increase of motivation among the sales associates (table 12-2).

In terms of revenue earnings, the amount of dollars earned from new account sales increased 19 percent, from $20,000,000 to $23,800,000. The participants and their managers estimated that the revised sales academy contributed to 70 percent of the new account sales with a confidence level of 65 percent. The amount gained from cross-selling was $120,000,000. The participants and their managers estimated that the revised sales academy contributed to 45 percent of the cross-selling earnings with a confidence level of 25 percent. The two revenue figures were converted to profit margin using a 30 percent margin rate, according to the financial averages of the company (table 12-3).

$$BCR = \frac{\$5,990,484}{\$4,995,800} = 1.2$$

Table 12-2. Level 4 results of the sales academy program.

Level 4 Evaluation Item	Results
Hours reduced in training per sales associate	56-hour reduction
Annual revenue	13 percent increase
New prospects contacted	10 per week
Needs assessment conducted	80 percent of the time
Number of sales proposals generated based on those analyses within 30 days	22 percent increase
Number of new accounts opened	32 percent increase
Number of customers retained	8 percent increase
Dollars earned from new accounts	19 percent increase ($20,000,000 to $23,800,000)
Dollars earned from cross-selling	$120,000,000

$$ROI = \frac{\$5,990,484 \text{ (Benefits)} - \$4,995,800 \text{ (e-Learning program costs)}}{\$4,995,800 \text{ (e-Learning program costs)}} \times 100$$

$$= 19.9\%$$

Table 12-3. Benefits adjusted for isolation and confidence estimates.

Hours Reduced in Training	Amount Saved	Isolation Adjustments	Final Result
56	$3,124,800	70% Estimate 65% Confidence	$ 1,421,784
Amount of *increased* dollars generated from new account sales	$3,800,000 ($23,800,000 – $20,000,000)	70% Estimate 65% Confidence 30% Profit margin	518,700
Amount of *increased* dollars earned from cross-selling	$120,000,000	45% Estimate 25% Confidence 30% Profit margin	4,050,000
		Total Benefits	**$ 5,990,484**

An ROI of 19.9 percent means that for every $1 invested in the program, there is a return of $1.2 in *net* benefits, after costs are covered. These benefits are representative of annual benefit, showing the amount saved or earned for one year following the launch of the e-learning sales academy program. The benefits will continue after the first year and are likely to increase in the case of this program. Although the impact sometimes decreases in traditional learning settings after the first year, this is not always true for e-learning programs. Given the upfront technology and development expenses in e-learning, the benefits may increase significantly after year one.

This case study shows annual benefits, but ROI practitioners should consider the multiyear impact of e-learning programs. Accountants frequently use depreciation and amortization to spread out the costs of assets during the years a company intends to use the assets. Companies often use a conventional straight-line method of depreciation, which depreciates the same each year rather than depreciating more during the first few years after the purchase of a major asset. Overall, the straight-line method results in lower expenses, and, consequently, higher profits in the first few years after the purchase. Another method, which is used particularly for technology investments, is the accelerated method. It is strongly recommended that ROI practitioners partner with the financial analyst within the company to follow the preferred method of depreciation. When consider-

ing long-term impact, the shelf-life of the e-learning program in its current format must be determined (Groppelli & Nikbakht, 1995).

Communication

Communication of the results is a critical step in the ROI process. It is also important to remember to customize communication according to the needs of the recipient. This particular study required three different forms of reporting. Figure 12-3 outlines the medium and the target audience for communication of the ROI results from this study (Phillips & Phillips, 2001).

Figure 12-3. Communication plan for evaluation reporting.

Communication Approach	Recipient of Communication
Detailed report of the ROI study	❏ Project sponsor ❏ Project team
Executive summary	❏ Executive team ❏ Program participants
Summary of findings	❏ Future participants ❏ Future managers

Lessons Learned

The process of designing and evaluating an ROI study is not all smooth sailing. In fact, there are several areas to highlight as lessons learned in the hope that other ROI practitioners can learn from these and avoid unnecessary work in their projects:

1. *Get early executive support.* The HR or learning group often feels ownership of employee development processes and is hesitant to let them be developed independently. Initial barriers occurred because the project was begun ahead of collaboration. Early partnership and consensus building is critical to the success of the project. Without the early and intermittent involvement of key business executives, the project is doomed to failure.

2. *Partner with the financial analyst within the client organization.* This partnership provides the ROI practitioner with a couple of advantages: First, it helps establish credibility with the organization's chief financial officer early in the project, and second, it helps the ROI practitioner learn about the preferred method of depreciation.

3. *Assemble a cross-functional project team.* Early credibility suffered during this project because it was initially seen as another HR initiative. Create a project team that comprises the right mix of functional representatives and skills to complete the study in a timely and credible manner.

4. *Enlist an expert in the ROI process.* Whether internal or external, this person's skills are a must for developing a credible ROI study. Without such expertise, confidence levels could weaken.

 ## Questions for Discussion

1. What steps would you take to ensure executive support in your ROI project?

2. What accounting approach does your company take when calculating the costs of assets during the years a company intends to use the assets?

3. Would you have shown the results in terms of annualized benefits from a single year or multiple-year results?

4. How could you ensure that you had the right mix of team members (skills and function) on your project team?

5. Are there other impact measures that you would have included in this study?

6. What would you have done differently in this study?

About the Author

Lizette Zuniga is the CEO of LCZ Integrated Solutions, a consulting firm focused on organizational improvement and accountability. With more than 15 years' professional experience, she has expertise in leadership and organizational development, culture assessment, program evaluation, ROI, and survey design. She has served as an internal as well as an external consultant for *Fortune* 500 companies. Zuniga holds a master's degree in psychology from Georgia State University and a doctorate in leadership and HRD from Barry University. She has contributed to the HRD literature by publishing several articles on leadership development and program evaluation. You may reach her at lcz_inc@bellsouth.net.

References

Chapter 1

Drimmer, A. (2002). *Reframing the Measurement Debate: Moving Beyond Program Analysis in the Learning Function.* Washington, DC: Corporate Executive Board.

Kirkpatrick, D.L. (1975). "Techniques for Evaluating Training Programs," *Evaluating Training Programs.* Alexandria, VA: ASTD Press.

Phillips, J.J. (2004). "The ROI Certification Process." www.roiinstitute.net.

Phillips, J.J. (2003). *Return on Investment in Training and Performance Improvement Programs,* 2nd edition. Boston: Butterworth-Heinemann.

Sibbet, D. (September–October 1997). "75 Years of Management Ideas and Practice 1922–1997." *Harvard Business Review,* supplement.

Training. (2004, March). "Top 100 Training Organizations." http://www.trainingmag.com/training/reports_analysis/top100/2004/rankings.jsp.

Chapter 4

Phillips, J.J. (2003). *Return on Investment in Training and Performance Improvement Programs,* 2nd edition. Boston: Butterworth-Heinemann.

Chapter 5

Mortgage Bankers Association of America. (1998). *Residential Mortgage Banking Basics.* Washington, DC: Real Estate Finance Press.

Phillips, J.J. (series editor). (1997). *Measuring Return on Investment,* volume 2. Alexandria, VA: ASTD Press.

Wachovia Corporation. (2004). *Foundations for Assessment, Measurement and Evaluation,* 1-12.

Chapter 6

Bloom, B. (editor). (1956). *Taxonomy of Educational Objectives: The Classification of Educational Goals, Handbook I: Cognitive Domain.* New York: David McKay Company.

Kirkpatrick, D.L. (1994). *Evaluating Training Programs: The Four Levels.* San Francisco: Berrett-Koehler.

Phillips, J.J. (1997). *Handbook of Training Evaluation and Measurement Methods,* 3rd edition. Boston: Butterworth-Heinemann.

Robinson, D.G., and J.C. Robinson. (1996). *Performance Consulting: Moving Beyond Training.* San Francisco: Berrett-Koehler.

Chapter 9

Phillips, J.J. (2003). *Return on Investment in Training and Performance Improvement Programs,* 2nd edition. Boston: Butterworth-Heinemann.

Phillips, J.J., R.D. Stone, and P.P. Phillips. (2001). *Human Resources Scorecard.* Boston: Butterworth-Heinemann.

Chapter 10

Hodges, T.K. (2002). *Linking Learning and Performance.* Boston: Butterworth-Heinemann.

Phillips. J.J. (2003). *Return on Investment in Training and Performance Improvement Programs,* 2nd edition. Boston: Butterworth-Heinemann.

Chapter 12

Groppelli, A., and E. Nikbakht. (1995). *Finance,* 3rd edition. Hauppauge: Barron's Educational Series.

Phillips, J.J. (2003). *Return on Investment in Training and Performance Improvement Programs,* 2nd edition. Boston: Butterworth-Heinemann.

Phillips, J., and P. Phillips. (2001). *In Action: Measuring Return on Investment,* volume 3. Alexandria: ASTD Press.

Additional Resources

Many other resources are available to help you understand, use, and implement evaluation in your organization. The materials listed below are available directly from the listed publishers, or they may be purchased from Amazon.com or other bookstores.

Other ROI Books

Bottomline on ROI. P.P. Phillips. Atlanta, GA: CEP Press, 2002.

The Consultant's Scorecard: Tracking Results and Bottom-Line Impact of Consulting Projects. J.J. Phillips. New York: McGraw-Hill, 2000.

The Human Resources Scorecard: Measuring the Return on Investment. J.J. Phillips, R.D. Stone, and P.P. Phillips. Woburn, MA: Butterworth-Heinemann, 2001.

Investing in Your Company's Human Capital: Strategies to Avoid Spending Too Little or Too Much. J.J. Phillips. New York: AMACOM, 2005.

Project Management Scorecard: Measuring the Success of Project Management Solutions. J.J. Phillips, T.W. Bothell, and G.L. Snead. Woburn, MA: Butterworth-Heinemann, 2002.

Proving the Value of HR: How and Why to Measure ROI. J.J. Phillips and P.P. Phillips. Alexandria, VA: SHRM, 2005.

Return on Investment in Training and Performance Improvement Programs, 2nd edition. J.J. Phillips. Woburn, MA: Butterworth-Heinemann, 2003.

Implementation Books

ROI Fieldbook. P.P. Phillips, J.J. Phillips, H. Burkett, and R.D. Stone. Woburn, MA: Butterworth-Heinemann. In press, 2005.

The Handbook of Training Evaluation and Measurement Methods, 3rd edition. J.J. Phillips. Woburn, MA: Butterworth-Heinemann, 1991.

Case Studies

In Action: Measuring Return on Investment, Volume 1. J.J. Phillips, Series Editor. Alexandria, VA: ASTD Press, 1994.

In Action: Measuring Return on Investment, Volume 2. J.J. Phillips, Series Editor. Alexandria, VA: ASTD Press, 1997.

In Action: Measuring Return on Investment, Volume 3. P.P. Phillips, Editor; J.J. Phillips, Series Editor. Alexandria, VA: ASTD Press, 2001.

In Action: Measuring ROI in the Public Sector. P.P. Phillips, Editor; J.J. Phillips, Series Editor. Alexandria, VA: ASTD Press, 2002.

In Action: Implementing Evaluation Systems and Processes. J.J. Phillips, Series Editor. Alexandria, VA: ASTD Press, 1998.

In Action: Measuring Learning and Performance. T.K. Hodges, Editor; J.J. Phillips, Series Editor. Alexandria, VA: ASTD Press, 1999.

In Action: Transferring Learning to the Workplace. M. L. Broad, Editor; J.J. Phillips, Series Editor. Alexandria, VA: ASTD Press, 1997.

In Action: Measuring Intellectual Capital. P. P. Phillips, Editor; J.J. Phillips, Series Editor. Alexandria, VA: ASTD Press, 2002.

In Action: Conducting Needs Assessment. J.J. Phillips and E.F. Holton, III, Editors. Alexandria, VA: ASTD Press, 1995.

In Action: Performance Analysis and Consulting. J.J. Phillips, Series Editor. Alexandria, VA: ASTD Press, 2000.

In Action: Implementing E-learning Solutions. C. Pope, Editor; J.J. Phillips, Series Editor. Alexandria, VA: ASTD Press, 2001.

The *Infoline* Series

Infoline, ASTD's series, is a how-to reference tool for training and performance professionals. This publication offers a variety of tools, templates, and job aids. The following *Infoline* issues focus on the five levels of evaluation discussed in this book.

Issue 258612: "Surveys From Start to Finish." L. Long, Author; G. Spruell, Editor, 1986.

Issue 258907: "Testing for Learning Outcomes." D.G. Hacker, Author; C. Sharpe, Editor, 1989.

Issue 259705: "Essentials for Evaluation." A.K. Waagen, Author; C. Sharpe, Editor, 1997.

Issue 259709: "Evaluating Technical Training: A Functional Approach." S.V. Falletta and W.L. Combs, Authors; C. Sharpe, Editor, 1997.

Issue 259813: "Level 1 Evaluation: Reaction and Planned Action." (1999). J.J. Phillips, Author; C. Sharpe, Editor, 1999.

Issue 259814: "Level 2 Evaluation: Learning." J.J. Phillips, Author; C. Sharpe, Editor, 1999.

Issue 259815: "Level 3 Evaluation: Application." J.J. Phillips, Author; C. Sharpe, Editor, 1999.

Issue 259816: "Level 4 Evaluation: Business Results." J.J. Phillips and R.D. Stone, Authors, C. Sharpe, Editor, 1999.

Issue 259805: "Level 5 Evaluation: Mastering ROI." J.J. Phillips and P. Pulliam, Authors; 1998, 2000.

Issue 250111: "Managing Evaluation Shortcuts." P.P. Phillips and H. Burkett, Authors, C. Sharpe, Editor, November 2001.

Issue 250304: "Evaluation Data: Planning and Use." P.P. Phillips, C. Gaudet, and J.J. Phillips, Authors, C. Sharpe, Editor, April 2003.

Software

Software has been developed to support evaluation as described in this book. The most complete system of measurement that provides various ways to analyze data at Levels 1 through 5 relies on a trademarked process called Metrics that Matter. This is a comprehensive measurement tool to bring accountability to the overall training and learning function.

Another option is a variety of routines and features to develop specific impact studies. This version can also be used for impact studies as a stand-alone product. Both products are available on a subscription basis. Additional details can be obtained from KnowledgeAdvisors (www.knowledgeadvisors.com).

Because of the variety and constantly changing nature of software to support evaluation, a complete list of software is not provided here. An updated list of current tools is available directly from the authors.

About the Editors

Jack J. Phillips

Jack J. Phillips, a world-renowned expert on human capital measurement and evaluation, is chairman of the ROI Institute. Through the Institute, Phillips provides consulting services for *Fortune* 500 companies and major organizations in 41 countries. He conducts workshops for major conference providers throughout the world. Phillips is also the author or editor of more than 30 books and more than 100 articles.

His expertise in human capital measurement and evaluation is based on almost 30 years of corporate experience in five industries (aerospace, textiles, metals, construction materials, and banking). Phillips has served as training and development manager at two *Fortune* 500 firms, senior HR officer at two firms, president of a regional bank, and management professor at a major state university.

His background in human resources led Phillips to develop the ROI Methodology—a revolutionary process that provides bottom-line figures and accountability for all types of training, performance improvement, human resources, learning, coaching, consulting, quality, and technology programs.

Books most recently written by Phillips include *Investing in Your Company's Human Capital: Strategies to Avoid Spending Too Little or Too Much* (AMACOM, 2005); *Proving the Value of HR: When and How to Measure ROI* (Society for Human Resource Management, 2005); *The Leadership Scorecard* (Elsevier Butterworth-Heinemann, 2004); *The Human Resources Scorecard: Measuring the Return on Investment* (Butterworth-Heinemann, 2001); *The Consultant's Scorecard* (McGraw-Hill, 2000); *Managing Employee Retention* (Butterworth-Heinemann, 2003); *Return on Investment in Training and Performance Improvement Projects*, 2nd edition (Butterworth-Heinemann, 2003); *The Project Management Scorecard* (Butterworth-Heinemann, 2002); and *Performance Analysis and Consulting* (ASTD Press, 2000). Phillips is series editor for ASTD's *In Action* casebook series and also serves as series editor for Butterworth-Heinemann's *Improving Human Performance* series. His books have been published in 25 languages.

He has undergraduate degrees in electrical engineering, physics, and mathematics; a master's degree in decision sciences from Georgia State University; and a doctorate in human resource management from the University of Alabama. In 1987 he won the Yoder-Heneman Personnel Creative Application Award from the Society for Human Resource Management.

Jack Phillips may be reached at: jack@roiinstitute. net.

Patricia Pulliam Phillips

Patti Phillips is an internationally recognized author, consultant, and researcher. She is president and CEO of the ROI Institute, the leading source of ROI evaluation education, research, and networking. She is a chairman of the Chelsea Group, an international consulting organization supporting organizations and their efforts to build accountability into their training, human resources, and performance improvement programs. She helps organizations implement the ROI Methodology in countries around the world including South Africa, Singapore, Japan, New Zealand, Australia, Italy, Turkey, France, Germany, Canada, and the United States.

Her interest in accountability and evaluation began at an early age when purpose and results were even then measures of success. This interest followed her throughout academia and 13 years in corporate life. During her tenure as a corporate manager who observed performance improvement initiatives from the client perspective, she learned that results are imperative. As manager of market planning and research, she was responsible for developing marketing programs for residential and commercial customers. In this role, she played an integral part in establishing Marketing University, a learning environment that supported the needs of new sales and marketing representatives.

In 1997, Phillips took advantage of an opportunity to pursue a career in a growing consulting business that introduced her to training, human resources, and performance improvement from a new perspective that directly reflected her values of accountability—ROI evaluation. Since 1997, she has embraced the ROI Methodology by committing herself to ongoing research and practice. To that end, Phillips has implemented ROI in private- and public-sector organizations. She has conducted ROI impact studies on programs such as leadership development, sales, new hire orientation, human performance improvement programs, as well as K–12 educator development, a National Board Certification mentoring program for educators, and faculty fellowship programs. She works with corporations, government, and academia to broaden the application of ROI evaluation to programs directly influencing the economic growth of communities around the world.

Her academic accomplishments include a doctoral degree in international development and a master of arts degree in public and private management. She is certified in ROI evaluation and has been awarded the designation of certified performance technologist.

Phillips has written a number of publications on the subject of accountability and ROI. Among her most recent publications are *Proving the Value of HR: How and Why to Measure ROI* (Society for Human Resource Management, 2005); *The Bottomline on ROI* (Center for Effective Performance, 2002), which won the 2003 award of excellence from the International Society for Performance Improvement; ASTD's *In Action* casebooks, *Measuring Return-on-Investment, Volume 3* (2001), *Measuring ROI in the Public Sector* (2002), and *Retaining Your Best Employees* (2002); the ASTD *Infoline* series including *Planning and Using Evaluation Data* (2003), *Mastering ROI* (1998), and *Managing Evaluation Shortcuts* (2001); and *The Human Resources Scorecard: Measuring Return-on-Investment* (Butterworth-Heinemann, 2001). She is published in a variety of journals, serves as adjunct faculty teaching training evaluation, and speaks on the subject at conferences including ASTD's International Conference and Exposition and the ISPI International Conference.

Patti Phillips may be reached at: patti@roiinstitute.net.

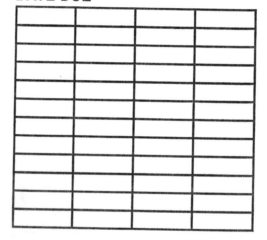

DATE DUE

HF Phillips, Jack J., 1945-
5549.5
.T7
P4344 ROI at work
2005